Coping with Global Institutional Change

Increased governance of international trade through supra-national institutions such as the World Trade Organization (WTO) has meant that national trade policies and organisational strategies need to be compatible with the norms of global institutions. Global institutional change impacts national economies and necessitates adaptation in ways that balance adherence to emerging norms while meeting socio-economic objectives.

This book focuses on two sector-specific global institutional changes initiated and implemented by the WTO in 2005 and examines how India's textile and pharmaceutical industries coped with these changes through coordinated efforts in the multi-level national institutional system comprised of the state, industry and individual business organisations. The findings of the book, which show both convergence and divergence across the two industries in the processes and outcomes of dealing with global institutional change, would be of interest to national policymakers as well as to scholars in multiple disciplines interested in the study of institutions and institutional change.

Preet S. Aulakh is Professor of Strategy and the Pierre Lassonde Chair in International Business at the Schulich School of Business, York University, Canada.

Raveendra Chittoor is Associate Professor of Strategy and International Business at the Gustavson School of Business, University of Victoria, Canada.

Coping with Global Institutional Change

A Tale of India's Textile and Pharmaceutical Industries

Preet S. Aulakh
Raveendra Chittoor

CAMBRIDGE
UNIVERSITY PRESS

CAMBRIDGE
UNIVERSITY PRESS

University Printing House, Cambridge CB2 8BS, United Kingdom

One Liberty Plaza, 20th Floor, New York, NY 10006, USA

477 Williamstown Road, Port Melbourne, vic 3207, Australia

314 to 321, 3rd Floor, Plot No.3, Splendor Forum, Jasola District Centre, New Delhi 110025, India

103 Penang Road, #05–06/07, Visioncrest Commercial, Singapore 238467

Cambridge University Press is part of the University of Cambridge.

It furthers the University's mission by disseminating knowledge in the pursuit of education, learning and research at the highest international levels of excellence.

www.cambridge.org
Information on this title: www.cambridge.org/9781009176330

First published 2022

Printed in India by Thomson Press India Ltd.

A catalogue record for this publication is available from the British Library

Library of Congress Cataloging-in-Publication Data

Names: Aulakh, Preet S., 1962- author. | Chittoor, Raveendra, author.
Title: Coping with global institutional change : a tale of India's textile
  and pharmaceutical industries / Preet S. Aulakh, Raveendra Chittoor.
Description: New York, NY : Cambridge University Press, 2022. | Includes
  bibliographical references and index.
Identifiers: LCCN 2022009506 (print) | LCCN 2022009507 (ebook) | ISBN
  9781009176330 (hardback) | ISBN 9781009176347 (ebook)
Subjects: LCSH: Textile industry–India. | Pharmaceutical industry–India.
  | World Trade Organization.
Classification: LCC HD9866.I42 A95 2022 (print) | LCC HD9866.I42 (ebook)
  | DDC 338.4/76770954–dc23/eng/20220330
LC record available at https://lccn.loc.gov/2022009506
LC ebook record available at https://lccn.loc.gov/2022009507

ISBN 978-1-009-17633-0 Hardback

For
Dr Sougata Ray and
Dr Mitrabarun (MB) Sarkar

Contents

List of Figures   ix

List of Tables   xiii

List of Appendices   xv

Preface   xvii

1.   Introduction: The Challenge of Global Institutional Change   1

2.   Conceptual Foundations and an Organising Framework   16

3.   National Policy Choices   38

4.   Industry Evolution: Tale of Two Industries   66

5.   Strategic Renewal and Firm-Level Responses   113

6.   Conclusion: Implications for Theory and Policy   162

Bibliography   190

Index   218

Figures

1.1   Global Rank of India's Pharmaceutical, Textile and Clothing Exports   7

2.1   The National Institutional System: An Organising Framework   24

4.1   India Exports and Imports of Goods and Services   68

4.2   India Textile and Clothing Exports and Imports   69

4.3   India Pharmaceutical Exports and Imports   70

4.4   India Textile and Pharmaceutical Exports as a Percentage of World Exports   73

4.5   Segment-wise Textile Exports from India   74

4.6   Segment-wise Share of Total Textile Exports from India   75

4.7   Segment-wise Share of Total Textile Imports into India   76

4.8   India Pharmaceutical Segment-wise Exports and Imports (Average Per Year during Each Period)   77

4.9   Total Inward and Outward Foreign Direct Investments, India   81

4.10   Inward Foreign Direct Investments in India's Textile and Pharmaceutical Industries   82

4.11   Outward Foreign Direct Investments in India's Pharmaceutical and Textile Industries   86

4.12   Textile Industry Fixed Capital and Number of Factories (Organised Sector)   88

4.13   Loans Sanctioned in the Textile Sector under TUFS   89

4.14   Pharmaceutical Industry Fixed Capital and Number of Factories   90

4.15   Total R&D Expenditures in India's Pharmaceutical Industry   90

4.16   Textile Industry: Investments in Plant and Machinery, R&D
        and Marketing   92

4.17   Pharmaceutical Industry: Investments in Plant and Machinery,
        R&D and Marketing   92

4.18   Textiles and Pharmaceuticals Value Added to Total
        Manufacturing in India   93

4.19   Textile Industry: Index of Industrial Production (1994–2005);
        Base Year: 1993–1994 = 100   94

4.20   Textile Industry: Index of Industrial Production (2005–2016);
        Base Year: 2004–2005 = 100   95

4.21   Textile and Pharmaceutical Industries: Index of Industrial
        Production (2012–2020); Base Year: 2010–2011 = 100   96

4.22   Textile Industry Profitability   97

4.23   Pharmaceutical Industry Profitability   97

4.24   Segment-wise Cloth Production   99

4.25   Textiles: Organised Sector Factories and Employment   100

4.26   Textiles: Organised Sector Average Annual Output and Wages
        Per Worker   100

4.27   Decentralised Power Loom Sector: Production, Units and
        Employment   101

4.28   Decentralised Power Loom Sector: Per Capita/Per Unit
        Production (Average Per Year)   102

4.29   Handloom Sector: Production, Units and Employment   103

4.30   Handloom Sector: Per Capita/Per Unit Production   103

4.31   Pharmaceutical Patents Filed and Granted in India   105

4.32   India-Origin Pharmaceutical Patents Granted by Foreign Patent
        Offices   106

5.1   Trends in Export Intensity (1990–2016)   115

5.2   Plant and Machinery Assets   124

5.3   Marketing Expenses   124

5.4   R&D Expenses   125

5.5   Conceptual Model: Resources, Capabilities and Product-Market
        Internationalisation   131

5.6   Pharma Industry: Average Sales, Exports and Imports Per Firm   138

5.7   Textile Industry: Average Sales, Exports and Imports Per Firm   139

Tables

3.1   Summary of Policy Choices in the Indian Textile and
       Pharmaceutical Industries, 1970–2020   60

3.2   Industrial Policy Framework for Indian Textile and
       Pharmaceutical Industries   63

4.1   Compound Annual Growth Rates in Exports and Imports   72

5.1   Sample Characteristics: Pharmaceutical and Textile Firms   138

5.2   Panel Estimation Results: Direct Effects of Investments in
       Capabilities on Foreign-Sales Intensity   141

5.3   Panel Estimation Results: Pharmaceutical Industry Mediating
       Effects of Imports   142

5.4   Panel Estimation Results: Textile Industry Mediating Effects of
       Imports   144

5.5   Panel Estimation Results: Determinants of Foreign-Sales
       Intensity—Moderating Effect of Business Groups in the
       Pharmaceutical Industry   145

5.6   Panel Estimation Results: Determinants of Foreign Sales
       Intensity—Moderating Effect of Geographic Clusters in the
       Textile Industry   147

5.7   Scale Effect for International Firms in the Pharmaceutical and
       Textile Industries   149

5.8   Segment-wise Data Summary of the Textile Industry   151

6.1   Comparing National Institutional Systems of India's Textile and
       Pharmaceutical Industries   164

Appendices

5A.1   Means, Standard Deviations and Correlations for the
        Pharmaceutical Industry Sample   154

5A.2   Panel Estimation Results: Determinants of Foreign Sales
        Intensity—Pharmaceutical Industry   155

5A.3   Panel Estimation Results: Determinants of Foreign Sales
        Intensity—Pharmaceutical Industry across Business Group
        Affiliated and Non-Affiliated Firms   156

5A.4   Means, Standard Deviations and Correlations for Textile
        Industry Samples   157

5A.5   Panel Estimation Results: Determinants of Foreign Sales
        Intensity—Textile Industry   158

5A.6   Panel Estimation Results: Determinants of Foreign Sales
        Intensity—Textile Industry across Geographic Cluster and
        Non-Cluster Firms   159

Preface

The last two decades of the twentieth century brought a remarkable consensus among the nations of the world in the way they conducted commerce. Erstwhile communist nations such as Russia and China as well as protectionist democracies such as India and Brazil, compelled by differing circumstances, have all embraced economic reforms and opened their borders for trade and foreign direct investment. The last word is not out on the overall effect of such liberalisation policies, with some countries like China dramatically benefitting from world trade and managing to lift millions of people out of poverty, while others (for example, in Latin America and Eastern Europe) severely affected with domestic players almost wiped out by foreign competition, and yet others like India positioned somewhere in between with some sectors benefitting from reforms and others losing out. But there was one critical factor that was common to all the firms located in these reforming nations—their business landscape has been dramatically transformed with the rules of the game in business radically redefined. How do firms from developing economies, saddled with resource deficiencies and underdeveloped institutions, cope with sweeping institutional changes triggered outside their country borders? This is the question that motivated the two of us to embark on a research programme for over fifteen years using the empirical context of Indian industries and firms with which we have been closely associated both as researchers and practitioners. This book is our best attempt to answer this question by taking a multi-level institutional perspective and drawing from the combined evidence of India's textile and pharmaceutical industries that have had varied results in successfully coping with global institutional changes initiated under the auspices of the World Trade Organization.

This book is dedicated to Dr Sougata Ray and Dr MB Sarkar, two phenomenal individuals who, during a chance meeting at one of the Academy of Management meetings around fifteen years ago, envisioned the necessity of collaborative research efforts between scholars located in India and abroad to study the growing participation of Indian organisations in global markets. Both of them pursued the realisation of this vision with tremendous energy, starting with a seminar at the Indian Institute of Management, Calcutta, during which we, the authors of this book, met for the first time. The seminar led to the beginning of a long and delightful research journey with the blessings of Drs Ray and Sarkar, the outcome of which was a set of papers on different aspects of strategy and internationalisation of Indian firms published in prominent international journals such as *Organization Science, Journal of International Business Studies, Global Strategy Journal, Long Range Planning, Management International Review* and *Journal of International Management*, among others. We are grateful to these two individuals for bringing us together, but more importantly, for their vision and guidance that have led to a long-term creative collaboration between the two of us. Dr Sarkar passed away a few years ago but his ideas, enthusiasm and passion for novel and cutting-edge research lives with us. In particular, we would like to acknowledge our co-authored paper (Raveendra Chittoor, M. B. Sarkar, Sougata Ray and Preet S. Aulakh, 'Third-World Copycats to Emerging Multinationals: Institutional Changes and Strategic Transformation in the Indian Pharmaceutical Industry', *Organization Science* 20, no. 1 [2009]: 187–205) that was the beginning of our intellectual journey together, and the core ideas developed in this paper were the springboard for the current book project.

We acknowledge the financial support provided by the Social Science and Humanities Research Council of Canada (SSHRC) through Grants 864-2007-0263 and 435-2017-1337. This support helped us in collecting data from India, hiring research assistants to collate and code the data at multiple levels of analysis, and disseminating our findings to varied audiences over the past few years. We would especially wish to acknowledge the research assistance provided by Maya Taishidler, Matthew Borinsky, Shilpi Tripathi, Puneet Bhargava and Padmalaya Mallick in helping us collect data, review the relevant literature, and make sense of the industry- and policy-level changes in the two industries over a thirty-year period. We also wish to thank our respective institutions, York University and the University of Victoria, for providing us with the necessary support to work on and complete this manuscript.

We also wish to thank Anwesha Rana and Aniruddha De at Cambridge University Press. Anwesha's enthusiastic support for the project over the last few years and Aniruddha's eye for detail during the production process were instrumental in the completion of this book.

1

Introduction

The Challenge of Global Institutional Change

What will happen to textile industries in ... more than 40 ... countries with thriving clothing industries based on exports. They are bracing for the scheduled elimination ... of quotas that have governed their exports to the world's two biggest markets: America and the European Union. The quotas have restrained some countries' exports, but in others, they have created an export industry that might not otherwise have existed.
—'The Looming Revolution: The Textile Industry',
The Economist, 13 November 2004, 76

India has become the world's supplier of cheap ... drugs because it has the necessary raw materials and a thriving and sophisticated copycat drug industry made possible by laws that grant patents to the process of making medicines, rather than to the drugs themselves. However, when India signed the World Trade Organization's agreement on intellectual property in 1994, it was required to institute patents on products by Jan. 1, 2005. These rules have little to do with free trade and more to do with the lobbying power of the American and European pharmaceutical industries.
—'Editorial: India's Choice', *New York Times*, 18 January 2005, A20

First January 2005 is an important date in the history of the governance of international trade. It is on this day that two global institutional changes took effect that, taken together, altered the trajectory of trade flows in textiles and pharmaceuticals, two industries that play salient roles in different ways in the economies of a large number of developing and developed countries.[1] Negotiated as a part of the General Agreement on Tariffs and Trade's, or GATT's, Uruguay Round of talks during the 1986–1994 period, member countries agreed to adopt the Textiles and Clothing (ATC) and Trade Related Intellectual Property Rights (TRIPS) agreements on 1 January 1995, which were to be phased in over the next ten years. The Agreement on Textiles and Clothing abolished the Multi-Fibre Agreement (MFA), which had governed global trade in textiles since 1974. The MFA endorsed bilaterally negotiated agreements on import quotas by developed countries on the exports of textile products from developing countries. Under the new arrangement after 2005, global trade in textiles and clothing would no longer be subject to protectionist quotas but would be governed by the general rules and disciplines embodied in the multilateral trading system. The TRIPS agreement called for a common global regulatory framework for intellectual property protection that required member countries to provide protection for product and process patents for a twenty-year period.[2] *The objective of this book is to explore, through a comparative method, how these two changes in the global trade regime adopted by the World Trade Organization (WTO) in 1995 and implemented in 2005* (a) *impacted and reshaped India's textile and pharmaceutical industries and* (b) *the various pathways by which firms, industries and national governments strategically responded to such globally originated institutional changes.*

As can be ascertained from the quoted editorials of two major international news outlets at the time of their implementation, the two agreements were negotiated based on specific interests and objectives of different country groups, and it was expected that the provisions of these agreements would differentially impact the trade positions of individual economies. In particular, it has been suggested that the negotiations behind the two agreements in the Uruguay Round of talks were part of a 'North–South grand bargain', whereby the developing economies would gain concessions in industries or sectors such as textiles and agriculture where they had natural historical advantages, and in turn, these countries will accommodate the needs of developed countries in new areas of intellectual property and services (Ostry 2002; *The Economist* 1997). Intellectual property protection in the pharmaceutical sector was a priority for developed countries given the vast investments made by their multinational corporations in new drug discoveries and who sought adequate patent protection to recoup and profit from their investments. Abolition of country quotas in the import of textiles and clothing by developed countries and the establishment and enforcement of strict national patent regimes by developing economies were part of this grand bargain (Lohr 2002; *The Economist* 1990).[3]

India was one of the handful of countries that had a substantial presence in global trade in both the textile and pharmaceutical sectors prior to 1995. Historical advantages in India's textile industry were built on the strength of the country being a major producer of raw materials and the availability of cheap labour to convert the materials into yarn and cloth. On the other hand, the Indian pharmaceutical industry grew due to a domestic regulatory intervention in 1970 that recognised process rather than product patents, thus allowing local firms to reverse-engineer existing drugs through different processes. Both industries were of critical importance to the Indian economy on multiple fronts. The textile industry provided employment to large numbers of people, while the pharmaceutical industry contributed to societal health by providing affordable access to crucial drugs for the domestic population as well as for people in other developing economies. The export success of both industries was also essential for the state to maintain foreign currency reserves.[4]

Institutional changes imposed by the WTO, which prioritised efficiency-based competition in textile trade and product-innovation-based intellectual property rights in pharmaceuticals, changed the 'rules of the game', and the implementation of the two agreements had the potential to disrupt India's existing advantages in the two industries and its position in global trade. Accordingly, the impending changes triggered a search in India for adequate strategic responses at the organisational and industry levels to cope with tectonic shifts in the global institutional and competitive landscapes and appropriate policy interventions to support organisational needs while maintaining the economic and social contributions of these industries. *Probing this interplay between organisational, industry and policy choices in response to global institutional change is of primary interest in this book.*

Given the importance of both the pharmaceutical and textile industries to the Indian economy, each of these has been studied extensively, as reflected in numerous monographs published in the aftermath of the global institutional changes of interest. Much of the interest in the pharmaceutical industry has revolved around the welfare implications of the WTO-imposed patent regime on the affordability and accessibility of drugs. For example, Chaudhuri (2005) examined the historical evolution of India's pharmaceutical industry in terms of its numerous welfare effects and critically assessed its sustenance in the aftermath of India acceding to the new patent-protection regime. Halliburton (2017) used the context of India's pharmaceutical industry to outline the global social implications of the increased spectrum of public knowledge and practices being claimed and institutionalised as private property. Bhaskarabhatla (2018) focused on the history of price controls of drugs before and after this global institutional change and the effectiveness of the various policy interventions in enhancing the affordability of essential drugs for Indian consumers. Other book-length studies have focused on understanding the structural changes in India's pharmaceutical industry in the post-TRIPS period (for example, Mitsumori 2018), the shift in the aggregate position of the industry's imports and exports across different product segments (for example, Joseph 2016), and sources of heterogeneity in the export performance of firms in the industry (Mazumdar 2013). The post-quota regime of the Indian textile industry has also been analysed at the aggregate industry level for changes in terms of export performance, productivity and employment generation (for example, Oberoi 2016; Dhiman and Sharma 2020).

Collectively, the aforementioned set of studies reinforces the continuing importance of both industries to India's economy at various levels in the post-reform period, including generating export earnings for the country, being large generators of employment in the manufacturing sector, fulfilling social functions such as regional development and employment of marginalised groups, and making available important drugs at affordable prices for the domestic market. Furthermore, depending on their respective domain or level of interest (that is, policy choices, industry structure or firm strategies), these studies also emphasise the challenges faced at each level in coping with the global institutional change and its associated competitive dynamics emerging in each industry.

Our book builds upon the existing literature to advance this body of research on three fronts: (*a*) observing and analysing changes over a thirty-year period (1990–2019) encompassing the different stages of national and global institutional changes in the two industries; (*b*) focusing on multi-level responses to institutional changes that include firm-, industry- and country-/policy-level choices and analysing whether their intersectionality enabled or constrained appropriate responses in each industry; and (*c*) using an inter-industry comparative approach to understand the sources of convergence or divergence of multi-level responses and their effectiveness within the same national context.

At the most basic level, this study expands the time period of observing the impact of institutional changes on the two industries and the associated multi-level responses. Most of the existing published studies were conducted in temporal proximity to the implementation of the TRIPS and ATC agreements, and, thus, their findings or arguments were either conjectural (that is, the likely impact of institutional changes on the global competitiveness of the two industries and the welfare implications) or preliminary (that is, based on data from the period between the adoption and implementation of the two agreements [1995–2005] and the few years in the immediate aftermath). Since the impact of institutional changes on economic activities and adjusting to them are evolutionary processes that take time to play out (Mahoney and Thelen 2010; Nelson and Winter 1982), the extended time period (1990–2019) of our study allows for a fuller examination of the processes of institutional change in the two industries and the efficacy of various choices made at the firm, industry and policy levels to cope with the new global institutional contexts. It should also be noted that the two global institutional changes were initiated during the period when India's economy was adjusting to the national institutional changes underway since 1991 as part of India's economic liberalisation. Examining the intersection of national and global institutional changes and the adjustments of the two industries to broad-scope economy-wide and narrow-scope sector-specific reforms (Gubbi, Aulakh and Ray 2015) has the potential to provide a more nuanced understanding of how industries and organisations cope with institutional change.

In addition to the extended time framework of our study, a more important extension to the existing literature is the consideration of multi-level responses to global institutional changes. The core mechanism through which adaptation was to happen was the development of the capabilities of firms in their respective industries to catch up with global leaders (that is, firms from other developed countries with better innovation capabilities in the case of the pharmaceutical industry and those from other developing countries with cost and productivity advantages relative to those in India in the case of the textile industry). There is a growing recognition that catch-up by firms and countries necessitates a system-level coordinated effort. As argued by Lee and Malerba (2018: 206), 'firms' learning and capability have to be supported by effective national and sectoral systems. These systems complement domestic firms in various ways and with a variety of actors and institutions, … and it is the successful combination and integration of capable firms and strong national and sectoral systems that generates a catch-up'. In particular, firm-level capability development necessitates the augmentation of tangible and intangible resources that lie outside firm boundaries. A supporting institutional environment at the industry and country levels enables access to the required resources for capability development. In addition to the enabling role of country- and sector-level institutions, there is also evidence that these institutions can constrain adaptation to external pressures, especially if there are incompatible implications of the choices made at different levels (Oliver 1991). Our study, by explicitly considering firm-, industry- and policy-level interventions in each industry, is attentive to the various enabling and constraining aspects of inter-level interactions and their implications for the paths taken to respond to institutional changes.

A third feature of our book is the study of the phenomenon of global institutional change through an inter-industry comparative approach. There is a robust tradition in inter-country comparative research across disciplines, including that of comparing institutions (for example, Hall and Soskice 2001), business systems (Witt et al. 2018), sectoral systems (for example, Malerba and Nelson 2011), business-group effects on firm-level performance (Hu, Cui and Aulakh, 2019) and innovation inputs and outputs (for example, Chang, Chung and Mahmood 2006), among others. While this body of research has provided useful insights regarding the ways national systems influence various economic activities across different countries, the path of inter-industry comparison within a single national context is relatively less undertaken in existing research. The choice of this approach in the current study is guided by two factors: First, a basic analysis of the relative global position of exports from India in the two industries of interest, textiles (which includes textiles and clothing) and pharmaceuticals, during the fifteen-year periods before and after the two global institutional changes show interesting patterns. As seen in Figure 1.1, the Indian pharmaceutical industry lost, as expected, its global position in the aftermath of the adoption of the TRIPS agreement (declining from a ranking of sixth in global exports to eighteenth between 1995 and 2005). However, the industry was able to adapt quickly to the new patent regime and regained some of its lost position, climbing back to tenth by 2015.[5] In the textile industry, the gradual dismantling of the quota regime between 1995 and 2005 saw immense gains for the textile subsegment (that is, production of fibre, yarn and cloth), which experienced a continuation of the upward trajectory initiated by India's economic reforms of 1991, going from a ranking of sixteenth all the way to second by 2015 (with China ranked first in textile exports). This trend of larger countries benefitting from the quota-free global trade regime by achieving greater-scale economies was in line with expectations underlying the global institutional change. However, Figure 1.1 also shows that India did not see substantial gains in the value-added clothing sector (which includes ready-made garments), ranking sixth in the post-2005 period. More importantly, two much smaller developing countries (Vietnam and Bangladesh) overtook India in global exports in this segment. These trends, taken together, suggest heterogeneity across the industries (and their subsegments) in terms of their ability to respond to externally imposed institutional changes but within the same national context. Examining the sources of this heterogeneity has the potential to provide interesting insights.

Second, and from a theoretical point of view, the comparative approach adopted in this study hopes to contribute to a better understanding of how global institutional change triggers national-level policy responses to facilitate adaptation by impacted industries and local firms within these industries to the 'new rules of the game' and the relative efficacy of the policy interventions in achieving global competitiveness for the firms and industries. An inter-industry comparison allows us to observe divergence and convergence of development trajectories in the textile and pharmaceutical industries within homogenous national institutional preconditions. Insights from two industries that are very different in terms of their sources of competitiveness, technology and know-how, life cycles and their underlying operating logics can contribute to a better understanding of the interplay between institutional change and industry renewal (Moodysson and Sack 2016). As suggested by Schmalensee (1989: 1000),

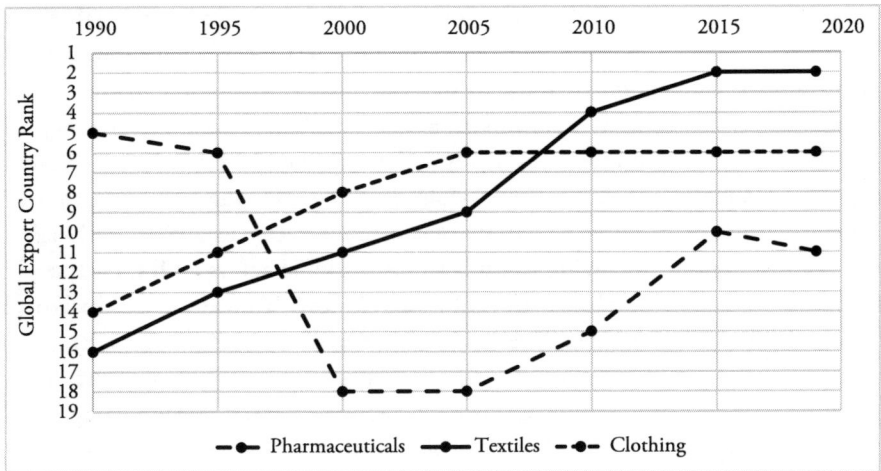

Figure 1.1 Global Rank of India's Pharmaceutical, Textile and Clothing Exports

Source: World Trade Organization (www.data.wto.org). The rankings are based on individual country data. The WTO also gives combined exports under the category 'European Union', which is not included in calculating the rankings.

descriptive inter-industry research can uncover 'robust empirical regularities that can be used to evaluate and develop theoretical tools'.

Conceptual and Methodological Approach of the Book

This study undertakes a comparative analysis to probe the ways in which India's textiles and pharmaceutical industries coped with two contemporaneous global institutional changes that altered the rules of the game in international trade for these two industries and necessitated a reassessment of each industry's traditional competitive advantages. The central focus of this comparative approach is to understand the transformation of private organisations in each industry in terms of their reconfigurations of resources and capabilities to compete in a new global context. Furthermore, the ability of each industry to maintain and/or enhance its presence in global markets had implications for India's export-led economic development model, and the paths taken by each industry to achieve that success had to be attentive to the sustenance of the respective historical socioeconomic and welfare contributions. Accordingly, the state, through its policy-making function, had an important role in ensuring that firm- and industry-level responses to enhance competitiveness and success in international markets were balanced with their important socio-economic development goals in the domestic or national space. The multi-level involvement of different institutions in India to global institutional changes leads to a modified research question that is of interest in this book: How and to what extent were organisational-, industry- and policy-level responses coordinated in the two industries in a way that the complementarities facilitated the export success of Indian firms while ensuring that the two industries at aggregate levels contributed to national socio-economic goals and aspirations?

These questions, involving multi-level institutional actors with their specific objectives and contributions, are addressed in the context of an analytical framework built around three streams of research: international competitiveness of firms from developing or emerging economies; national and firm-level catch-up; and institutions and institutional change. In the following paragraphs, we briefly outline the three building blocks of the analytical framework (or conceptual approach) used in the book. These are subsequently developed in greater detail in the following chapter.

Exporting firms are significant contributors to the creation of jobs, the generation of trade revenues, and the balance of trade. The globalisation of markets due to the lowering of trade barriers has increased the appeal of export-led growth both in country-level policy discourses and firm-level strategic choices, and, accordingly, through various incentives and export-promotion schemes, national governments encourage local firms to participate in international markets. In addition to contributing to national socio-economic aspirations, firms derive numerous benefits from exporting (Hitt et al 2006). First, there are efficiency gains. By exploring new markets, firms can achieve economies of scale and scope. Given the increasing costs of developing new products and technologies, the minimum efficient scale in various value-chain activities has increased to a level that is difficult to achieve with sales in a single market (Gupta and Govindarajan 2000). Targeting diverse customer segments with adaptive products and technologies can have scale and scope advantages for core technology development, especially when exporters enhance product or technology life cycles with research and development (Aw, Roberts and Winston 2005) or target customer segments in different phases of their developmental cycles (Aulakh, Kotabe and Teegen 2000).

Second, there are growth benefits (Autio, Sapeinza and Almeida 2000). Although risky for many, exporting can help some firms grow faster than their competitors (Sapienza et al. 2006) and improve their competitive position by arbitraging country differences in economic cycles, currency fluctuations, and administrative and trade regulations (Aulakh, Kotabe and Teegen 2000). Exporters can also cross-subsidise value-chain activities among countries to ward off competitive pressures from rival firms (Gupta and Govindarajan 2000) and negotiate more favourable terms with governments, suppliers, distributors and customers. Third, there are learning opportunities (Zahra, Ireland and Hitt 2000). Firms exposed to a range of environmental contexts develop more adept mental models (Barkema and Vermeulen 1998), develop the capabilities required to flexibly adapt to new markets (Sapienza et al. 2006), and thus decrease the cost and increase the benefits of subsequent market entry. Because exporters gain broader exposure to diverse institutional contexts, competitive conditions and customer behaviour, they can leverage knowledge from one market context to another and improve their innovation prospects (Salomon 2006).

Despite the potential firm-level gains from exporting, firms rarely achieve all these benefits because of the costs of internationalisation: coordination costs related to managing dispersed operations and entry costs of setting up in and learning about institutionally distant markets (Barkema and Vermuleun 1998; Abdi and Aulakh 2019). These costs are accentuated for exporting firms from developing economies for two reasons: first, they face a higher liability of foreignness and newness in global markets (Hymer 1976); second, and more importantly, the assumed benefits of exporting materialise only if developing economy firms have products or services that are competitive in international markets. Accordingly, the literature on the internationalisation process of firms from developing economies has converged on the idea that these firms face a unique problem in that they need to first overcome significant knowledge and resource hurdles to internationalise in the first place by acquiring appropriate technological knowledge and financial resources (Chittoor et al. 2009). In the light of the objectives of this book, the relevant insight from the relevant existing literature is that success in foreign markets in an era of market-based (textiles) and knowledge-based (pharmaceuticals) competition after the implementation of the two global institutional changes requires access to critical resources and the development of capabilities to catch up and compete with other global firms with superior capabilities and international experience.

How could firms located in resource-poor developing economies such as India access such critical resources and capabilities? Here, we build on insights from the literature on economic catch-up. While originally applied to inter-country catch-up in economic development, this literature has evolved to study the process of catch-up by developing economy (laggard) firms with those from developed countries (leading) firms (Lee 2013, 2019; Malerba and Lee 2021). This literature identifies multiple paths that laggard firms from developing economies can take to close the gap with leading firms.[6] More importantly, it recognises the importance of various types of resources at the organisational level and, as mentioned in the previous section, sees a system-level (which includes the state, industry and firms) coordinated approach between institutional actors to ensure the availability of these resources. This process can take the form of firms' ability to tap into tangible resources directly made available by the state or indirectly from outside domestic and international sources whose access is facilitated by regulatory changes negotiated between the state and industry associations.[7] However, this literature takes a structural viewpoint in the sense that it assumes that once an institutional system is established, firms will have the requisite resources needed for catching up. However, since the system consists of multiple actors, the availability and allocation of resources, and the targeted prioritisation of activities are a function of the compatibility or convergence in the shifting or evolving goals of the different actors. To understand these dynamics, we tap into the literature on institutional change and institutional logics.

The state, industries and organisations in a country can be thought of as separate institutions but are tightly coupled to protect broader societal interests within the confines of national boundaries. However, each of these operates within its own norms of behaviour and obligations, or institutional logics, defined as organising principles through which various actors construct meaning for their social reality and which constrain or enable behaviour by prescribing appropriate means and ends. Institutional change impinges on existing belief systems and taken-for-granted rules and often introduces competing logics that guide the behaviour of various actors (Thornton, Ocasio and Lounsbury 2012). Relative attention to one or the other of the competing logics has implications on how institutional actors within and across levels negotiate for the allocation of resources to cope with the new rules of the game. Our analytical framework uses insights from institutional change and institutional logics literature to identify various competing logics introduced by global institutional changes in the two industries and explores ways in which these logics are reconciled at different institutional levels (that is, policy, industry and firm). In this regard, much of the existing literature on coping with competing logics considers their resolution at a single level of decision-making (that is, the *intra-institutional* level) and identifies structural separation or strategic solutions as ways to accommodate their conflicting and contradictory prescriptions (Thornton and Ocasio 2008; Smith and Tushman 2005). While the applicability of the existing approach is assessed and applied at each level in the current study, its unique context allows us to move beyond a single-level analysis and explore *inter-institutional* possibilities for dealing with institutional changes and competing logics. The intrusion of global institutional changes in the pre-existing logics of each of the three institutions could promote greater interactions between them to forge a coordinated response to embrace, accommodate or confront some of the imposed logics. The proposed framework for this book foregrounds the various types of intersectionality that are possible and evaluates their applicability within the empirical context of this study.

A multi-level national institutional system framework based on the aforementioned literature streams and encompassing both intra- and inter-institutional approaches to navigating institutional complexity is subsequently applied to examine the policy, industry and firm responses across the two industries. The methodological approach of the book entails an examination of policy choices, industry evolution and firm-level strategies over the 1990–2019 period, a period that includes different stages in national and global policy regimes faced by the two industries. Assessment of these responses at the three levels necessitates different analytical approaches. Accordingly, a multi-method approach is used in this book.[8] Policy choices are examined through the method of descriptive historical analysis, which includes a close reading of the texts of legislated policies and understanding the political and industry contexts in which these policies were implemented, as well as how specific policy instruments attempted to reconcile often competing logics connected with economic efficiency and socio-economic welfare. The industry-level investigation is accomplished through an analysis of aggregate data released by the relevant ministries in India, international agencies (for example, WTO, the World Intellectual Property Organization [WIPO], the United Nations Conference on Trade and Development [UNCTAD] and so on), industry associations, independent consulting organisations and official government statistical bodies in India. The firm-level analysis of organisational responses to institutional changes is performed through quantitative analyses of thirty-year panel data of firms in each industry extracted from the Prowess Database compiled by the Centre for Monitoring of Indian Economy (CMIE).[9] For the organisational level analysis, a formal theoretical model is developed and empirically tested.

Structure of the Book

In Chapter 2, we elaborate on the literature introduced above and develop an organising framework around these conceptual foundations related to the internationalisation of developing economic firms, catch-up mechanisms and institutional logics. The main argument underlying the framework is that since global institutional changes impact various institutions within a country, coping with external changes necessitates a coordinated effort by the national institutional system comprising the state, the sector that is impacted by global institutional change, and the organisations within that sector. Being attentive to the fact that each of the institutions within this system operates on its own logic, the framework incorporates possibilities of an emergence of competing logics at each institutional level because of the external pressures; dealing with these competing logics requires both intra- and inter-institutional coordination and solutions. The framework is primarily descriptive, and the hope is to use an inductive approach to probe the different components of the framework in subsequent chapters.

Chapter 3 foregrounds the historical importance of the textile and pharmaceutical industries for the Indian economy, both as generators of much-needed foreign exchange reserves during the import-substitution regime and facilitators in achieving welfare goals of providing employment and affordable drugs to the population. It then explores the ways in which global institutional changes had the potential to disrupt the contributions of these two industries. Using a variety of policy documents (that is, specific acts and policies, annual reports of the relevant ministries and industry associations) and secondary academic articles and research reports, it identifies and critically evaluates specific policies and programmes instituted by successive Indian governments over four distinct policy regimes that are classified as follows: import-substitution industrialisation (1947–1985); economic liberalisation (1985–1995); preparation for global institutional change (1995–2005); and coping with institutional change (2005–2020). Focusing on the different policy regimes (some before the global institutional changes) allows for an understanding of the competing logics that emerged at the level of the state and the challenges of reconciling them in the light of the external pressures and demands at industry and organisational levels. The chapter subsequently links India's policy choices with existing industrial policy frameworks and evaluates the implications for the structural evolution of the two industries and the strategic choices of firms.

Chapter 4 assesses the evolution of the industries from 1990 to 2020, punctuated by the global institutional changes in 1995 (adoption of the agreements) and 2005 (implementation of the agreements) and national institutional changes emanating from the specific policy interventions in each industry. More specifically, this analysis incorporates (*a*) the overall and subsegment positions of the two industries in global trade, as well as their contributions to India's export-led growth model; (*b*) participation in international resource markets, including through inward and outward foreign direct investment, and their implications for know-how transfer and industry value-chain upgradation; and (*c*) investments in downstream and upstream activities. The final part of the chapter assesses the respective performance outcomes in each industry on production output, employment generation and innovation. The objective of this chapter is to emphasise both similarities and differences in the transformation of the two industries in response to institutional changes and to understand the different paths taken by each industry to incorporate the new logics of global competition while simultaneously accommodating the national aspirations of export growth and welfare. This chapter is attentive to heterogeneity in performance outcomes within subsegments of each industry.

Chapter 5 examines organisational-level responses to institutional changes. It investigates how Indian pharmaceutical firms (which faced a discontinuous institutional change related to the international property protection regime of product patents), and textile firms (that faced an environment of increased market-based competition) undertook strategic renewal by accessing international resources and entering foreign markets. Drawing from evolutionary economics and institutional theory, an analytical model that links investments by firms in a variety of resources and capabilities and organisational-level export success is developed. Furthermore, our model assesses the role of network resources provided by business groups and geographical clusters in moderating the relationships between investments in capabilities and export success. This model is empirically tested through panel data of firms included in the CMIE Prowess Database.

The concluding chapter (Chapter 6) compares the findings from the previous four chapters on local responses to global institutional changes at each of the three levels of analysis for the two industries: policy, industry structure and firm. The purpose is to identify both the commonalities and differences to explore the specific implications for theories of institutional change and institutional logics, normative insights for organisations navigating institutional complexity, and lessons for policymakers attempting to balance economic and social goals.

Conclusion

The book intends to make four contributions, and its findings would be of interest to different audiences. First, the study draws attention to the efficacy of different types of resources (firm, national and global levels) used by individual organisations to navigate and respond to global institutional change and their differential implications for export growth and global competitiveness in the two industries. These findings would be of interest to organisations contemplating strategic renewal through a reconfiguration of their resources and capabilities and to policymakers developing programmes that provide direct support to enhance the organisational capabilities of indigenous firms. In this regard, the book adds to a growing body of research interested in understanding the phenomenon of emerging economy multinationals because of their unconventional approaches to globalisation in terms of the speed, destination and modes of internationalisation (for example, Cuervo-Cazurra and Ramamurti 2014; Grosse and Meyer 2019; Sauvant and Pradhan 2010). By examining the combined roles of policy choices, industry structures and firm strategies in developing global advantages in very different types of industries, the findings from the current study complement and add to existing research whose primary focus has been to probe firm-level strategic choices.

Second, the study contributes to theories of institutional change and logics. There has been a growing call by scholars for further research that delves into multi-level and comparative studies to understand how seemingly contradictory logics at a given level can be accommodated through inter-level accommodations and to understand heterogeneity in outcomes of institutional change within similar contextual conditions (Greenwood et al. 2011; Thornton and Ocasio 2008; Thornton, Ocasio and Lounsbury 2012). Findings from our comparative and multi-level method address this research gap.

Third, by critically evaluating the effectiveness of different policy instruments (for example, direct support through subsidies and indirect support through domestic regulatory changes) to enhance competitiveness in global markets of local firms and industries while at the same time preserving their contributions to economic and social welfare, this study provides useful insights for public policy choices in finding an ideal balance between the local and global markets, and between welfare and efficiency.

Fourth, and more broadly, the study contributes to a resurgent interest in understanding new models of state intervention and their effectiveness in influencing the competitive advantages of national firms and their implications for globally negotiated trade and investment agreements (Hu, Cui and Aulakh 2019).

Notes

1. Another change in the governance of global trade in 1995 was the institutionalisation of the General Agreement in Tariffs and Trade (GATT) into the World Trade Organization (WTO), which had the power to adjudicate trade disputes between countries.

2. The agreement had provisions for the protection of various types of intellectual property, including trademarks, copyrights and trade designs. Patents are the relevant intellectual property protection concerns in the pharmaceutical industry, and thus the main focus in the current study. For detailed provisions of both agreements, see WTO Agreements, www.wto.org. For the implications of TRIPS to various economies, see Taubman, Wager and Watal (2020).

3. Scholars have pointed out the asymmetry in concessions given by developed and developing countries in this bargain (Hamilton 1997). As argued by Srinivasan (2002: 347), the 'TRIPS agreement as well as other commitments that poor countries undertook as part of the Uruguay Round agreement was more costly to them than the uncertain gains from the concessions of the developed countries including the MFA phase-out'.

4. For details on the importance of each industry to India's economy, see the annual reports of the respective ministries (http://texmin.nic.in; https://pharmaceuticals.gov.in), and India's five-year plans (https://niti.gov.in/planningcommission.gov.in/docs/plans/planrel/fiveyr). For instance, according to the Ministry of Textiles Annual Report of 2001–2002, the Indian textile industry contributed 14 per cent to industrial production and 27 per cent to the country's export earnings. After the agriculture sector, it was the largest employer—employing approximately 35 million workers—and, more importantly, the industry was a major source of employment for the weaker socio-economic sections of the society. India's pharmaceutical industry was able to satisfy more than 70 per cent of the local demand with affordable drugs and was a source of numerous essential drugs for the rest of the developing world.

5. According to the Department of Pharmaceuticals, Government of India (Annual Report 2020–2021), India's pharmaceutical industry is the world's third largest by volume and fourteenth largest by value. India is the largest supplier of generic drugs in world markets and, owing to its position as a substantial producer of important life-saving drugs and vaccines, prides itself as the 'Pharmacy of the World' (https://pharmaceuticals.gov.in/annual-report).

6. This literature is discussed in greater detail in Chapter 2.

7. These include easing of import controls for technology, know-how and intermediate products, allowing inward and outward foreign direct investment, among others. These are discussed in more detail in Chapter 3.

8. The level-specific methods are discussed in more detail in their respective chapters (Chapters 3, 4 and 5).

9. The CMIE Prowess database is one of the most comprehensive databases of Indian firms. It contains detailed financial data from 1990 of approximately 50,000 Indian firms, including all firms traded on India's major stock exchanges and several others, such as the central public sector enterprises. The database covers most organised industrial activity in India, and the firms in Prowess account for 75 per cent of all corporate taxes and more than 95 per cent of the excise duties collected by India's government (Chittoor et al. 2009).

2

Conceptual Foundations and an Organising Framework

> Organizations face institutional complexity whenever they confront incompatible prescripts from multiple institutional logics.... To the extent that the prescriptions and proscriptions *are* incompatible, or at least appear to be so, they invariably generate challenges and tensions for organizations exposed to them.
>
> —Greenwood et al. (2011: 318, italics in original)

Institutions and institutional change have attracted considerable scholarly interest in numerous disciplines given their primacy as rules of the game in society that structure exchange between various societal actors (for example, Greif 2006; North 1990; Scott 2014).[1] Research has scrutinised the process of institutional change, whether it is narrow or broad in scope, incremental or discontinuous, and exogenously or endogenously determined, among other characteristics (for example, Campbell 2004; Mahoney and Thelan 2010). There is a general agreement among scholars that irrespective of the process, institutional change encompasses shifting the rules of the game and imposes institutional complexity on the actors. Institutional changes emanating from evolving political and economic landscapes within individual countries and pressures from supranational bodies such as the World Trade Organization (WTO), the International Monetary Fund (IMF) and the World Bank have been instrumental in triggering economic reforms and liberalisation programmes of developing economies and their integration into the global economy (Gereffi 2010). Increasing integration into the global economy has transformed the competitive landscapes for developing country firms, thus necessitating organisational transformations to deal with new competitive dynamics.

In the context of a variety of local and global institutional reforms, understanding how indigenous firms in developing economies worldwide respond to challenges presented by a radically changed competitive environment has been the subject of vigorous research in the past two decades (for example, Aulakh and Kotabe 2018; Newman 2000; Malerba and Lee 2021; Peng 2003; Uhlenbruck, Meyer and Hitt 2003; Zahra et al. 2000).[2] The objective of this chapter is to use this body of research and its underlying theoretical approaches to develop an analytical framework through which the global institutional changes of interest in this study and the multilevel national responses (at the level of the state, industries and organisations) in the Indian textile and pharmaceutical industries can be evaluated in subsequent chapters. An underlying assumption in this chapter is that the end objective of multilevel national responses to global institutional changes is to maintain and enhance the competitiveness of these two industries in international markets. The challenge is how to achieve this objective given the underlying resource constraints and competing institutional logics at each level of analysis.

Institutional Change and Pathways to Organisational Transformation

First- and Second-Order Organisational Change

In their seminal article on organisational changes in the context of shifting market and institutional pressures, Greenwood and Hinings (1996: 1024) distinguish between convergent and radical organisational change. While the former consists of 'fine-tuning the existing orientation', radical organisational change or 'frame bending' involves the breaking loose from an existing 'orientation' and 'transformation of the organization'. This distinction closely resonates with the first- and second-order change dichotomy proposed by Meyer, Goes and Brooks (1993). According to this view, first-order change is incremental and merely entails 'adjustments in systems, processes or structures, but does not involve fundamental change in strategy, core values, or corporate identity' (Newman, 2000: 604). Second-order change, however, is 'transformational, radical, and fundamentally alters the organisation at its core' (Newman 2000: 604). While the aforementioned distinctions in organisational change have their antecedents in different variants of institutional theory, a third distinction has its roots in the evolutionary theory of the firm (Nelson and Winter 1992). Focusing on the imperative of reconfiguring resources, product markets and capabilities in response to external shifts and discontinuities (Teece, Pisano and Shuen 1997; Helfat and Peteraf 2003), the evolutionary view in strategy research has emphasised the role of deliberate search processes in organisational morphing (Barnett and Burgelman 1996; Helfat and Lieberman 2002; Zollo and Winter 2002). Such a search, which is a critical concept that undergirds how firms adapt and grow, distinguishes between two broad patterns of learning behaviours. Exploration is associated with distant search involving 'variance-increasing activities, learning by doing, and trial and error' (Smith and Tushman 2005: 522). On the other hand, exploitation is associated with local search involving 'refinement, choice, production, efficiency, selection, implementation, execution' (March 1991: 71).

How do these models of organisational change apply to developing economy firms facing externally imposed discontinuities? Several of studies have found evidence of first-order change involving local searches by firms from developing economies in response to regulatory reforms and foreign competition. This has entailed refining their product and services in a way that exploits their home countries' unique resources and capabilities and includes leveraging cost-oriented, commodity approaches such as component or private-label manufacturing for established multinationals (Craig and Douglas 1997; Dawar and Frost 1999). Furthermore, when faced with competition from foreign multinationals on their domestic turf, developing economy firms that were especially capable of serving markets with underdeveloped infrastructures and institutional voids have tended to move into other developing country markets that had similar institutional environments (Khanna and Palepu 2006). The common findings, therefore, are that firms from developing economies, when faced with liberalising reforms in their domestic markets, respond with strategies that exploit their existing resources and capabilities, which have been honed by operating in unique home-market institutional contexts. This perspective on focusing on existing capabilities has also been supported by recent research, which suggests that in the light of institutional voids in domestic factor markets, firms from developing economies must take detours 'to build a new path in building their innovation capabilities instead of replicating practices employed in advanced economies' (Lee 2019: xvii). These detours include 'petit patents and trademarks instead of promoting and strengthening regular patent rights', participating in existing global value chains, and 'specializing first in short-cycle technology-based sectors and products (Lee 2019: xvii–xviii). The implication here is that the response to radical institutional change in developing economies should be incremental, both in terms of the product and technology upgradation and the foreign markets targeted for expansion.

While the internationalisation of developing economy firms in similar markets conforms to the dominant idea that firm internationalisation exploits the existing advantages abroad (Buckley and Casson 1976; Dunning 1988), there is also growing evidence of developing economy firms internationalising for exploration purposes to augment their asset base, including technology and managerial know-how, branded products, and to access globally dispersed vertical and horizontal linkages (Luo and Tung 2007). High-profile foreign acquisitions of marquee companies and brands and aggressive growth of exports to advanced markets have been linked to developing economies' attempts to undergo second-order change through a strategic renewal of their resources and capabilities (Gubbi et al. 2010).[3]

Strategic Renewal and Catch-Up

Renewal is an evolutionary concept that emphasises the acquisition of new knowledge-based resources and productive assets as a route to effect a concomitant change in a firm's product-market domains and generate new competencies (Floyd and Lane 2000). By recognising how firms engage in path-dependent adaptations over time, the notion of renewal mirrors the dynamic capabilities argument that changing environments require firms to engage in activities that enable them to reconfigure their resources, product markets and capabilities (Teece, Pisano and Shuen 1997; Eisenhardt and Martin, 2000; Danneels, 2002). The twin notions of renewal and dynamic capabilities, therefore, focus attention on the ability to engage in 'continuous morphing' as an antidote to technological and market discontinuities (Rindova and Kotha 2001). The dominant focus of such research has been on the effect of technological shifts on incumbent firms (for example, Abernathy and Utterback 1978; Tushman and Anderson 1986). However, there is also evidence that strategic renewal helps organisations respond to institutional transitions; that is, a distant (or exploratory) search in knowledge bases, product markets and organisational practices from sources distinct from those that existed in the past (Katila and Ahuja 2002; Kriauciunas and Kale 2006; Rosenkopf and Nerkar 2001) helps organisations in developing economies transform themselves in the face of institutional changes (Peng 2003; Newman 2000; Filatotchev et al. 2003), and catch up with leading global firms (Lee 2019; Malerba and Lee 2021).

In its initial scope, catch-up, which is defined as the narrowing of a country's gap in productivity, income or technology vis-à-vis a leading country, was studied at the level of national economies (Lee 2013). For instance, a body of research has focused on understanding catch-up processes amongst advanced countries with different levels of economic and technological capabilities (for example, Abramovitz 1986; Gerschenkron 1962), while more recent research has expanded the domain to understand how some developing economies have been able to catch up (Nayyar 2013) and sometimes leapfrog advanced countries in certain sectors and technologies (Lee 2019). An important mechanism of the catch-up is participation in global resource markets to access internationally developed knowledge and applying such knowledge to local contexts (Bell and Pavitt 1993; Lall 1992). According to Nelson (2008: 14–15),

> for countries aiming to catch up, the basic challenge is to learn to master new ways of doing things…. The innovation in catching up involves bringing in and learning to master ways of doing things that may have been used for some time in the advanced economies of the world, even though they are new for the country or region catching up.

Two aspects from this body of research on catch-up are relevant for the current study. First, although the phenomenon was studied primarily in the context of catch-up between countries, recent work has seen the applicability of the underlying principles in the catch-up process between firms (Lee and Malerba 2018). Malerba and Lee (2021:3), for instance, define firm-level catching-up 'as an evolutionary process of closing the gap between latecomers and forerunners, in uncertain, context-specific and changing environments'. The second aspect relates to the type of participation in international resource markets, especially for developing economy firms that aim to develop new capabilities to compete with 'leading firms' in both domestic and foreign markets in a liberalised global trade environment.

Accumulative and Assimilative Learning

While there is a general consensus that global markets provide learning opportunities for firms from developing economies, which in turn can provide the impetus for strategic renewal and catch-up, there is divergence in the literature regarding the mechanisms through which external learning is internalised and applied for indigenous innovation (Nelson 2005; Lall 1992). The source of this divergence is the underlying assumption of the two schools of thought explaining the process of technological learning and economic growth in developing economies, namely accumulation and assimilation (Kim 1997; Lall 1992; Nelson and Pack 1999; Nelson 2005). The two viewpoints build upon two dimensions of knowledge, namely explicit and tacit (Polanyi 1966) or objective and experiential (Penrose 1959). Explicit knowledge can be codified and acquired through books, technical specifications, designs and machinery. On the other hand, tacit knowledge is deeply rooted, hard to codify and can be acquired primarily through experience that includes observation, imitation and practice (Kim 1997).

The accumulation view, rooted in neoclassical economics, considers learning and the associated economic growth, coming primarily through investments in physical and human capital (for example, Abramovitz 1986; Amsden 1989;

Kim and Lau 1994). It assumes that technological knowledge is largely embodied in machinery and codified documents and thus can be gained through investments to acquire them. Accordingly, high rates of investment in physical and human capital along with imports of technology allow firms in developing economies to improve the production function (Kim and Lau 1994).

The assimilation perspective, with roots in evolutionary economics (Dosi 1988; Nelson and Winter 1982; Nelson and Pack 1999; Nelson 2005; Lall 1992; Bell and Pavitt 1993), emphasises 'assimilation' processes that stress learning by doing, entrepreneurship and innovation, in addition to accumulation through investments (Nelson and Pack 1999). While accumulation is necessary, it is not sufficient to achieve technological learning. According to this view, competitiveness is seldom achieved through the simple accumulation of technology without concomitant investments in technology upgrading, improvement and innovation (Evenson and Westphal 1994). It is argued that only a small portion of technology is codified in the form of blueprints; therefore, learning is accomplished as much by doing and using as by reading and studying. To use the acquired know-how effectively, new sets of skills and organising principles are required, which can be achieved when firms pursue product-market internationalisation in global markets and interact with advanced market firms and customers (Nelson 2005).

Both the accumulative and assimilative perspectives establish the importance of learning through distant search (that is, foreign markets) as an important mechanism for catch-up in developing economies. There are two mediums to accomplish this, namely through direct import of technology and an endogenous process of learning by doing through product-market internationalisation. As accumulation theorists have argued, developing economy firms leverage inflows of foreign technology to improve their technological base (Pack and Saggi 1997). The import of technologies from industrially advanced countries has been a primary means for firms from newly industrialising economies in their quest to catch up technologically. Foreign-technology transfer can provide new dimensions by raising the knowledge level and can serve as a catalytic source of technological change (Kim 1997). However, there are many elements of experiential learning from foreign markets that cannot be acquired by accumulation through imports alone. From the perspective of assimilation scholars, venturing into international markets through exports or other modes stimulates and supports learning (Pack and Westphal 1986; Nelson 2005). Internationalisation necessitates firms to pay attention to world standards and meet the high performance demanded by international customers, which stimulates learning (Nelson, 2005). This view is supported in the international business literature, which has highlighted the multitude of learning opportunities that product-market internationalisation offers (Johanson and Vahlne 1977; Ghoshal 1987; Doz, Santos and Williamson 2001). The very process of internationalisation has been conceptualised to involve gradual acquisition, integration and use of knowledge about foreign markets and operations.

Organisational Constraints

In the preceding paragraphs, we have outlined the underlying principles and approaches of different theoretical traditions (that is, renewal and dynamic capabilities, distant and local search behaviours, accumulation and assimilation of external know-how to catch-up) that explain second-order organisational transformation in developing economies in response to externally imposed institutional changes. A common aspect underlying these different approaches is the requirement of substantial resource commitments. Furthermore, the reconfiguration of organisational resource and product markets associated with strategic renewal and catch-up necessitates exploratory or distant search, which tends to be risky, given uncertain outcomes. These two conditions thus require organisations contemplating second-order transformation to possess the resources required for distant search and have a propensity to take on the enhanced risk associated with such search behaviour (Sitkin and Pablo 1992).

The literature has identified several factors that constrain developing economy firms' ability to undergo second-order change in response to external pressures. The first is related to their inherent resource disadvantages in developing front-line capabilities that are required to compete in demanding foreign markets (Chittoor et al. 2009). It has been shown that firms from developing economies differ from Western firms in how they embark on their internationalisation process (Mathews 2006). A fundamental assumption typical of Western models of international expansion is that the firm in question already possesses the technology and product-related knowledge it needs to cater to the demands of foreign markets, and internationalisation serves to exploit this stock of existing capabilities (Hitt et al. 2006). However, an alternative model suggests that even before to moving into international markets, a firm must upgrade its technological and scientific know-how to be able to offer products commensurate with the more advanced needs of international markets. Due to underdeveloped strategic-factor markets in the domestic space, developing economy firms often face difficulties in acquiring resources to overcome the initial resource hurdle to become globally competitive.[4]

Second, and somewhat related to resource constraints, is what is referred to as 'capability failure', conceptualised as the difficulty in building base capabilities needed to start the catch-up process. According to Lee (2019: 36–37),

> the stark reality is that economic actors, especially firms, have extremely weak levels of capability. In several developing countries, private firms are unable to pursue and conduct in-house R&D, which they consider an uncertain endeavour with uncertain returns. Thus, the problem is not one of less or more R&D but of 'zero' R&D.

While resource disadvantage and capability failure have to do with inherent resource constraints that limit developing economy firms from undertaking second-order organisational change, a third factor is associated with the embeddedness of an organisation within an institutional context. This creates resistance to change, especially for organisations more firmly embedded in existing institutional arrangements. A large body of research on organisational adaptation, anchored in organisational ecology and institutional theories (Hannan and Freeman 1984; Greenwood and Hinings 1996), suggests that close coupling of an organisation with a given institutional context constrains the organisation's ability to adapt to environmental discontinuities, especially if adaptation necessitates an exploratory search of 'alternate routines, technologies, and purposes' from those that existed in the past (Sorenson 2002: 76). Organisations embedded in a set of pre-existing institutionalised beliefs, norms, rules and cognitive systems *imprint* themselves into their structures, policies and practices, and form the basis of how they understand and interpret different situations and environments (Scott 2014).[5] Imprinting often leads to inertia 'because the old organizational rules and routines are enmeshed with the interests and identity of individuals' in entrenched power networks (Nee 2005: 61).

The preceding discussion can be summarised as follows: global institutional change impacts the rules of the game, thus making it difficult for organisations to continue with existing ways of doing business. The way to respond is through the strategic renewal of resources and capabilities, the acquisition of which involves costly and risky exploratory search. However, firms may either not have the resources (resource constraint) or the willingness (embeddedness constraint) to undertake second-order transformation with risky and uncertain outcomes, which together impinges on their ability to adequately respond to external changes. The pertinent question then becomes how these constraints can be overcome or minimised for organisations to adapt to externally imposed institutional changes. We use some of the emerging arguments in the catch-up and

Figure 2.1 The National Institutional System: An Organising Framework

Source: Authors.

institutional logics literature to understand this question. The common element in both these approaches is to look beyond organisational-level adaptation and see the problem within the system in which the firm is embedded. We call this the 'national institutional system', which includes the state, the field or sector to which an organisation belongs, and the organisation itself. We suggest that the multi-level system with possibilities of inter-institutional interactions has implications for second-order learning needed to respond to global institutional changes and achieve global competitive advantage. The main components of this analytical framework are summarised in Figure 2.1, which are elaborated upon in the subsequent sections.

National Institutional System

In addition to the accumulation and assimilation mechanisms discussed previously, the literature also emphasises the key role played by a wide range of institutions in developing an infrastructure to support and orient innovation in organisations (Coriat and Weinstein 2002; Nelson 2008). Common institutions supporting the development and maintenance of this innovation infrastructure include the financial system, industry associations, technical societies, universities, legal institutions, public policy groups, and organisational structures that facilitate firms in learning and undertaking innovation activities (Nelson 2005). However, Malerba and Nelson (2011) also foreground differences across sectors in terms of respective sources of competitive advantage (for example, scale and scope, vertical linkages, intellectual property protection, and so on), and thus point out the need for sector-specific public policy instruments and regulatory regimes. In recent work, Lee and Malerba (2018) and Malerba and Lee (2021) adapt the underlying mechanisms of the national innovation system in the context of catch-up by developing economies and suggest that 'domestic firms' capability building must go hand in hand with system factors (national and sectoral)' (Lee and Malerba 2018: 174).[6] The overall objective of national and sectoral systems is to make institutional resources available to domestic organisations to incentivise them to pursue firm-level innovation and capability-development activities, and these institutional resources include direct financial and technological support, as well as a facilitating regulatory environment (for example, strong intellectual property protection regime, ease of access to global product and resource markets, and filling institutional voids in labour, product and capital markets, among others) (Malerba and Lee 2018; Khanna and Palepu 1997).

Based on the aforementioned literature, our proposed sector-specific National Institutional System is comprised of organisations, their respective industry sectors, and states as three levels of institutions.[7] Our argument is that the interaction of these three eventually determines success in navigating global institutional changes. An important point to note here is that much of the literature on national innovation systems takes a static approach in the sense that it is assumed that organisations' ability to innovate is dependent upon the existing state of development in the innovation infrastructure, and organisations adapt to the given state of things. One point of departure of our framework is that we see the whole national system being influenced by global institutional changes. That is, instead of just assuming that global institutional changes impact local organisations that then adapt to institutional discontinuities based on the given state of national and sectoral resources, our framework explicitly allows higher-level institutions to respond to external pressures. Such an approach accomplishes two things. First, it incorporates the evolutionary perspective, which suggests that the effective deployment of capabilities by developing economy firms involves the coevolution of technologies employed, industry structure and broader economic institutions (Nelson 2008). Second, and more importantly, by examining how global institutional changes separately impact each of the three institutional levels, we can identify the types of institutional complexity emerging at each level and their implications for coping with these changes.

Institutional Complexity and Competing Logics

To understand institutional complexity at the three levels, we use the literature describing the concept of institutional logics. According to Thornton, Ocasio and Lounsbury (2012: 2), the 'institutional logics perspective is a metatheoretical framework for analysing the interrelationships among institutions, individuals, and organizations in social systems. It aids researchers in questions on how individual and organizational actors are influenced by their situation in multiple social locations in an inter-institutional system'. The institutional logics perspective has been used to explain the creation, maintenance and sustenance of organising principles of a particular realm of social life. These aspects are defined as 'the socially constructed, historical patterns of material practices, assumptions, values, beliefs, and rules by which individuals produce and reproduce their material subsistence, organize time and space, and provide meaning to their social reality' (Thornton and Ocasio 1999: 804). The literature views these organising principles manifesting at multiple levels (Besharov and Smith 2014; Thornton 2004), and institutional theorists have identified how several key institutions, such as the capitalist market, the bureaucratic state, corporations, professions, community, family and religion, are each guided by their own institutional logics (Friedland and Alford 1991; Thornton, Ocasio and Lounsbury 2012).

Our interest in this study is on three hierarchically ordered institutions (that is, state, industry [field] and organisations) and the associated logics relevant in the context of global institutional change. In most economies, the state plays a role in coordinating economic activity and possesses 'extraordinary constitutive powers to define the nature, capacity, and rights enjoyed by political and economic actors, including collective actors' (Scott 2014: 120). In particular, when an internally consistent and well-established system of formal market institutions is absent (that is, when institutional voids are present), the functioning of the economy and the behaviour of organisations are coordinated by the state, which provides alternative mechanisms or encourages their development to fill the absence of market-supporting institutions (Hu, Cui and Aulakh 2019). The state, as a national-level institution, has its own logic, defined as the 'basic orientation of the state in securing social and political order' (Greenwood et al., 2010: 523) that guides the behaviour of organisational actors and manifests itself in issues such as the organisation and institutionalisation of private economic activity (Jackson and Deeg 2008), the degree and scope of government intervention (Nee and Opper 2007), competition and cooperation amongst economic actors (Hall and Soskice 2001), and the composition and transformation of market participants (Whitley 1999), among others.

The intermediate-level institution in our framework is the industry associated with a given organisation.[8] An organisational field has been defined as 'a recognized area of institutional life: key suppliers of resources and customers of products, regulatory agencies and other organizations that produce similar services or products' (DiMaggio and Powell 1983: 148) or as 'the existence of a community of organizations that partakes of a common meaning system and whose participants interact more freely and fatefully with one another than with actors outside of their field' (Scott 1994: 207–208). Existing research considers this level to be the most important in institutional analysis because the 'nature and extent of institutional complexity facing organizations is fundamentally shaped by the structure of the organizational fields within which they are located ... [and] it is also at this level that referent audiences, such as accreditation agencies and professional associations, are especially active' (Greenwood et al. 2011: 334). Examples of different industry logics studied in prior research include editorial and market logics in the publishing industry (Thornton and Ocasio 1999), market and state logics in the Islamic banking sector (Gumusay, Smets and Morris 2020), and the left-leaning and conservative logics of labour unions in the global apparel industry (Anner 2009), among others. Our framework incorporates industry (or sector) as the field-level institution.[9]

Overcoming Resource and Embeddedness Constraints in the National Institutional System

Countries that have succeeded in growing the competitiveness and scale of their manufacturing sectors have adopted different policy approaches. However, a common element in their approaches has been a close coordination between producers and government policymakers, with governments playing an active role in providing incentives for domestic industrial growth and in relieving constraints on industrial competitiveness.

—*Twelfth Five Year Plan, 2012–2017* (Government of India 2012: 55)

India's manufacturing ... strategy must be built around three components. The first are *capabilities and processes* that go across many, if not all sectors.... The second component has to be the plans to *strengthen the performance of selected sectors*. The selection of these sectors is done by a combination of top-down and bottom-up analysis.... Sector strategies should be formulated jointly by the associations of producers in the sector... and relevant government departments.... The third ... component ... is the *institutional ability for effective consultation and collaboration* between producers and public policy makers....

—*Twelfth Five Year Plan, 2012–2017* (Government of India 2012: 57–58, italics in original)

How does the proposed national institutional system overcome the resource and embeddedness constraints of developing economy firms in their pursuit of second-order change to cope with institutional change? We suggest that the national institutional system works in two fundamental ways. First, the system can either directly provide resources to domestic organisations to upgrade their capabilities or indirectly facilitate access to the needed resources through regulations that ease their international flows. Second, inter-institutional interactions within the system can overcome embeddedness constraints. However, the necessary conditions for the two mechanisms to work are (*a*) the coordination of responses to external pressures between the state, industry associations and organisations (as reflected in the aforementioned extracts from India's policy document) and (*b*) the presence of some form of compatibility in the means and/or ends of dealing with institutional complexity at the three levels (Besharov and Smith 2014). We elaborate on these in the following section.

Organisational-Level Competing Logics

A starting observation is that externally initiated institutional change creates complexity not only at the organisational level but also at higher-order societal and field levels (Greenwood et al. 2011; Thornton, Ocasio and Lounsbury 2012). We have previously discussed how external institutional change related to economic liberalisation in developing economies and their global integration necessitates organisational-level strategic renewal through distant search, which is limited because of resource and embeddedness constraints. The latter can also be understood within the framework of institutional complexity and competing institutional logics because the conundrum facing these organisations is whether to continue with proximate search (that is, refining existing capabilities and competing in similar foreign markets, often referred to as 'exploitation') or pursue distant search (that is, developing new capabilities and competing in advanced country markets, or 'exploration'). While the former enables a firm to refine its existing knowledge and enhance its expertise regarding existing products and markets, the latter involves a higher-order capability to identify, evaluate and incorporate knowledge about new product/customer domains into the firm (Rosenkopf and Nerkar 2001; Danneels 2002). A problem arises, however, because of an inherent paradox in their relationship: while excessive focus on any one mode of search is detrimental, it is palpably difficult for organisations to simultaneously execute both (Levinthal and March 1993). The threat of obsolescence due to excessive exploitation and the risk of short-term failure due to a singular focus on exploration point towards the need to pursue both strategies. However, these search strategies appear to be not only internally inconsistent in their requirement of facilitating structures and systems but also competing in nature in that they tend to drive each other out (March 1991). In their pursuit of maintaining or attaining competitiveness in global markets in the light of institutional changes, the organisational challenge for developing economy firms is thus to deal with institutional complexity arising from competing logics of local versus distant search.

State-Level Competing Logics

Global institutional changes also engender institutional complexity for the state. For instance, external pressures have led numerous countries to undergo institutional transitions encompassing fundamental changes in norms and values underlying economic and political systems, legal and regulatory frameworks and financial infrastructure (Newman 2000). Erstwhile socialist economies have moved from redistributive to market focus (Nee 1989), market economies of developed countries have shifted away from the principles of the welfare state (McLaughlin, Osborne and Ferlie 2002), and other countries have adopted political and economic reforms to deregulate, liberalise and globalise their economies (Hoskisson et al. 2000). These changes in the national economic systems bring about institutional complexity for the state because the objectives and the means to achieve them often lead to the emergence of logics different from the ones previously prevalent. In redistributive economies, for instance, 'goods and services are collected and distributed from a centre in accordance with the customs, regulations, ideology, and ad hoc decisions of those social groups that hold redistributive power.... [The] institutional logic of redistributive economies differs substantively from market economies where goods are exchanged directly between buyer and sellers' (Nee 1996: 909). Relatedly, state-owned organisations and private enterprises have their respective operating logics, and the substantive presence of both in an economy creates complexity for the state in terms of resource allocation, competition policy, public versus private goods, and so on (Hu, Cui and Aulakh 2019; Kornai 1979; Nee 1989).

In the context of this study, the two global institutional changes in the textile and pharmaceutical industries shifted the bases of global competition for each industry (that is, production efficiency in the former and product innovation in the latter). This, in turn, brought about new institutional logics that were fundamentally different from the prevalent norms under which the two industries operated (that is, employment in the textile and affordable drugs in the pharmaceutical industry). Thus, although the overall objective of the state had been to ensure that the two industries remain globally competitive, the new means for achieving this objective (that is, increased economic efficiency) were in conflict with those prior to (that is, welfare) the externally imposed institutional changes.

Industry-Level Competing Logics

The field, or industry, is also impacted by global institutional changes as an intermediate-level institution between the national or state and local organisations. A nation's economy is composed of different sectors (which could be categorised broadly, such as agriculture, manufacturing and services) or more specifically in terms of industries (for example, mining, pharmaceuticals, textiles, steel, and so on), and the overall performance of the economy on different parameters (for example, gross domestic product, employment, productivity, trade competitiveness, and so on) is determined by the performance of its different sectors. Thus, the importance or 'weight' of a sector in a national economy is determined by its relative contribution to these aggregate quantitative measures. In addition, an industry can also have a 'voice' in a country's economic policy because of its strategic (for example, national or food security) and/or socioeconomic (for example, regional development, employment access) role in the economy. The weight and voice of an industry allow it to have, through its representative associations or trade bodies, a greater influence in shaping public policy.[10]

Global institutional changes have the potential to influence the weights and voices of the specific sectors, which in turn impacts the attention they receive from the state.[11] Therefore, the industry objective in response to externally induced changes is to maintain or enhance its weight and voice in the country's economy. However, institutional changes can provide opportunities for an industry in terms of easier access to global resources and product markets and fewer regulatory constraints, among others. These, along with a new basis of competition, lead to the intrusion of new industry logics. At the industry level, therefore, organic (that is, domestic resources and markets) and inorganic (that is, international resources and markets) mechanisms of growth are present, and often these can compete with each other, given the vehicles through which these are implemented. International resource and market access in developing economy industries often entail becoming part of established global production or value-chain networks or through inward foreign direct investment. In these cases, although the industry can achieve second-order transformation and maintain its weight in the economy, it could lose its voice because it may have to sacrifice its social or welfare contributions as the condition of entry into existing global networks.[12]

Managing Competing Logics in the National Institutional System

In the preceding paragraphs, we identified the sources of institutional complexity at the three levels and specific institutional logics that emerge at each level and which are often competing with pre-existing ones. The literature from different contexts provides some guidance as to how institutional actors manage competing logics, and we use some of this literature to propose how these can be adapted in the context of the current study. Much of this work examines the response to institutional complexity and the resolution of associated competing institutional logics at a single level of analysis, primarily at the organisational and field levels. In this regard, two approaches have been considered, structural and strategic (Greenwood et al. 2011). The structural approach assumes that competing logics are necessary for the functioning of the organisation/field and, therefore, both should be adopted. However, their underlying characteristics make it difficult for simultaneous adoption. An example of this conundrum is the accommodation of exploration and exploitation as alternate search behaviours to deal with external discontinuities discussed previously. Organisational responses entail the continued exploitation of existing assets while starting an exploration of new assets. However, due to implicit tensions, it is difficult for a firm to accomplish a balance. Exploratory behaviours, which are characterised by discovery, experimentation and risk-taking, are fundamentally different from exploitative behaviours characterised by refinement and efficiency (Cheng and Van de Ven 1996). Exploitation's reliance on existing routines impedes adjustment to novel situations and forecloses a firm's ability to perceive new strategic options (Cyert and March 1992). The structural approach to this dilemma suggests task partitioning, temporal detachment and separation of the organisation into disparate, unconnected business units as a way to resolve the tension (Duncan 1976; Christensen 1997) with different units either focusing on variation-reducing processes within the scope of the current strategy or on variation-inducing processes outside the prevailing strategy (Burgelman 1991, 2002; He and Wong 2004; March and Simon 1958).

Structural separation to accommodate competing logics involves redesigning an organisation into specialised units. Examples of such separation include spinoffs in high-tech firms to manage exploitation and exploration (Christensen 1997) or matrix structures in multinational corporations to manage the dual needs of efficiency and adaptability to compete in global markets (Bartlett and Ghoshal 1989). These structural solutions require high resource commitments, thus making this approach difficult for firms from developing economies, especially if they do not have the scale (size) to develop complex organisational structures. Structural separation in the developing economy context is more probable at the state- and field-level institutions. The state plays an important role in directing and coordinating economic activities in quite a few economies, especially in developing countries. This form of state participation, referred to as 'state capitalism', is defined as melding 'powers of the state with powers of capitalism. It depends on the government to pick winners and promote economic growth. However, it also uses capitalist tools such as listing [state-owned enterprises] on the stock market and embracing globalization' (*The Economist*, 2012:3). Similarly, Musacchio and Lazzarini (2012: 3) view 'state capitalism as the widespread influence of the government in the economy, either by owning majority or minority positions in companies or through the provision of subsidized credit and/or other privileges to private companies'. Differences in state capitalisms across developing economies (as reflected in relative support for public- versus private-sector firms) (Musacchio, Lazzarini and Aguilera 2015) and in the political context within which the state interacts with organisational actors (as reflected in a unitary-versus-pluralistic political system) (Kohli 2004) lead to unique state logics that inform organisations' practices and behaviours.

In their typology, Musachhio, Lazzarini and Aguilera (2015) differentiate types of state capitalism in terms of government ownership and the control of organisations. At one extreme are state-owned enterprises (SOEs), which are directly funded by governments and are usually established to fulfil developmental goals. At the other extreme are private organisations, which operate independently of the state but potentially receive indirect support through preferential capital access, tax breaks and subsidies. Between these two extremes, governments can also participate in economic activities by being the majority or minority investors in different organisations. Apart from the level of ownership and control, state capitalism can be distinguished in terms of the importance of SOEs and private enterprises as engines of economic growth (Kohli 2004). For instance, in erstwhile communist economies in Eastern Europe, SOEs were the primary vehicles of economic growth. The SOEs received monopolies in different sectors, and their goals were to pursue import-substitution industrialisation and to fulfil the welfare goals of the state without being subjected to internal and external competition. In contrast, the South Korean economic growth model of the 1960s and 1970s relied on the private sector as the engine of growth. According to Kohli (2004: 13), South Korea's growth model encompassed a 'realization that maximizing production requires assuring the profitability of efficient producers but not inefficient ones'. Such a growth model is more 'pro-capitalist' rather than 'ideologically pro-market'. In both types of growth models, domestic firms were promoted through direct and indirect state support, limitations on international (through trade barriers and investment restrictions) and domestic (through sector monopolies) competition to cushion their economic functioning, and encouragement and support of inter-organisational relationships through the formation of business groups. These cases are examples of structural separation within a given sector (that is, some organisations are expected to fulfil the welfare function while others are encouraged to be globally competitive through an increase in efficiency) or across sectors (that is, assigning specific roles for the whole industry, for example, generating employment or generating exports). In economies where the state coordinates economic activities, field-level institutions adhere to the expectations of the state and adopt logics compatible with the expectations, that is, activities are focused on the specialised role accorded to the sector or organisations within that sector.

The strategic approach, on the other hand, sees the resolution of institutional complexity through a contestation within the organisation for the primacy of one logic over the other. Seen through the lens of intra-organisational power dynamics and resource dependencies (Oliver 1991), this approach sees the adoption of the institutional logic supported by the dominant group with more voice and power (Pache and Santos 2010). In the context of exploratory search and adaptation to institutional changes, Greenwood and Hinings (1996: 1038) posit that 'organizationally defined groups vary in their ability to influence organizational change because they have differential power. Some groups or individuals are listened to more keenly than others. Some have more potential or less potential for enabling or resisting change'. Moreover, '… when members of an organization have diverse interests, organizational outcomes depend heavily on internal politics, on the balance of power among the constituencies' (Hannan and Freeman 1984: 151). Although institutional complexity is resolved at the level of the organisation, this approach nonetheless sees possibilities of inter-institutional alignments. According to Greenwood et al. (2011: 349), the 'response of an organization to competing logics … is partly a function of how logics are given voice within the organization; but the ability of a voice to be heard is linked to the influence of that logic's field-level proponents over resources—including legitimacy—that they control'. We believe this inter-institutional-level approach is highly relevant in the context of our study.

The underlying assumption in managing complexity in an inter-institutional system is that 'institutions operate at multiple levels of analysis and that actors are nested in higher-order levels—individual, organizational, field, and societal' (Thornton, Ocasio and Lounsbury 2012: 13) because of which there are possibilities of interaction and coordinated action between actors at different levels.

Furthermore, levels of hierarchy and multiple domains play important roles in devising ways to deal with competing logics, as they may facilitate the division of labour and allocation of resources in a manner that allows oppositional forces to be reconciled (Gupta, Smith and Shalley 2006). In this regard, Besharov and Smith (2014) identify compatibility in the means and ends of competing logics as an important determinant of an organisation's ability to reconcile, accommodate and adopt multiple logics. Defining compatibility 'as the extent to which the instantiations of logics imply consistent and reinforceable organizational actions', Besharov and Smith (2014: 367) argue that consistency regarding goals of competing logics is more important than means, 'because goals reflect core values and beliefs … [which] are hard to challenge or modify. In contrast, means are evaluated based on a logic of consequence and are therefore more malleable'. These arguments regarding the compatibility of logics at the organisational level can be extended to the inter-institutional level.

As discussed before and summarised in Figure 2.1, global institutional changes that are the focus of this study influenced the three levels of the national institutional system, introduced new logics at each level and triggered searches for ways to respond to the externally imposed new rules of the game for competing in international markets. In search of adequate responses, the goal at each level (that is, state, industry and organisations) was to achieve competitiveness in global markets, and, in that sense, there was compatibility with the goals of the three levels. However, the means to achieve this were less compatible because of different competing logics at each level (that is, balancing distance versus local search at the organisation level, organic and inorganic growth at the field level, and efficiency and welfare at the level of the state). Interactions between levels can allow for malleability in means. For instance, it was argued before that organisational adoption of second-order change is hampered by resource and embeddedness constraints. Given that the state's goals are tied to local organisations' ability to undertake risky and distant search, it may be willing to provide the resources to organisations for this search, thereby influencing the latter's ability and motivation for adopting the newer logics necessitated by global institutional change. Similarly, field-level institutions, as intermediaries between organisations and the state, can play multiple roles at both ends to bring about compatibility in the means to achieve common goals. At the field level, industry associations can use a combination of acquiescence (that is, complying with the state's policy expectations) and manipulation (that is, shaping the state's policies) to effectively deal with institutional processes (Oliver 1991). This can take the form of negotiating access to resources for organisations within the industry or, more importantly, through favourable regulations that facilitate second-order organisational change. Furthermore, as suggested by Papapioannou et. al. (2006:76), 'industry associations as key intermediary actors' shape industry development through 'evolutionary processes of conflict, negotiation and knowledge diffusion'. The ability to use inter-institutional interactions for the resolution of competing logics and/or the adoption of one logic over the other will eventually depend upon the relative power of constituents in the national institutional system as well as the structure of the industry.

Conclusion

The main premise of the current study is that global institutional change introduces new rules of global competition and thus has the potential to disrupt not only organisations' competitive advantages but also the trade positions of nation states. Responding to or coping with externally imposed changes necessarily entails a coordinated effort at various levels, which we term the 'national institutional system', comprising the state, the field or industry, and organisations. Drawing from various theoretical perspectives dealing with institutional change, institutional logics, catch-up and emerging market firm internationalisation, we propose an organising framework to allow us to understand the different processes and interactions in play within the institutional system. We have elaborated on some possibilities of adaptation to global institutional change at intra- and inter-institutional levels. In the following chapters, we dig deeper into the three levels of the national institutional system for India's textile and pharmaceutical industries. We compare and contrast the ways through which the system worked for each industry.

Notes

1. There are definitional distinctions about institutions across various theorists. The purpose here is not to delve into these and choose one definition over the other. A common aspect from the various elaborations in the literature that is used in the current study is that institutions denote some norms or rules of game.
2. Research has focused on economic reforms through privatisation in former Soviet bloc countries as well through market liberalisation in countries in Asia, Africa and South America.
3. Asset augmentation as the primary motivator for developing economy firms' aggressive international expansion speed and paths has also been shown in the new theoretical models of 'springboard' (Luo and Tung 2007) and 'linkage-leverage-learning' (Mathews 2006).

4. Underdevelopment of factor markets in developing economies is often attributed to institutional voids or lack of market-supporting institutions. Such voids then give rise to various non-market alternatives that coordinate economic activities, such as the economic planning mechanisms of the state (Kohli 2004; Nee and Opper 2007), the informal institutions supporting relationship-based (as opposed to rule-based) transactions (Peng 2003), and business groups as an organisational form that internalises transactions (Khanna and Yafeh 2007). In subsequent chapters, we examine how some of these alternative sources influence organisational adaptation in the two industries of interest.

5. Imprinting and its impact on inertia have been observed in organisational forms such as business groups (Gubbi, Aulakh and Ray 2015), business systems (Whitley 199) and market-coordination mechanisms (Hall and Soskice 2001).

6. While firms are embedded in broad institutional contexts, they are also simultaneously connected with quasi-level institutions, which affect their ability to appropriate institutional resources. In the context of developing economies, however, certain unique organisational forms such as business groups could act as supra-firm institutions, substituting for some of the functions that are typically provided by stand-alone institutions in developed economies (Mahmood and Mitchell 2004; Chang, Chung and Mahmood 2006). Similarly, organisations could be part of geographical clusters that provide access to resources and know-how. We consider the influence of these two quasi-institutions on organisational responses to institutional changes in Chapter 5. However, given the idiosyncratic nature of these institutions to specific national contexts, we do not include these in the more general framework proposed here.

7. Our proposed system differs from the National Innovation System (NIS) that has been prevalent in the innovation literature (see Watkins et al. 2015 for a review) in the sense that it can accommodate different types of objectives beyond just innovation. As an example, the two industries under consideration in the current study have different innovation imperatives. While the strategic renewal in the pharmaceutical industry entails innovation activities, that in the textile industry necessitates competitive actions that go beyond innovation.

8. In institutional theory, this is the intermediate level of institution (that is, above organisational level but below national or state level) and is often referred to as a 'field' (Greenwood et al. 2011). Among catch-up scholars, the equivalent is a 'sector' (Malerba and Lee 2021).

9. Much of the empirical research on institutional logics is at the field level, often operationalised in terms of an industry. For instance, research has examined the emergence and reconciliation of multiple logics in the global mobile industry, health care industries in various countries, and financial sectors, among others (for a review of this research, see Greenwood et al. 2011: Table 1, 325–331).

10. The literature on weight and voice has its origins in understanding power dynamics in organisations that are structurally separated into different units, or are part of a network or a business group, each vying for attention and resources from the centralised coordinating body. The underlying argument is that a sub-unit's weight and voice is a source of power that it can leverage to access critical resources (Bouquet and Birkinshaw 2008). This logic can be applied to the country level as well where different sectors are vying for the state's attention.

11. A case in point is India's automobile industry. During the import-substitution industrialisation regime, the domestic auto industry was considered strategic because of its technological base and network externalities potential. Accordingly, it had influence in shaping India's trade policies. However, economic liberalisation in 1991 opened up the auto sector to foreign players, including through equity joint ventures. The domestic players rapidly lost their influence in shaping policy, and the Indian industry now has a substantial presence of foreign companies, some through joint ventures with Indian partners.

12. These aspects are discussed in more detail in Chapter 4.

3

National Policy Choices

The global institutional changes initiated in 1995 and implemented in 2005 impacted India's pharmaceutical and textile industries, both of which were of immense strategic importance to the Indian economy. To sustain these industries and improve their competitiveness under new institutional regimes, successive Indian governments have initiated numerous policies that continue to evolve. The purpose of this chapter is to outline the industry-specific policy initiatives promulgated to cope with global institutional changes. However, to understand the underlying logics and the various components of the policy choices, one has to look at the national institutional context within which these industries historically evolved prior to 1995, as the respective trajectory of each industry in the previous periods impacted the policy constraints and opportunities in dealing with global institutional changes. Accordingly, before detailing the post-1995 policy initiatives, this chapter first discusses the historical context of these industries, especially in relation to policy regimes. Given their importance to the Indian economy, each of these industries has been extensively studied by numerous scholars, and these studies have critically evaluated numerous policy interventions over the years. The purpose of this chapter is to highlight the broad and evolving thrust of policy choices in a comparative framework rather than attempt to be comprehensive in detailing all policy interventions before or after global institutional changes impact each industry.[1] The chapter divides the policy regimes into four periods: (*a*) import substitution industrialisation, 1947–1985; (*b*) economic liberalisation, 1985–1995; (*c*) preparing for global institutional change, 1995–2005; and (*d*) coping with global institutional change, 2005–2020. After discussing the evolving policy choices in each of these periods regarding their applicability to the two industries, these choices are placed within an appropriate industrial policy framework. This framework will then guide analyses in subsequent chapters in terms of the impact of policy interventions on the evolution of the two industries and the implications of firm strategic choices within each industry in response to the two global institutional changes.

Import Substitution Industrialisation and the Licence Raj (1947–1985)

Akin to much of the developing world, India followed an import-substitution industrialisation model for economic growth for almost forty years after its independence from the British in 1947 (Kohli 2004). This model was implemented through state-directed development, whereby state-owned enterprises dominated industrial sectors which required high levels of capital investments. India's first prime minister, Jawaharlal Nehru, termed these public sector enterprises 'the temples of modern India'. On the other hand, the private sector participated in a few sectors that were protected from foreign competition through a variety of restrictions related to inward foreign direct investment (FDI), tariff and non-tariff barriers and onerous administrative requirements. This period is often referred to as the 'licence raj' (Chittoor and Aulakh 2015). The logic of 'self-reliance' and 'redistribution' pervaded much of the policy decisions during this period, including those aimed at the pharmaceutical and textile industries. The availability of and accessibility to affordable drugs were the primary objectives for the pharmaceutical industry, while increased employment, especially in rural regions and amongst historically marginalised segments of society, underlaid the policies for the textile industry.

Pharmaceutical Industry: For the pharmaceutical industry, the immediate need after independence in 1947 was the ability to meet local demands for essential drugs. The government undertook a few initiatives by setting up a number of public sector units (PSUs), such as Hindustan Antibiotics Limited and Indian Drugs and Pharmaceuticals Limited (Joseph 2016), to meet this demand. However, given the limited production capacity of these state-owned enterprises, the government also provided incentives to multinational corporations to set up manufacturing facilities in India. Foreign companies imported their patented bulk drugs into India, which were then processed and sold locally. This process had two implications for India. First, the prices of these drugs were relatively high, thus making them inaccessible to a vast majority of Indian consumers. Second, foreign multinationals acquired a dominating position in India and held almost an 80 per cent share of the market by 1970. Thus, the policies produced neither increased self-reliance for India, as there were bulk drug imports that continued to drain the limited foreign exchange reserves, nor enhanced accessibility to cheap drugs for Indian consumers. This situation led to important policy interventions in this industry in 1970, and two landmark legislations shaped the development of the industry over the next two decades (for more details, see Ramanna 2002; Pingali and Chatterjee 2015; Joseph 2016).

The Patents Act of 1970 was based on the objectives that the 'patents are granted to encourage inventions and to secure that the inventions are worked in India on a commercial scale ... [and] are not granted merely to enable patentees to enjoy a monopoly for the importation of the patented article' (Section 83 of the Patents Act, 1970). It further allowed for compulsory licensing and the use of patents in the country on considerations of public interest. Section 5 of the act provided for 'process patenting' for inventions relating to 'substances intended for use, or capable of being used, as food or as medicine or drug, or substances prepared or produced by chemical processes'. This clause provided legal sanctions to process patents for pharmaceutical products (Racherla 2019; Raghavan 2006). That is, instead of granting patents to end products, as was done in developed countries, this act allowed patents for the manufacturing process. Indian companies could produce the same molecules that were under product patent in other countries at a fraction of the original costs by simply altering the manufacturing process. The act also reduced the period of patent protection to between five and seven years from the earlier period of sixteen years and allowed for compulsory licensing after three years of the patent. This act, in combination with increased public investments in research and development (R&D), emphasis on the production of bulk drugs, and restrictions on the size of pharmaceutical firms through the monopolistic practices act, helped to encourage the entry and growth of private Indian pharmaceutical firms (Joseph 2016). These firms used 'reverse engineering' to produce drugs at a fraction of the costs and established a strong domestic market position (that is, the market share of the domestic Indian pharmaceutical sector went from 20 per cent in 1970 to 52 per cent in 1980 and almost 80 per cent in 2006 (Narayanan G. 1984; Haley and Haley 2012)).

In addition to indigenising local production, the government also wanted to ensure accessibility to these drugs. Accordingly, the Drug Price Control Order (DPCO) of 1970 was passed with the purpose of controlling drug prices so that they were within reach of the average consumer. This drug order hoped to balance the welfare of consumers and producers by reducing the prices of essential drugs while also ensuring reasonable profits for the growth of the industry. The former was achieved by the government acquiring the rights to fix the maximum selling prices of eighteen essential bulk drugs and freezing the sale prices of other bulk drugs at the level that prevailed immediately before the issue of the order. Reasonable profits for the manufacturing firms were ensured by allowing the inclusion of various costs (for example, prices of materials, conversion cost from bulk to formulations, packing charges, mark-up, excise duty and sales tax) in the calculation of the retail price of a formulation.

The aforementioned policy interventions were further strengthened in the following years to foster more self-reliance in drug manufacturing and keep the drug prices accessible.[2] Related measures included the discouragement of the import of bulk drugs by multinational corporations through onerous foreign exchange regulations and restrictive equity ownership, the inclusion of a greater number of drugs categorised under the 'essential' category and thus subject to price controls, and the encouragement of local firms to produce generic drugs for both domestic consumption and exports (which had been facilitated by regulatory change in the United States (US) under the 1984 Hatch–Waxman Act) (Joseph 2016; Sahay and Gordhan 2008). Because of a combination of these policy interventions, the two decades after 1970 witnessed an exponential growth of the Indian pharmaceutical industry, with a compounded annual growth rate (CAGR) of over 14 per cent between 1970 and 1994 (CRIS INFAC 2004).

Textile Industry: While much of the pharmaceutical industry developed in India after the country's independence, the textile industry played an important role in the country's economic history and underwent a structural transformation during British colonial rule. In essence, the traditional handloom industry declined because of colonial trade policies and competition from English machine-made textiles that started at the beginning of the nineteenth century. From a less than 1 per cent share of the Indian market in 1820, British textiles increased their share to more than 60 per cent by 1890 (Broadberry and Gupta 2009). A nascent but important indigenous textile mill industry developed in western India during the first half of the twentieth century, particularly during the war years when international trade was disrupted. According to Kohli (2004: 253), World War I 'enhanced India's strategic importance in British global designs and suggested that continued defence and other public expenditures required new sources of revenue. Since the land revenue could not be increased readily ... the state sought instead to get revenue by taxing imports....' A number of domestic industries, including textiles, received import protection, which gave a 'boost to the emerging Indian industry right through the end of the second World War' (Chittoor and Aulakh 2005: 292).

Thus, in 1947, an independent India inherited a textile industry consisting of a large unorganised handloom sector composed of small-scale units spread across the country and an organised sector of industrial mills set up through the import of modern technology. However, the long period of neglect by the colonial rulers of the former sector had become a political issue during the nationalist struggle, and this played an important role in policy choices made by the Indian government after independence. As argued by Kohli (2004: 269),

> the issue of the destruction of small-scale household-based textile production at the hands of modern textiles played a central role in India's nationalist imagination. With this political inheritance, it would have been very difficult to unleash modern textile manufacturing against small-scale production. Add to this [were the government's] socialist proclivities, which inclined [it] to argue in favour of producing cheap cloth for mass consumption.

Thus, until the 1980s, textile policies in India were geared to protect small-scale producers at the expense of the industrial sector.[3]

The policy to protect the handloom sector took many forms: a large number of textile products were reserved for production by firms in the handloom sector; restrictions were put on capacity expansion in the organised sector, which included mills and power looms; and the import of technology was discouraged through high tariff and non-tariff barriers. In addition, the government put price controls on the outputs of this sector to provide subsidised inputs for the handloom sector. The government then went further and nationalised a large number of private mills in 1974 to curb the role of the organised textile sector in India's economic growth (for extended analysis, see Kohli 2004; Desai 1983; Ganesh 2002). In the meantime, government policy had to deal with the Multi-Fibre Agreement (MFA) on textiles in 1974, under the auspices of the General Agreement on Tariffs and Trade (GATT). The MFA initiated a quota regime whereby international trade between developed and developing countries was to be guided through bilateral quotas negotiated between the countries concerning what and how much could be exported from developing countries to individual Western markets. The objective of this agreement was to protect the textile and apparel producers in developed countries who were losing market shares in their domestic markets to low-cost producers from the Global South (Yoffie 1983).

Most of the policy interventions in the Indian textile industry up until the 1980s were thus guided by the need to protect the small-scale sector and effectively allocate the country quotas to various segments of the organised and unorganised sectors. Since the competition for these quotas was intra-country, rather than inter-country, there was not much attempt made to increase the productivity of the domestic textile industry. The main aim was to protect the handloom sector and ensure a cheap supply of materials to this sector from the largely nationalised mill sector.

Economic Liberalisation (1985–1995)

By the early 1980s, the limitations of the import-substitution industrialisation policy of the previous four decades had become clear to the Indian government, as '[n]either state-led growth nor political efforts at redistribution and poverty alleviation' had proven to be successful (Kohli 2004: 279). Domestic production capacity in various industries, including the pharmaceutical and textile sectors, was not enough to meet the growing domestic demand. Although the much-heralded economic liberalisation and the associated pro-market orientation were formally introduced in 1991, the mechanisms through which future development was to be accomplished started taking shape in the mid-1980s when successive Indian governments moved towards promoting economic growth over redistributing policy objectives (Kohli 2004; Rodrick and Subramaniun 2005). This transformation was implemented through a pro-business orientation that focused 'on raising the profitability of the established industrial and commercial establishments' and 'tended to favor incumbents and producers' (Rodrick and Subramanian 2005: 195).[4]

Pharmaceutical Industry: To increase the availability of quality drugs to meet domestic demand, a new drug policy was initiated in 1986 under the title 'Measures for Rationalisation, Quality Control and Growth of Drugs Pharmaceuticals Industry in India'; this policy had the objectives of (*a*) ensuring abundant availability at reasonable prices of essential and life-saving and prophylactic medicines; (*b*) strengthening the system of quality control over drug production; (*c*) creating an environment conducive to channelising new investment into the pharmaceutical industry to encourage cost-effective production with economic sizes; and (*d*) introducing new technologies and new drugs (Government of India, Drug Policy 1986). Major reforms were initiated to achieve these objectives, including the abolition of licensing requirements for all bulk drugs, the easing of importing rules for intermediate products, the allowing of 51 per cent foreign investments in Indian drug firms, and streamlining the drug price control system. These policies reflected an attempt to wean the economy away from the 'self-sufficiency' of import-substitution industrialisation to achieve growth of the domestic industry, even if doing so entailed a dependence on foreign technology and know-how. Furthermore, Indian pharmaceutical firms in the private sector were seen as the engine through which the policy objectives could be met.

Textile Industry: While a lack of appropriate indigenous know-how was the reason behind the pharmaceutical industry's inability to meet local demand, the low production capacity of the small-scale handloom sector in the textile industry was seen as the reason for the unmet demand. The government made a major shift in its Textile Policy of 1985. According to the policy document,

> 'the multiplicity of objectives has inhibited the achievements of the main task of the textile industry, that is to increases the production of cloth at reasonable prices to meet the clothing requirements of a growing population. Henceforth, the approach to the textile industry would be guided by this main objective.... [I]n pursuit of this main objective, the employment potential of the industry shall be kept in view. (Textile Policy of 1985, cited in Srinivasulu, 1996: 3199)

The new policy sought to increase the efficiency of the sector through the removal of capacity restrictions on industrial mills. Furthermore, the government provided cheap lines of credit and reduced import controls to allow industry technology modernisation through the use of foreign textile machinery.[5]

To protect the handloom industry, with its vast employment potential, the government passed a parallel act, namely the Handloom (Reservation of Articles for Production) Act of 1985, which promised to preserve the distinctive and unique role of handlooms and accordingly reserved twenty-two varieties of textile products for exclusive production in this sector (Srinivasulu 1996). The overall effect of both the new textile policy and the handloom act was to the benefit of the power loom sector, which increased its production of fabric from 5,886 million metres in 1985–1986 to 13,338 million metres in 1990–1991. The mill sector remained flat during these years, while the production of handlooms saw slower growth from 3,236 to 4,295 million metres during this period (Srinivasulu 1996).

The aforementioned policy changes of the mid-1980s in both the pharmaceutical and textile industries saw a shift in the government's position regarding the reliance on foreign technologies to improve innovation and productivity to meet domestic demand; thus, in both sectors, import controls were relaxed. However, by the end of the decade, this approach of accessing foreign know-how was threatened by the foreign exchange reserve crises and led to a more drastic policy shift for the whole economy, that is, one predicated on export-led growth. In 1991, the Indian government ended the 'licence raj' and implemented major economic liberalisation measures to establish stronger linkages with the global economy and 'to unshackle the Indian industrial economy from the cobwebs of unnecessary bureaucratic control' (Government of India 1991). Triggered externally by a balance-of-payments crisis, these 'reforms by storm' (Bhagwati 1993) primarily aimed to increase local productivity and international trade, attract foreign investments and promote the global competitiveness of Indian firms. A few notable changes in this connection were the deregulation of industries to permit private enterprises, the abolition of import licensing for capital goods and intermediates and the significant reduction in import duties for tradable goods and services, the implementation of currency convertibility within a flexible exchange-rate regime, the reform of the capital market to liberalise equity pricing and access to offshore equity and debt, and the de-licensing of industrial investments, thereby permitting majority foreign ownership in all industries, except for banks, insurance, telecommunications and airlines (Ahluwalia 2002). These broad-scope reforms affected most sectors of the economy, including the pharmaceutical and textile sectors.[6]

In line with economy-wide liberalisation measures, the pharmaceutical industry also underwent significant de-licensing and the liberalisation of imports and foreign investments. Some of the key measures included reductions in the import tariffs on pharmaceutical ingredients from a high of 85 per cent in 1993 to a maximum of 30 per cent in 2004, the elimination of industrial licensing requirements for most products, the ability of foreign companies to hold majority equity stakes in their Indian ventures, and new guidelines for the control of drug prices (Gubbi, Aulakh and Ray 2016; Joseph 2016). Similarly, the new industrial policy de-licensed the textile industry, thereby abolishing the prior government requirement of approval to set up textile units, including power looms. Thus, by the early 1990s, the overall policy thrust in India had shifted from import-substitution industrialisation to export-led growth, and the new national institutional regime facilitated the entry of foreign firms into the Indian market and encouraged firms in both industries to not only meet growing domestic demand but also contribute to the country's exports. However, this trajectory would change fundamentally soon after, when in 1995 global institutional changes in the pharmaceutical and textile industries altered the basis of global competition for both the industries. National policies had to reorganise again to cope with these impending changes.

Preparing for Global Institutional Change (1995–2005)

The World Trade Organization (WTO) formally came into existence in 1995 at the end of the Uruguay Round of trade negotiations (which had begun in 1986), and the principles governing global trade through the General Agreement on Tariffs and Trade (GATT) since the end of World War II were integrated into the WTO. In addition, several new trade policies were negotiated during the preceding trade talks, and two important agreements, which are of interest in the current study, were formally adopted on 1 January 1995, namely the Agreement on Trade-Related Aspects of Intellectual Property Rights (TRIPS) (which impacted the Indian pharmaceutical industry) and the Agreement on Textile and Clothing (ATC) (which had potential implications for the Indian textile sector). For both agreements, the WTO allowed a transition period of ten years and expected them to be fully implemented by 1 January 2005.[7] Before evaluating their impact on the two industries in India and the specific policy interventions, it may be useful to provide a brief context of the two agreements and their main provisions.

TRIPS Agreement

The Uruguay Round of international trade negotiations was launched in 1986. One of the most divisive issues in these negotiations was the insistence of developed countries, led by the United States (US), for improved intellectual property protection through the enactment of appropriate laws by member states and their strict enforcement. Given their traditional advantage in technology and know-how and the ideological bent in seeing these as 'private' benefits of their innovative firms, the developed countries wanted to link any liberalisation in international trade to strong intellectual property rights (IPR). However, developing countries 'decried the inclusion of intellectual property in negotiations on lowering trade barriers as "forum-shopping" by the United States after proposals of uniform patent laws failed to gain traction at the World Intellectual Property Organization (WIPO)' (Daemmrich 2011: 4). These countries considered intellectual property to be more of a public good, and instead of seeing strong intellectual property laws as a means for development, they believed in achieving a certain level of development before thinking about protecting intellectual property. Despite opposition from developing countries, the Trade-Related Intellectual Property Rights (TRIPS) agreement came into effect on 1 January 1995; however, there were a few transitional arrangements made in order for member states to enact the appropriate laws and enforcement mechanisms over the following ten years (for critical analysis of the agreement, see Reichman 1996; Hamilton 1996; Ragavan 2006). Except for a few of the least-developed countries, the full agreement was to be in force by 1 January 2005 (World Trade Organization 1995c). The agreement covered different kinds of intellectual property (including copyrights, trademarks, industrial designs, patents, and so on) and outlined the minimum standards for each of these as well as the enforcement and dispute-settlement mechanisms (World Trade Organization 1995c).

The relevant part of the TRIPS agreement for the Indian pharmaceutical industry is related to the minimum standards regarding patents. As discussed earlier, the Patents Act of 1970 provided 'process' rather than 'product' patents for the pharmaceutical industry. Section 5 (Patents) of the TRIPS agreement negated this distinction:

> The TRIPS Agreement requires Member countries to make patents available for any inventions, whether products or processes, in all fields of technology without discrimination, subject to the normal tests of novelty, inventiveness and industrial applicability. It is also required that patents be available and patent rights enjoyable without discrimination as to the place of invention and whether products are imported or locally produced. (World Trade Organization 1995c)

The agreement stated a twenty-year period for the patents but did allow for the exclusion of some items from patentability that were 'necessary to protect *ordre public* or morality, including to protect human, animal or plant life or health or to avoid serious prejudice to the environment, provided that such exclusion is not merely because the exploitation is prohibited by their law' (Section 5, Item 2). The agreement also established a process (Article 31) of compulsory licensing of patented products or processes for domestic use in the 'case of a national emergency or other circumstances of extreme emergency or in the cases of public non-commercial use', with 'adequate remuneration … taking into consideration the economic value of the authorization'.

The requisite patent protection needed to be compliant with the TRIPS agreement had severe implications for the Indian pharmaceutical industry. First, reverting to the product patent regime would provide the protection sought by international pharmaceutical firms to bring their best products to India and would result in a steep increase in competition. Second, Indian firms had built their competitive advantage in both domestic and international markets through the manufacturing and selling of knock-offs of patented drugs, including generics, by exploiting the prevailing process patent regime. Product patents would protect a chemical entity, not a manufacturing process, thus making the kind of reverse engineering practised by Indian firms illegal. Third, various interest groups in India cautioned the government about the welfare implications of patent protection for pharmaceutical products in India, in particular the pricing and affordability for domestic consumers. However, due to the necessity of being part of the WTO, the Indian government reluctantly signed the TRIPS treaty in late 1994 and effectively committed itself to intellectual property protection reform that would eventually produce a patent act consistent with the agreement.

Agreement on Textiles and Clothing (ATC)

During the trade negotiations of the Uruguay Round, the major objective of the trading nations was to bring more sectors within the general principles (that is, reciprocity, transparency and non-discrimination) of GATT. One of the important sectors that had been exempt from these principles was trade in textiles. Since 1974, global trade in textiles and clothing had been regulated by the Multi-Fibre Agreement (MFA). The MFA was initiated at the behest of developed countries, especially North America and western Europe, to protect their respective textile industries. As suggested by Yoffie (1983: 2), since 'textiles and apparel were among the oldest industries in industrial countries, firms were often concentrated in declining regions ... and most textile workers had limited mobility and few alternative job opportunities'. Given that these industries employed a large workforce, textile firms and their unions had tremendous political clout. 'The emergence of low-cost competitors in the Third World led textile and apparel producers in the industrial nations to lobby hard for protectionism' (Yoffie 1983: 3). Accordingly, the MFA agreement was initiated in 1974, through which developed countries negotiated bilateral quotas with individual developing countries; this arrangement allowed the developed countries to offer some protection to their domestic textile industries. For developing countries, the MFA had mixed implications. Some of the smaller countries developed their nascent textile industries by receiving preferential treatment based on historic connections with individual developed countries (that is, colonial connections, development aid objectives, and so on) that awarded them with quotas, even if they did not possess comparative advantages. For developing countries with large textile industries, the MFA restricted growth in exports to advanced markets as their bilateral quotas were much below their potential to export given their relative cost advantages.

Thus, along with the objectives of the world community to streamline the underlying principles governing trade as it was moving to institutionalise the GATT into the WTO, the push to dismantle the MFA also came from some of these developing countries with large and growing textile industries and their new export-growth model of development in the 1980s. These countries wanted flows in the textile trade to be a function of the country's comparative advantages rather than artificially determined through preferential treatments and quota regimes (World Trade Organization 1995a).[8] Accordingly, the Agreement on Textiles and Clothing (ATC) was put in place on 1 January 1995 with the objective of dismantling the quota system within ten years (through four stages) and facilitating increased competition in global and national markets (Smeets 1995). For developing countries with a significant presence in the global textile trade, such as India, the ATC was both an opportunity, as it removed quantitative restrictions on the extent of exports to large developed country markets, and a threat, since these markets could only be accessed through the development of competitive advantages rather than via taken-for-granted bilateral quotas (Dhiman and Sharma 2021). In the competition for access to the global market, the Indian textile industry now had to compete with other developing countries with similar (or lower) labour costs.

The aforementioned global institutional changes related to pharmaceuticals and textiles changed the competitive landscape for Indian firms operating in both industries and necessitated policy changes by the Indian government to facilitate the development of legal frameworks and competitive conditions to align with these new realities. The following decade (1995–2005) was thus used to initiate appropriate policies to prepare both sectors to cope with the full implementation of the two agreements at the beginning of 2005.

Pharmaceutical Industry: The most immediate need was to make India's intellectual property regime adhere to the TRIPS agreement. Given numerous concerns in India about the social welfare aspects of the new patent requirements and its potential implications for the competitiveness of Indian pharmaceutical firms, the government took a phased approach to amending the Patents Act of 1970. Through incremental amendments made in 1999, 2002, and 2005, the Patents (Amendment) Act of 2005 was enacted in early 2005.

The main provisions of the 2005 Indian Patents Act incorporated the requirements of the TRIPS agreement (Patents [Amendment] Act, 2005). In particular, Section 5 of the Patents Act of 1970, which was meant to provide limited conditions of 'process patenting' for inventions relating to 'substances intended for use, or capable of being used, as food or as medicine or drug, or substances prepared or produced by chemical processes', was omitted in the amended act of 2005 and now included 'products' in the patentable subject matter category. Furthermore, the act made 'reverse-engineering or copying of patented products without requisite licence from the patent holder illegal', retroactive to 1 January 1995, but 'allowed the manufacture of generic versions of drugs patented prior to 1995' (Racherla 2019: 283). In addition, in line with the TRIPS agreement, the Indian act provided a twenty-year guaranteed period for the protection of patents.

However, the 2005 act included two provisions to protect India's generic pharmaceutical industry and the broader objective to provide accessibility to drugs necessary for public health.[9] One was related to preventing evergreening by multinational corporations, which encompasses the use of legal loopholes to extend the monopoly period of the patent through the application of a secondary patent based on minor modifications (Racherla 2019). Section 3(d) of the act tried to minimise this evergreening by qualifying what would be considered patentable:

> [T]he mere discovery of a new form of a known substance which does not result in the enhancement of the known efficacy of that substance or the mere discovery of any new property or new use for a known substance or of the mere use of a known process, machine or apparatus unless such known process results in a new product or employs at least one new reactant.

The second provision used the flexibility afforded in the TRIPS agreement about compulsory licensing in the case of national emergency or public health crises to incorporate in the act. According to Section 92A,

> compulsory licence shall be available for the manufacture and export of patented pharmaceutical products to any country having insufficient or no manufacturing capacity in the pharmaceutical sector for the concerned product to address public health problems, provided compulsory licence has been granted by such country, or such country has, by notification or otherwise, allowed the importation of the patented pharmaceutical products from India.

Compliance of intellectual property protection in the pharmaceutical industry with the requirements of the TRIPS agreement was just one of the challenges for policymakers in India. For both industries, the global institutional changes due to TRIPS and the ATC also necessitated policy choices to prepare them to meet new competitive challenges that would take full effect in 2005. Accordingly, the government undertook various policy initiatives during the 1995–2005 period to prepare the Indian industries for new competitive challenges that would be fully in place after 2005. In the following paragraphs, the thrust of these initiatives is discussed.

Along with developing an appropriate intellectual property protection regime related to TRIPS, the Indian government was also aware of the potential implications of the new regime to the Indian pharmaceutical sector and was thus simultaneously considering options to support the industry after the impending changes in 2005. The government set up a number of committees and, based on their analyses and recommendations, developed a new pharmaceutical policy in 2002 (Government of India, Department of Pharmaceuticals 2002). In its introduction, the policy report acknowledged the importance of Indian pharmaceuticals in meeting the domestic social goals of providing accessible drugs, as well as contributing to the export-led growth development model of the post-liberalisation era. However, it noted that

> two major issues have surfaced on account of globalization and implementation of our obligations under TRIPS which impact on long-term competitiveness of Indian industry: a) the essentiality of improving incentives for research and development in the Indian pharmaceutical industry, to enable the industry to achieve sustainable growth particularly in view of anticipated changes in the Patent Law, and b) the need for reducing further the rigours of price control particularly in view of the ongoing process of liberalization. (Government of India, Department of Pharmaceuticals 2002)

Accordingly, the new policy objectives for the pharmaceutical industry were to strengthen indigenous capability for the production of quality drugs, reduce barriers to trade to facilitate their exports, and create an incentive framework to encourage R&D investments for new technologies and new drugs while 'ensuring abundant availability at reasonable process within the country of good essential pharmaceuticals of mass consumption' (Government of India, Department of Pharmaceuticals 2002). Thus, most of the elements of the specific provisions in the policy related to balancing these objectives of innovation in pharmaceutical production and the availability of affordable drugs for domestic consumers.

To achieve the innovation objectives, the government initiated schemes to support drug development; however, this support was primarily targeted towards larger companies with existing investments of at least 5 per cent of turnover per annum in R&D, with a minimum investment of INR 10 crores (1 crore = 10 million) in new drug development, employing more than 100 research scientists, and having obtained at least ten patents for research done in India. Furthermore, the policy abolished industrial licensing for most bulk drugs, allowed foreign investment up to 100 per cent equity by foreign firms, and facilitated both technology agreements of Indian firms with foreign companies and importation of know-how and technology. These policy initiatives were geared to provide the necessary incentives and the facilitating infrastructure to increase innovation in the Indian pharmaceutical sector. Along with these provisions, the new policy proposed the further dilution of price controls.[10] The new guiding principle for the identification of specific bulk drugs for price control was to be the mass consumption nature of the drug and the absence of sufficient competition for such drugs. The bulk drug prices could be controlled under the new policy if the moving annual total value for any formulator was more than INR 25 crores. The exemption from price controls for drugs developed indigenously was extended to fifteen years or to the term of process patents for indigenous new drug-delivery system. With these changes, the scope of price controls was reduced to only 22 per cent of the total market (Government of India, Department of Pharmaceuticals 2002).

Textile Industry: The challenges posed by the global institutional change to the pharmaceutical industry emanated from a new intellectual property regime that necessitated a shift towards product innovation while controlling the prices for these innovations for the domestic market. Global change in the textile industry, on the other hand, required the Indian textile industry to improve its efficiency and productivity to compete with other developing countries in global markets. Indian policy challenges aimed to find ways to improve productivity while keeping in consideration the different segments of the industry and their relative conduciveness for productivity growth and implications for employment opportunities for a large workforce employed in the industry. Thus, policies initiated by the Indian government from 1995 to 2005 to prepare the textile sector for the impending implementation of the ATC were of a different nature than those made for the pharmaceutical sector.

The Government of India initiated a new policy, the National Textile Policy, in 2000, also known as the NTxP-2000 (Government of India, Ministry of Textiles 2000), to meet the challenges of global institutional change. The objectives of the new policy were to attain and sustain a 'pre-eminent standing in the manufacture and export of clothing' and equip the industry to withstand 'import penetration' in the post-ATC competitive environment. This would be accomplished through appropriate regulations that would incentivise investments in 'state-of-the art manufacturing capabilities' by domestic producers and through inward FDI. According to the NTxP-2000, this technology upgrading of the textile industry was to be achieved by simultaneously strengthening the 'traditional knowledge, skills and capabilities' of the informal and decentralised sectors of the industry, including expanding 'productive employment'. These policy objectives had an in-built paradox in terms of balancing technological modernisation with high employment (that is, efficiency versus employment [Ganesh 2002]).

This paradox arising from competing logics can be understood by closely examining the structure of the Indian textile industry in the 1990s (Government of India, Ministry of Textiles 2001–2002; Simpson and Shetty 2001). The textile industry was highly fragmented across the different stages of textile production (the production of fibre [natural and man-made], spinning, weaving, processing and apparel/garmenting). In 1995–1996, there were only 274 vertically integrated 'composite' mills that could perform spinning, weaving and finishing operations. Much of the industry was segmented into three 'interrelated but competing sectors—the organized mill sector and the "decentralized" handloom and powerloom sectors' (Simpson and Shetty 2001: Section 2, 1–3). The organised mill sector (consisting of approximately 1,200 large- and medium-sized mills and 900 small mills) spun yarn, which was sold for fabric production (through controlled prices) to the power loom and handloom sectors, with the former generating approximately 55 per cent and the latter generating 23 per cent of the total production in 1996 (Simpson and Shetty 2001). The processing of the fabric (that is, dyeing and finishing) was done by nearly 13,000 independent firms in hand-processing (80 per cent) and power-processing (20 per cent) units. Apparel production (which was reserved for the small-scale industrial units) was done by more than 30,000 units (Shetty and Simpson 2001). In terms of employment, out of the 35 million people who had direct employment in the textile industry, only 1 million people were employed in the organised mill sector, with the rest being employed in the different segments of the unorganised sector. The handloom sector was the largest employer, with over 12 million people (Government of India, Ministry of Textiles 2001–2002).

Out of the different sectors in the Indian textile industry, only the production of man-made fibres was consolidated, with three firms holding almost 90 per cent of the market share; this sector used state-of-the-art technology (Simpson and Shetty 2001). None of the other sectors upgraded their technologies throughout the 1990s. For the organised mill sector, restrictions on vertical integration and prices disincentivised investments in the upgrading of technology to increase productivity and efficiency, while the small size of individual units in the unorganised sector put constraints on the available funds for modernisation (Ganesh 2002; Roy 1998b). A number of studies conducted in the 1990s consistently highlighted the extent to which the Indian textile industry lagged behind competitors in other developing economies in terms of modernisation and the level of technology used (for example, Chandra 1999; Shetty and Simpson 2001).

The National Textile Policy of 2000 attempted to overcome these constraints of a fragmented industry in the hope of preparing it for the impending competitive challenges of the post-ATC era. One major thrust area in the new policy was technological upgrading in all sectors of the industry to enhance productivity and improve the quality of products. The Technology Upgradation Funds Scheme (TUFS) was launched in 1999 'to provide impetus' to the industry's modernisation. The scheme allocated INR 250 billion over five years (1999–2004) to be used for a 5 per cent interest subsidy (or interest reimbursement) on loans taken by firms from financial institutions for modernisation or technology improvement. Firms in the small-scale sector of the industry could opt for either this 5 per cent interest subsidy or take a 12 per cent credit-linked capital subsidy (Government of India, Ministry of Textiles 2001–2002).

In addition to the direct support given to individual firms to upgrade their technology, the Textile Policy of 2000 also attempted to improve the institutional infrastructure to support the industry in both upstream and downstream activities. Regarding the former, the main thrust was towards employment and human resource development. Anticipating the possibility that uncompetitive mills would be closed due to increased global competition and their inability to modernise, the policy provided for a Textile Workers' Rehabilitation Fund to support and retrain displaced workers. In addition, the policy organised and coordinated resources with state governments to train workers in the power loom and handloom sectors to use updated technologies and improve their work conditions. At the downstream level, the National Textile Policy objective was to increase textile and apparel exports from USD 11 billion in 2000 to USD 50 billion by 2010, with half of that share going to the finished garments. This was to be accomplished through increased inward FDI and alliances with foreign firms to allow know-how transfer and brand-building, inter-sector competition by de-reserving the garment industry from the small-scale industry segment, and restructuring export promotion through various councils and industry associations.

The aforementioned policy initiatives during the ten-year period of 1995–2005 were geared to prepare both the pharmaceutical and textile industries for the institutional changes that were to take effect on 1 January 2005. The competitiveness of both industries would depend on the extent to which each industry moved up the technology frontier (that is, product innovation for pharmaceuticals and technological upgrading for textiles) relative to their respective global competitors. However, social welfare considerations in India (that is, drug accessibility and affordability for pharmaceuticals and employment opportunities in textiles) had the potential to limit the technology frontier that could be achieved. Policy interventions attempted to address these conundrums, and their efficacy was determined during the period after the start of the new institutional regimes.

Coping with Global Institutional Change (2005–2020)

Textile Industry: The 2009–2010 annual report of the Indian textile sector highlighted the industry's importance to the country in terms of being the second-largest provider of employment (after agriculture) and contributing 14 per cent to the country's industrial production, 4 per cent to the gross domestic product (GDP) and 17 per cent to export earnings. It further lauded the 100 per cent increase in exports in textiles and clothing from USD 11 billion in 2000 to USD 22.4 billion in 2010 (Government of India, Ministry of Textiles 2009–2010). While the post-quota trade regime in the textile industry had provided new growth opportunities for developing countries, the export performance of India's textile industry was well short of the target of USD 60 billion that the government had set in the National Textile Policy of 2000. The 2009–2010 report attributed this failure to achieve its target to infrastructure constraints and the lack of state-of-the-art technology, among others (see also Hashim 2005; Narayanan G. 2005). Furthermore, a report commissioned by India's Ministry of Textiles performed a comparative input cost analysis of five textile-exporting developing countries (namely Bangladesh, Cambodia, China, India and Pakistan) and concluded that India's competitiveness in the industry had fallen behind that of its competitors. It recommended a need to increase productivity and reduce labour costs, in addition to improving the overall manufacturing infrastructure (Government of India, Ministry of Textiles 2014).

The major policy thrust for the textile industry during the post-ATC era, especially after 2010, focused on the modernisation of all segments of the industry, the necessary skill development required for upgraded manufacturing, and the supporting infrastructure needed to facilitate modernisation and skill development. The anchor in this policy thrust continued to be the TUFS, which was initially put in place for five years from 1999 to 2004 but has been continuously extended in modified forms until 2022.[11] As described earlier, the scheme provided a 5 per cent interest subsidy for loans taken, especially for upgrading manufacturing technology. The scheme had a slow start during the 1999–2006 period, with fewer than 1,000 applications on average per year, but it picked up steam starting in 2006, when the number of applications and the amount disbursed increased substantially.[12] The benefits of the TUFS expanded from 2004 onwards, with capital subsidies of between 10 and 30 per cent on technology or machinery investments expanded to all sectors, except the large-scale spinning mills (for details, see Government of India, Ministry of Textiles 2013–2014: Table 3.3, 36–38). Furthermore, to increase production and employment within the garment sector (with a projected export contribution of 50 per cent by this sector), the TUFS was amended in 2016 to provide an additional production- and employment-linked subsidy of 10 per cent, in addition to the 15 per cent capital subsidy. The new provision was an output-based subsidy, which would be paid after the achievement of production and employment targets by firms that had used the capital subsidy for technology modernisation (Government of India, Ministry of Textiles 2016).

Concerns about adequate employment opportunities in the textile sector, especially in the context of the skilled workforce needed to work technologically advanced manufacturing equipment, required skill-development efforts. From 2016 onwards, various schemes were initiated to provide the different sectors of the industry with a skilled workforce. This included the Integrated Skill Development Scheme (ISDS) to train 1.5 million workers and the Scheme for Capacity Building in Textile Sector (SAMARTH) to train an additional million workers. These schemes developed sector-specific training modules, and the workers were certified through a common National Skill Qualification Framework (for details, see Government of India, Ministry of Textiles 2016–2017, 2017–2018, 2018–2019, 2019–2020a; for other skill-development initiatives, especially in the garment sector, see Kuzhiparambil 2020).

In addition to the direct support to individual firms through interest and capital subsidies on the various iterations of TUFS and making a skilled workforce available to them, two other policy initiatives were put in place during the 2016–2020 period to improve the industry's competitiveness. The first, the Scheme for Integrated Textile Parks (SITP), was to be a partnership between the central government and groups of private entrepreneurs, industry associations and agencies of state governments, whereby the former would contribute 40 per cent of the total project cost, including that needed for land, infrastructure and buildings. The objective of the scheme was to provide 'financial assistance to a group of entrepreneurs to establish state-of-the-art infrastructure facilities in a cluster for setting up their textile units, conforming to international environmental and social standards and thereby mobilize private investment in the textile sector and generate fresh employment opportunities' (Government of India, Ministry of Textiles 2018). Fifty-six such parks were sanctioned across the country by 2020 (Government of India, Ministry of Textiles 2019–2020). The second sector-specific initiative encouraged the development of regional clusters in the handloom and handicraft sectors, both of which primarily consisted of small- and medium-sized firms that had a global competitive advantage in differentiated products but were not not competitive in terms of costs. The objective of these clusters was to provide, at very local levels, some infrastructure and marketing support to maintain their employment and export potential.

The aforementioned policy initiatives in the textile industry during the post-2005 period, along with aggressive across-the-board export promotion activities under the aegis of the Ministry of Commerce and Industry, attempted to address the shortfall in the export targets for the industry and rectify the technology and efficiency aspects identified by various reports as the reasons for the industry's lack of competitive advantage relative to India's competitors.[13] The underpinnings of the policy approach for the industry were to maintain a balance between technology upgrading and employment, and ensure the development of the industry across India's regions and the different segments of the industry, including the production of raw materials, spinning, weaving and garmenting.

Pharmaceutical Industry: The trajectory of the Indian pharmaceutical industry in the post-2005 period led to different policy choices.[14] The overall balance of trade in pharmaceuticals was favourable to India, increasing from USD 1 billion in 2002 to 3.9 billion in 2009 (Joseph 2012). Opening up of the economy in terms of trade and FDI facilitated resource internationalisation. In the post-2005 period, the industry attracted large investments from foreign multinationals through mergers and acquisitions and strategic alliances with local firms. Furthermore, the new IPR regime led to increased outlays in R&D by individual firms, which in turn garnered approval from international regulatory bodies. However, although the new patent regime pushed the industry towards higher value-added segments, the underlying structural changes in the industry were a cause for concern.

In analysing the structure of the industry, Chaudhuri (2012: 53) cautioned about the movement towards product monopolies and higher drug prices in the patent era:

> Imports of high priced finished formulations are expanding rapidly, with manufacturing investments lagging behind. The MNCs [multinational corporations] are ... expanding vigorously in the generic segments... and are trying to grow not only organically but through mergers and acquisitions and strategic alliance with Indian generic companies. The MNCs are on the way to dominate the industry again.

Furthermore, the negative balance of trade in bulk drugs, especially the increased imports from China (almost 52 per cent in 2009), caused concern about the competitiveness of indigenous Indian firms (Joseph 2012).

Large Indian pharmaceutical firms were increasingly perceived as merely performing contract-based functions of basic research and producing generics for foreign multinational corporations, which was reflected in the increasing trade surplus in the formulations or finished drugs (Joseph 2012; Gopakumar 2012).

Policy changes in India from 2010 onwards were geared towards rectifying the structural anomalies that were developing in the Indian pharmaceutical sector under the post-2005 institutional regime. The National Pharmaceutical Pricing Policy of 2012 (NPPP-2012) revisited drug pricing for the domestic market. In reassessing the history of price controls and the emerging conditions, the preamble to the policy acknowledged the challenges in balancing the interests of producers and consumers:

> [V]arious policies adopted from time to time have tried to cope up with the challenge of striking a balance between ... varying requirements of enabling the industry to grow and at the same time ensuring affordable ... medicines to the consumers. The balancing of diverse and conflicting interests is indeed a difficult task, as is the reconciling of short-term interests with long-term goals and concerns. (Government of India, Ministry of Chemicals and Fertilizers, Department of Pharmaceutical 2012: 14–15; see also Pingali and Chatterjee 2015)

The new policy prioritised the regulation of drug prices based on the 'essentiality' principle rather than the 'economic criteria/market share' principle that guided price controls under the existing drug policy of 1994. The new policy prepared a National List of Essential Medicines based on the criteria developed by local committees of experts and the World Health Organization (WHO).

Furthermore, the new price regulations applied only to drug formulations (that is, prices paid by consumers for the finished products prescribed and sold in the market) rather than bulk drugs, because the active pharmaceutical ingredient of the bulk drug 'may not fully reflect the "essentiality" of the actual drug formulation' (Government of India, Ministry of Chemicals and Fertilizers, Department of Pharmaceutical 2012: 18). The third component of the new policy was regulation through 'market-BASED' pricing of formulations, which would likely bring new competitors in the respective segment. According to the rationale for this provision, the existing cost-based pricing 'allows no space for the new entrant to come in at an uncovered price point. As a result, production activity and competition in the product segment tend to stagnate. This is neither good to the consumer-patient nor for industry growth' (Government of India, Ministry of Chemicals and Fertilizers, Department of Pharmaceutical 2012: 20).

In essence, the NPPP-12 simultaneously attempted to address concerns about an increase in drug prices in the post-2005 product-patent-centred IPR regime and the industry concentration of large domestic firms and foreign multinational corporations. Further incentives to support the growth of small- and medium-sized firms in both R&D and production activities have been initiated since 2018, which are quite similar to those made in the textile industry. These include the Pharmaceutical Technology Upgradation Assistance Scheme (PTUAS), which provides 6 per cent per annum interest subvention on loans for technology or infrastructure upgradation for small and medium enterprises (SMEs) and assistance in developing clusters and common facility centres through public–private partnerships (Government of India, Ministry of Chemicals and Fertilizers, Department of Pharmaceuticals 2018). Furthermore, new policies were announced in 2020 to support product diversification of the Indian pharmaceutical sector for the domestic market and expand the portfolio of products for exports. These aims include the production of medical devices (85 per cent of the local demand was met through imports in 2020) by establishing four special parks that provided a common infrastructure for this capital-intensive sector (Government of India, Ministry of Chemicals and Fertilizers, Department of Pharmaceuticals 2020) and the production of high-valued goods (that is, beyond generics) through the promotion of global champions (Government of India, Ministry of Chemicals and Fertilizers, Department of Pharmaceuticals 2021). Under this scheme, which is targeted towards all domestic firms, large and small, firms will get an incentive of up to 10 per cent on incremental sales of high-valued proprietary drugs and devices.

The preceding sections have outlined the policy initiatives in the Indian textile and pharmaceutical industries since the early 1970s and have attempted to place the development and evolution of different logics influencing policy choices in the context of national and global institutional changes impacting these industries. A comparative summary of this evolution of institutional changes and policy choices is provided in Table 3.1. The next section discusses these policy choices within the context of the existing frameworks related to economic growth in developing countries and instruments of industrial policy.

Table 3.1 Summary of Policy Choices in the Indian Textile and Pharmaceutical Industries, 1970–2020

Institutional Context	TEXTILE INDUSTRY		PHARMACEUTICAL INDUSTRY	
	Priorities	*Policy Choices*	*Priorities*	*Policy Choices*
1970–1985 Import-substitution industrialisation	• Domestic demand • Employment in the small-scale informal sector	• Price controls on output of mills • Capacity restrictions of the industrial sector • Import restrictions	• Accessibility • Affordability	• Price controls • Process patents
1985–1995 Economic liberalisation and export-led growth	• Unmet domestic demand • Preserve employment	• Capacity restrictions removed • Ease import controls including on machinery • Protect handloom sector	• Accessibility • Export growth	• De-licensing • Reduced all import controls including on bulk drugs • Inward FDI
1995–2005 Preparing for global institutional change	• Export growth • Increased efficiency and productivity • Scale economies through consolidation • Maintain/increase employment in all sectors	• Technology upgrading • Inward FDI for the garment industry	• Accessibility • Export growth	• Product patents • Compulsory licensing • Inward FDI • R&D support for large firms • Easing of price controls
2005–2020 Coping with global institutional change	• Create competitive advantage in global markets • Adopt modern technologies • Create skilled workforce	• Technology upgrading • Skill development • Infrastructure modernisation • Sector-specific clusters and parks	• Affordability • Exports of high-value products • Product diversification • Development of indigenous firms	• Price controls of 'essential drugs' • Technology upgradation for SMEs • Infrastructure support through clusters and parks

Source: Authors.

Tale of Two Industries within an Industrial Policy Framework

Understanding government interventions to promote national economic objectives has been and continues to be of immense interest across academic disciplines and to policymakers within national contexts, as well as to those governing international institutions (for extended reviews see Oqubay et al. 2020; Cherif and Hasanov 2019; Warwick 2013; Weiss 2015). Much of the earlier work focused on policy interventions in protected national markets (for example, import-substitution industrialisation, trade barriers, and so on) and evaluated economic growth through theories about infant industries and strategic trade policies. More recent work examines various types of government interventions in a liberalised global trade environment whereby export-led growth, catch-up and technological learning are some of the objectives underpinning these interventions (Oqubay 2020; Nayyar 2013). In the light of this shift in the aims of policy interventions, a few studies have attempted to develop new taxonomies or frameworks of 'industrial policy' to understand such interventions. According to Warwick (2013: 16),

> industrial policy is any intervention or government policy that attempts to improve the business environment or to alter the structure of economic activity towards sectors, technologies or tasks that are expected to offer better prospects for economic growth or societal welfare that could occur in the absence of such intervention.[15]

The objectives (or aims) of industrial policy are realised by targeting certain sectors of the economy (policy orientation) through specific instruments (policy domain) (Warwick 2013; Weiss 2015). More specifically, policy orientation can be 'horizontal' or 'selective', with the former being broad in scope and influencing vast swathes of the economy, while the latter is narrow in scope and targets specific sectors or tasks (Warwick 2013; see also Gubbi, Aulakh and Ray 2015). The policy domain includes various instruments related to product and factor (that is, capital, land, labour and technology) markets that offer 'different means of support for producers either by shifting relative incentives or providing various forms of direct support' (Weiss 2015: 7–8). An important element in designing the specific instruments is to ensure compatibility, coherence and synergy in the policies to accommodate competing pulls from different constituents (for example, large versus small firms, organised versus unorganised sectors of the economy) or different goals (for example, economic efficiency versus social welfare) (Oqubay 2020; Drez and Sen 2002).

These elements of industrial policy are used to map (see Table 3.2) the two industries of interest within the aforementioned framework. There are a few noteworthy aspects of this map. First, in both industries, we see a multilevel policy orientation. That is, these industries were first impacted by the horizontal policy orientation in 1991 when India initiated economy-wide reforms and moved towards an export-oriented economic growth strategy. The associated policy domains used to achieve this objective included the de-licensing of major sectors of the economy, removing barriers for trade and investment and initiating export-promotion policies. These policies were supplemented through selective policy intervention for each industry after 1995 because of the differential impact of the respective global institutional change.

Second, the focus of the global institutional changes and the locus of emerging competition in the subsequent period led to different types of policy orientation for each industry. The ATC eliminated the bilateral quota regime and heralded global competition in the industry, which provided greater access to markets, including lucrative markets. The new institutional context increased competition between developing countries to access global markets given the high labour intensity of the textile industry. Accordingly, the selective policy orientation entailed augmenting existing comparative advantages through modernisation and increasing efficiency and productivity to compete with other developing countries having similar advantages. On the other hand, the TRIPS agreement heralded a new institutional context that strengthened the IPR regime within which global trade would be conducted. For the global pharmaceutical industry, this meant a shift towards proprietary patented products as the basis for competition. Developing countries in this industry had to compete with developed countries for global market access, and since the latter had competitive advantages in producing innovative products, policy orientation in this industry for a developing country entailed 'catching up' through R&D investments and innovation.

Third, the implementation of the respective selective policy orientations to achieve economic objectives in the two industries (that is, productivity and innovation) had to be balanced by social welfare objectives for each industry (that is, employment and affordability). Accordingly, we see different instruments being used in the policy domain. For the textile industry, productivity gains through technology upgrading have to be accomplished with parallel instruments for skill development to maintain or increase employment opportunities. In the pharmaceutical industry, investments in R&D to produce high-value new drugs need to be balanced with appropriate policy interventions to ensure the affordability of these drugs for domestic consumers.

Table 3.2 Industrial Policy Framework for Indian Textile and Pharmaceutical Industries

	Textile Industry	*Pharmaceutical Industry*
Liberalisation and economy-wide horizontal policy orientation (1991 onwards)	Liberalisation of exports, imports and FDI; de-licensing economic activity; export promotion	Liberalisation of exports, imports and FDI; de-licensing economic activity; export promotion
Nature of global institutional change	Increased market-based global competition	Strong IPR regime and product patents
Locus of new competition	Developing economies	Developed economies
Selective (industry-specific) policy orientation (1995 onwards)	Augmenting comparative advantages through technology upgradation and skill development	Developing new competitive advantages through R&D investments and innovation
Competing logics	Productivity and employment	Innovation and affordability
Policy domains	Technology: Capital subsidy Labour: Skill development Capital: Interest rate subvention Infrastructure: Parks and clusters	Product: Patents and price controls Technology: Capital subsidy Infrastructure: Parks and clusters

Source: Authors.

Conclusion

The main objective of this chapter was to identify various policy interventions in the Indian textile and pharmaceutical industries that were initiated to cope with respective global institutional changes. The nature of the institutional changes and unique characteristics of each industry led to different policy orientations, as well as to different policy instruments. In addition, some of the policy instruments provided direct support to individual firms, while others did so indirectly through public goods such as improvements in the institutional infrastructure, the development of clusters and parks, and improvements in regulatory aspects. The following chapters incorporate the implications of these policy choices in shaping industry- and firm-level responses to global institutional change.

Notes

1. For extensive studies on the various policy interventions and their implications see Chaudhury (2005), Mitsumori (2018) and Joseph (2016) on the pharmaceutical industry, and Dhiman and Sharma (2020) and Oberoi (2016) on the textile industry. Furthermore, the *Economic and Political Weekly* has published numerous studies over the years that have analysed the rationale and implications of the specific policy initiatives. See also Majumdar (1996) for the general linkages between policies and performance in the Indian industrial sector.

2. These included the Drug Policy of 1978 and Price Control Order of 1979. The general thrust of these policies was to make the two acts of 1970 more effective; thus, these policies are not discussed in more detail here. For greater elaboration of the fine-grained policy changes, see Joseph (2016).

3. Cotton plays a dominant role in India's textile industry; however, the industry continues to have substantial components of silk, wool and jute as well. Most of the policy interventions discussed in this chapter relate to the cotton sector of the industry.

4. Under the pro-business orientation, the relative importance of the private sector vis-à-vis state-owned enterprises increased substantially, and private enterprises saw the gradual removal of constraints through de-licensing, the opening of new sectors to private enterprises, and new foreign direct investment (FDI) polices (Chittoor and Aulakh 2005; Kohli 2004).

5. The new textile policy was criticised for its abandonment of the handloom sector, with one critic calling it a 'liquidation of the handloom industry, which has been intimately woven into the history of India's freedom struggle and her crusade against underemployment in the post-independence period' (Jain 1985: 1121).

6. While the 1991 reforms were comprehensive and encompassed measures to fundamentally change the organisation of economic activity in India across all sectors, policy changes enumerated after the market liberalisation under periodic export–import policies have been industry specific (http://www.exim-policy.com). In both types of reforms, facilitating exports has been a salient objective.

7. The least developed countries were given until 2016 to implement the TRIPS agreement, and some countries in Africa were allowed to have preferential arrangements with Europe and the United States in the textile industry.

8. The agreement (Article 1, Section 2) made some exceptions to 'permit meaningful increases in access possibilities for small suppliers and development of commercially significant trading opportunities for new entrants in the field of textiles and clothing trade' (World Trade Organization 1995a).

9. Both these provisions were challenged by multinational pharmaceutical firms in India but were affirmed by Indian courts. For details of these cases involving Novartis and Bayer, see Racherla (2019).

10. The Price Control Order of 1995 scaled back the number of bulk drugs under price control to seventy-four drugs representing 40 per cent of the total market. Through successive orders, the number of drugs under price control had been brought down from 342 in 1978 (out of approximately 350–360 bulk drugs then in the market, virtually 100 per cent of the drugs) to 142 in 1986 (out of approximately 700 bulk drugs then in the market).

11. The scheme was revised in 2012 and 2016; these revisions are mentioned as Revised Restructured TUFS (RR-TUFS) and Amended TUFS (ATUFS). For its history, latest position and annual disbursements, see Government of India, Ministry of Textiles (2019–2020).

12. For example, in 2005–2006, the number of approved applications was 1,078, which went to 12,589 the following year. From 1999 to 2019, a total of 49,679 have been funded through a total cumulative subsidy of INR 26,828 crores (Government of India, Ministry of Textiles 2019–2020b).

13. Export-promotion policies, especially through subsidies, is the subject of ongoing contestation at the WTO. Since these issues apply to all sectors, a detailed discussion of these contestations is beyond the scope of the study.

14. The detailed structural changes in and performance of the Indian pharmaceutical industry are discussed in Chapter 4.

15. There are numerous definitions of industrial policy (Warwick 2015: 15). This particular definition is adopted in this chapter because it incorporates both economic and social objectives behind policy interventions. As has been made clear throughout this chapter, policies in both textile and pharmaceutical industries have necessitated a balancing of competing objectives.

4

Industry Evolution

Tale of Two Industries

[Use] foreign trade, i.e., imports and exports, for balancing internal production and demands in such a way that we tilt our structure of production more in favour of employment-intensive industries and exchange its products with imported products that are less employment intensive.

—'Development Perspective', in *Eighth Five Year Plan, 1992–1997*
(Government of India 1992)

Foreign trade policies ... must be tailored to the objective of accelerating growth in an environment in which the world is becoming increasingly integrated and globalised. The process of globalisation ... needs to be managed so that we can derive the maximum advantage from world markets. To do this, it is necessary to continue the process of opening up the economy to international competition, ... while making parallel efforts to strengthen the potential of Indian industry to compete effectively in world markets.

—'Development Strategy', in *Ninth Five Year Plan, 1997–2002*
(Government of India 1997)

The previous chapter outlined the evolution of India's policy choices associated with economy-wide national and sector-specific global institutional changes. In particular, new global rules of the game regarding international trade and global competition in the textile and pharmaceutical industries in 1995 overlapped with domestic economic liberalisation underway during the previous years. The subtle but important implications of this interaction of national and global institutional changes are reflected in the epigraph passages from the preamble to India's five-year plans. While the development path put in place in the Eighth Five-Year Plan (1992–1997) to further economic liberalisation was through specialisation (that is, focusing on domestic production in employment-intensive industries while allowing free imports in industries that are not employment-intensive), the path in the Ninth Five-Year Plan (1997–2002) recognised the need for integration with global markets and sought to improve the competitiveness of Indian industry so that it can effectively compete in international markets. Both the textile and pharmaceutical industries belonged to the group of key sectors that would anchor India's development strategy, and, accordingly, industry-specific policies were put in place to help achieve the international competitiveness of the two industries.

The objective of this chapter is to evaluate the evolution of the Indian textile and pharmaceutical industries within the context of the multilevel institutional changes. Drawing from the literature on institutional change, industrial policy, and industry structure and evolution (for example, Fatas-Villafranca, Sanchez-Choliz and Jarne 2007; Majumdar and Bhattacharjee 2014; Malerba and Pisano 2019; Mingo and Khanna 2013), this chapter assesses the response or adjustment to national and global institutional changes and the associated policy initiatives during the 1990–2018 period. The goal is not to establish causal linkages but to evaluate, in a comparative setting, how each industry evolved during the different stages of institutional change on key aspects related to the development objectives put in place by government policy. In particular, the previous chapter outlined how export growth and international competitiveness were some of the key objectives for each industry that were to be accomplished through both supply-side (for example, production efficiency and innovation) and demand-side (for example, value-added differentiated products, diversification of markets) changes. These objectives, however, needed to be accomplished while monitoring the welfare implications of industry changes, that is, employment and subsector growth in the textile industry and the affordability and accessibility of drugs in the pharmaceutical industry. This chapter examines the evolution of these two industries in light of these parameters.

Much of the data used here are at the aggregate industry level, and attempts have been made to access these data primarily from official sources, both outside (for example, the World Bank, the United Nations Conference on Trade and Development [UNCTAD], the Organisation for Economic Co-operation and Development [OECD], the World Intellectual Property Organization [WIPO]) and within India (for example, the Reserve Bank of India, ministry data, survey of industries, sectoral census data, and so on). Wherever possible, multiple sources were consulted to evaluate the accuracy of the data. Second, the data presented in the chapter are descriptive and intended to capture trends over the period of study. That is, we do not statistically test causal relationships or perform any statistical tests but provide a representation of the evolution in various aspects of each industry. The main objective in this chapter is to understand how the two industries evolved in the light of the interplay of multi-level institutional changes and how this evolution incorporated some of the objectives put in place through policy interventions outlined in the previous chapter. Firm-level heterogeneity in responding to institutional changes is subsequently evaluated for each industry through formal modelling in the following chapter.

International Trade: Exports and Imports

Overall Country-Level Trade

Export-led growth has been a major component of India's economic development since the early 1990s, and this growth model was supposed to achieve two objectives: At the minimum, it would alleviate the foreign exchange crisis experienced by the Indian economy at the time by generating much-needed foreign reserves. More importantly, participation in international product markets was an important mechanism that would incentivise industrial sectors to invest in physical and human capital to move up the global value chain (that is, the 'accumulative' view of neoclassical economics [for example, Abramovitz 1986; Amsden 1989]) and become more innovative through 'learning by doing' (that is, the 'assimilative' view of evolutionary economics [for example, Dosi 1988; Nelson and Winter 1982; Nelson and Pack 1999; Nelson 2005; Lall 1992; Bell and Pavitt 1993]). This section evaluates how far the two industries of interest contributed to overall trade since 1991. In this regard, it is useful to first see the overall trajectory of India's trade since the inception of economic liberalisation. As shown in Figure 4.1, throughout the 1990–2018 period, India had a negative

Figure 4.1 India Exports and Imports of Goods and Services

Source: World Trade Organization (WTO) International Trade Statistics, 1990–2018, https://stats.wto. org/ (accessed 15 April 2021).

trade balance, with the deficit increasing from USD 6 billion in 1990 to USD 136 billion in 2012 and stabilising from 2012 to 2018. The data show that although exports increased substantially (the solid line) and consistently during the thirty-year period, import growth remained consistent and faster than export growth for most of the period.

Industry-Level Trade: Textile and Pharmaceutical Industries

The pertinent question for this study is the contribution of the Indian textile and pharmaceutical industries to India's overall trade position. Between the two industries, textiles played an important historical role in India's exports, and the post-liberalisation expectation was that this industry would continue to be a salient anchor of the country's exports of manufactured products. This is reflected in the specific objectives for the industry in the government's five-year plan for 1992–1997:

> … greater emphasis will be laid on production of value-added, diversified and quality goods for export and increasing capacity utilisation, sophisticated design and product-mix and appropriate technology…. The textile exports are expected to be Rs. 28,000 crores in 1996–97 (approximately USD 7.5 billion). To achieve this, emphasis will be laid on exports of non-quota items, higher unit-value realisation and better marketing techniques.

Figure 4.2 provides the exports and imports of India's textile industry.

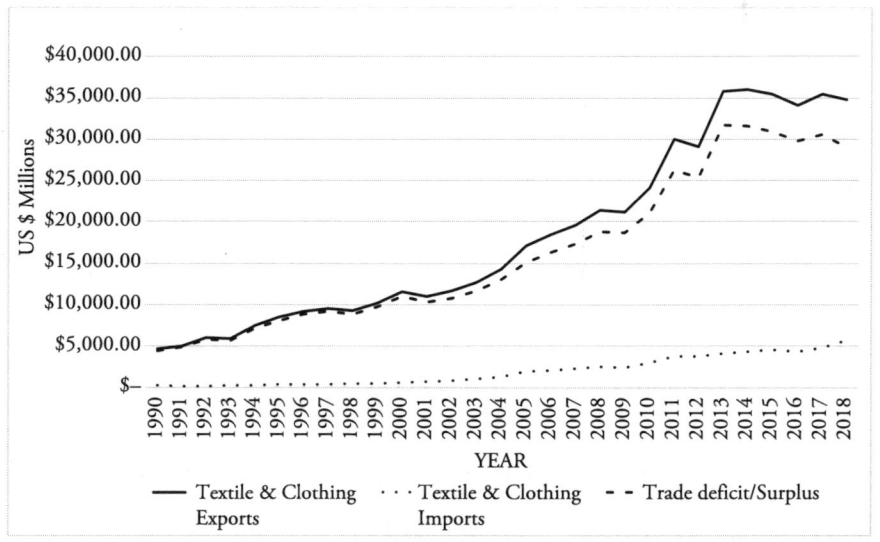

Figure 4.2 India Textile and Clothing Exports and Imports

Source: WTO, International Trade Statistics, 1990–2018, https://stats.wto.org/ (accessed 15 April 2021).

As seen in the figure, the textile industry has continued to positively contribute to the country's balance of trade, with a trade surplus throughout the period. Furthermore, textile exports increased seven-fold from 1990 to 2003 before stabilising during the 2013–2018 period. The greater integration of India's textile industry in global trade is reflected in increased imports of textiles from 2000 onwards, which escalated after 2005 when the global quota regime was abolished. A more fine-grained analysis of the sectoral (or segment-specific) growth in exports and imports will be carried out later in this chapter.

While textile exports had historically been a mainstay of India's international trade, the pharmaceutical sector was seen primarily as one that would meet domestic demand for affordable drugs. This is reflected in India's planning document of the post-liberalisation era. According to the Ninth Five-Year Plan (1997–2002), '[t]he domestic industry is in a position to meet about 70 per cent of [the] country's requirements of bulk drugs and almost the entire demand for formulations…. The public sector investment in the pharmaceutical industry has been the engine of growth for the industry as a whole….' It is only during the Tenth Five-Year Plan (2002–2007) that the export potential of the pharmaceutical industry was acknowledged, and the international orientation of the industry, anchored primarily by the private sector since India's liberalisation, has contributed to India's exports. The international trade data for this industry are provided in Figure 4.3.

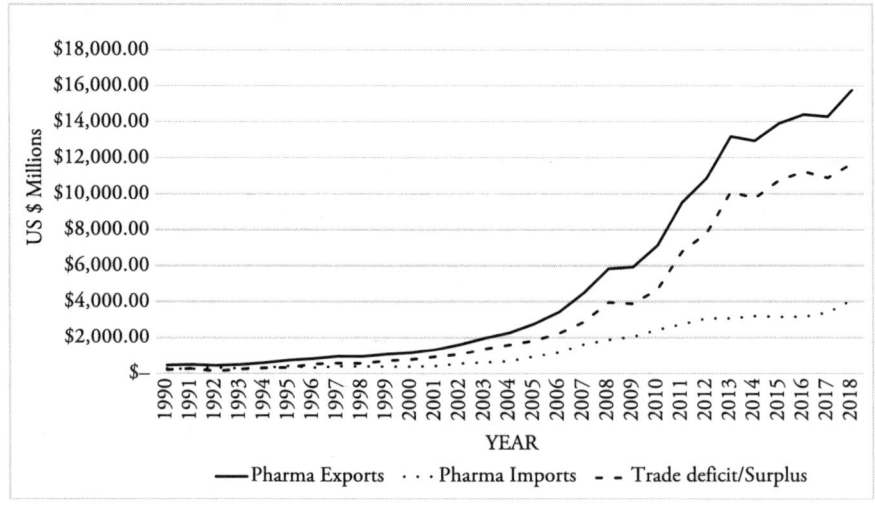

Figure 4.3 India Pharmaceutical Exports and Imports

Source: WTO, International Trade Statistics, 1990–2018, https://stats.wto.org/ (accessed 15 April 2021).

As shown in the figure, the Indian pharmaceutical industry was largely oriented towards the domestic market, with minuscule participation in global markets in the years prior to the economic liberalisation of 1991. Exports doubled in the first decade after liberalisation (1990–2000) but had exponential growth in the following decade, growing from approximately USD 1 billion in 2000 to more than USD 7 billion in 2010, which more than doubled again by 2016. There was also an increase in imports during this period, although the pharmaceutical industry in India has consistently maintained a trade surplus during the period of study. The growth in imports in the pharmaceutical industry closely tracks the growth in exports, thereby suggesting a close link between the two. It is clear from these data that the Indian pharmaceutical industry embraced globalisation, with initial internationalisation occurring in the context of national institutional changes heralded by India's economic liberalisation, which subsequently picked up speed as a response to the impending global institutional change related to the TRIPS agreement.

The data on India's overall trade flows in goods and services and those in the two industries show an overall increase in exports over the 1990–2018 period as well as an increase in imports. Both the textile and pharmaceutical industries show trade surpluses, thus contributing to reducing the country's overall trade deficit. A comparison of compounded growth rates in three specific post-liberalisation periods shows interesting contrasts between the two industries. As summarised in Table 4.1, the growth rates of pharmaceutical exports and imports during the three periods were very similar to India's overall trade growth rates. In the case of the textile industry, during the 1990–1995 period, exports grew at a faster rate than India's overall exports, while import growth was lower. However, export growth in textiles slowed considerably in the two subsequent periods (6.43 per cent during 1996–2005 and 4.97 per cent during 2006–2018), well below that of the pharmaceutical industry and India's overall trade export rates. Furthermore, textile imports increased substantially during the transition period at the end of the quota regime in global textile trade. While imports in the textile and pharmaceutical industry represented approximately 1 per cent each out of total imports during the 1990–2018 period, the share of textile exports in total India exports decreased from 23 per cent in 1990 to approximately 10 per cent during the 2008–2018 period, while the share of pharmaceutical exports increased from 2 per cent in 1995 to 5 per cent in 2018 (WTO, International Trade Statistics, 1990–2018, https://stats.wto.org/).

Table 4.1 Compound Annual Growth Rates in Exports and Imports

	Textiles and Apparel		Pharmaceuticals		Total India Goods and Services	
	Exports	Imports	Exports	Imports	Exports	Imports
1990–1995	10.27%	6.40%	8.13%	7.80%	8.8%	8.5%
1996–2005	6.43%	19.55%	13.00%	11.81%	13.6%	12.8%
2006–2018	4.97%	8.15%	12.48%	10.01%	9.3%	9.4%

Source: Computed by authors from the WTO, International Trade Statistics, 1990–2018, https://stats. wto.org/ (accessed 15 April 2021).

Although one cannot read too much from these trends without analysing the shifting trends in India's overall export basket,[1] it is at least clear that India's strategic dependence on the textile industry for earning its foreign exchange has decreased over the years, while the strategic importance of the pharmaceutical sector as an important contributor to India's trade surplus has increased. Overall, both industries continue to play an important role in India's export-growth aspirations, with the pharmaceutical industry showing greater export growth and increasing its contribution relative to the textile industry.

An additional trade-related aspect of the two industries is noteworthy. In addition to the contribution of each industry to India's trade balance, the two industries also increased their relative weights in their respective categories of world exports. As shown in Figure 4.4, the share of India's textile exports as a percentage of world textile exports increased from just over 2 per cent in 1990 to 2.75 per cent in 1995, 3.5 per cent in 2005 and to almost 4.75 per cent in 2015. That is, in line with predictions that larger textile-producing countries would gain from the abolition of the quota regime from 2005 onwards, the Indian textile industry increased its share in global exports in an era of increased competition in the industry. Data for the pharmaceutical industry are available from 2000 onwards, and, as shown in Figure 4.4, the pharmaceutical industry has also increased its share in the global export market from under 1 per cent in 2000 to 2.67 per cent in 2016, with most of the increase happening after the full implementation of the TRIPS agreement in 2005.

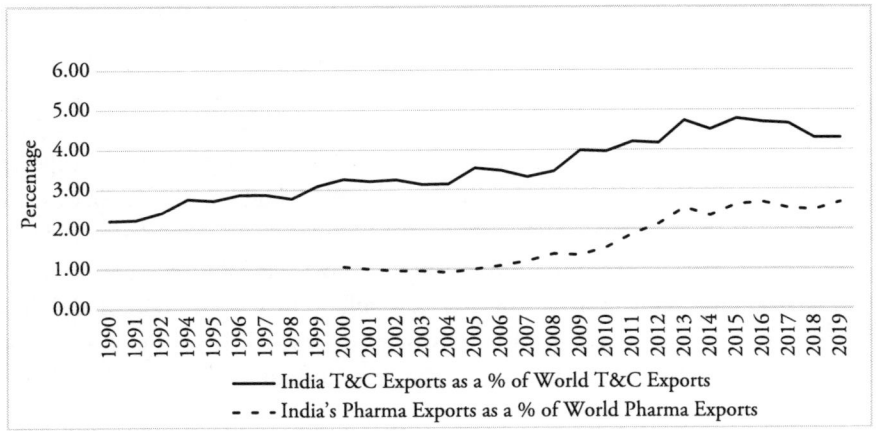

Figure 4.4 India Textile and Pharmaceutical Exports as a Percentage of World Exports

Source: Computed by authors from the WTO, International Trade Statistics, 1990–2018, https://stats. wto.org/ (accessed 15 April 2021).

Segment-wise Exports and Imports in the Two Industries

While the aforementioned data provide evidence about the ability of the two industries in India to cope with global institutional change by increasing industry exports and attaining a higher share in global export markets, whether this was achieved through a sustainable competitive advantage can be revealed by the nature of the products being exported and the export destinations of the products. In particular, the aspirations behind the various policy initiatives were to have a diversified portfolio of both products and markets for each industry. The following paragraphs evaluate these aspects through an analysis of the exports and imports within different subsegments (or sectors) of each industry as well as the geographical destinations and sources of the exports and imports respectively.

Although India's textile industry produces and exports manufactured materials from a variety of raw materials, the three segments comprising more than 80 per cent of total exports are cotton textiles, man-made textiles and ready-made garments.[2] The value-addition process of converting raw materials (both cotton and man-made fibres) to yarn is done in the organised mill sector, while the weaving of yarn to produce fabric and the subsequent conversion of fabrics to made-up items and ready-made garments is performed in the unorganised and decentralised handloom, power loom and garmenting sectors. The production data across the various sectors are provided in later sections in the chapter; here, the focus is on export data in the three primary segments.

As seen in Figures 4.5 and 4.6, ready-made garment exports constitute more than 40 per cent of the total textile exports from India, and the growth in exports has remained consistent throughout the period, with a growth spurt after 2005 when the Agreement of Textiles and Clothing (ATC) abolishing the quota regime came into effect. In the five years after the ATC, ready-made garment exports doubled from approximately USD 6 billion to USD 12 billion. Similarly, exports of man-made textiles have shown a consistent increase throughout the period but saw a similar spurt in export growth during the post-ATC five-year period, with exports doubling from approximately USD 2 billion in 2005 to more than USD 4 billion in 2010. Interestingly, the growth in the export of cotton textiles saw the greatest spurt from 2010 to 2015, when exports doubled from USD 5 billion to USD 11 billion.

What explains the sector-specific growth in different time periods? The end of the quota regime could have provided new market opportunities in the ready-made garment segment since a large part of these products were contract-manufactured for major international retail buyers. The end of bilateral quotas allowed these buyers to source their products from larger textile-producing countries. Man-made textiles may have benefitted from an increase in productivity because of technology upgrading. This will be discussed in more detail in the following sections. The lag in cotton textile export growth as a

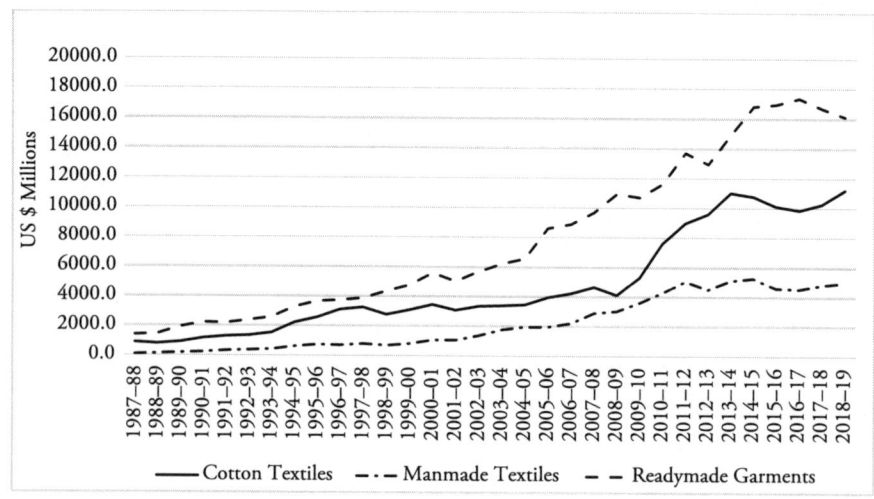

Figure 4.5 Segment-wise Textile Exports from India

Source: Reserve Bank of India trade data, https://dbie.rbi.org.in/DBIE/dbie.rbi?site=statistics (accessed May 2021).

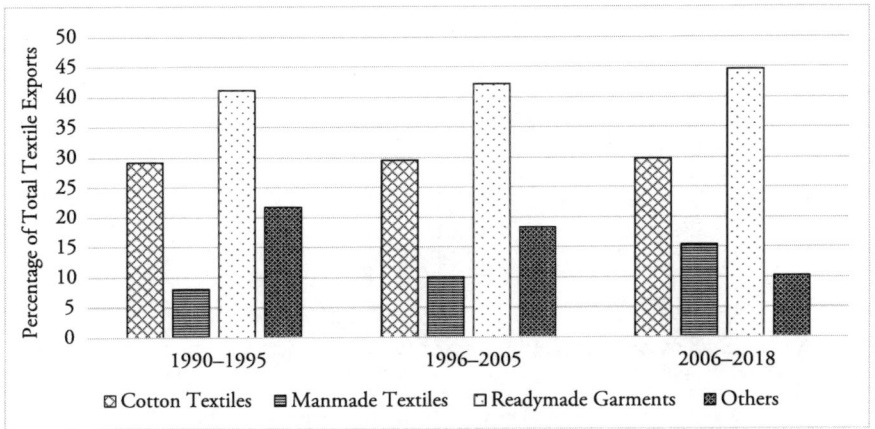

Figure 4.6 Segment-wise Share of Total Textile Exports from India

Source: Computed by authors from Ministry of Textiles Foreign Trade Statistics, 1990–2018, http://texmin.nic.in/textile-data (accessed 3 May 2021).

Note: 'Others' include wool, jute, silk and handicrafts.

response to the new global regime is somewhat puzzling, as it could connote the failure of the handloom and power loom sectors to enhance productivity in the light of impending institutional change. A further point of note from Figure 4.6 is the stable share of cotton textiles in total exports (approximately 29 per cent), while the share of ready-made garments increased from 41 to 45 per cent and that of man-made textiles from 8 to 15 per cent during the 1990–2018 period. Much of the increased share in these two segments came from other segments, which include wool, silk and jute.

Data for segment-specific imports in the textile industry are available in much less detail and for fewer years. While import of textiles continues to be a small part of India's textile trade, the growth rates in imports shown in Table 4.1 enable a noticeable trend. The noteworthy aspects of imports shown in Figure 4.7 are as follows: (*a*) the decrease in relative reliance on raw materials for total imports, which constituted almost 50 per cent of total imports during the 1990–1995 period and declined to approximately 20 per cent of total imports during 2006–2012; (*b*) the increase in the share of semi-raw materials from 11 per cent to 22 per cent during the same period—the most likely components of these imports are the intermediate materials for the production of man-made textiles—and (*c*) the increase in the share of imports of finished goods from 38 per cent to 55 per cent. This increase in finished goods imports could be due to intra-segment global trade for branded ready-made garments.

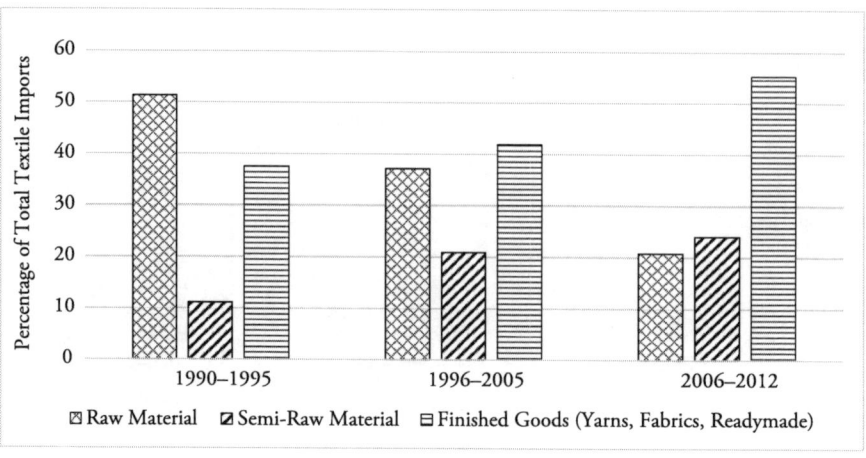

Figure 4.7 Segment-wise Share of Total Textile Imports into India

Source: Computed by authors from Ministry of Textiles Foreign Trade Statistics, 1990–2018, http://texmin.nic.in/textile-data (accessed May 2021).
Note: 'Others' include wool, jute, silk and handicrafts.

The major segments of the pharmaceutical industry in the manufacturing of drugs are (*a*) bulk drugs and active pharmaceutical ingredients (APIs) and (*b*) formulations. Formulations are final products, that is, drugs ready for consumption by patients, which can be sold in various forms, including tablets, capsules and injections (Greene 2007). Formulations are sold as branded (that is, protected through patents) or generic (that is, copies of off-patent branded drugs) products.[3] The input materials for creating the final products are bulk drugs and APIs (active chemical substances in powder form and having therapeutic value), which are manufactured from different chemicals. The Indian pharmaceutical industry is involved in the manufacturing of both formulations and bulk drugs, and, given its role as a major supplier of formulations of cost-effective generic drugs in world markets, India is often referred to as the 'pharmacy of the world'. The advantage in the production of bulk drugs and APIs is more cost-driven, given the requirements of economies of scale, while focus on formulations is more value-driven and success depends on both research and development (R&D) and marketing capabilities. In this regard, margins in the production of formulations are likely to be higher than those of bulk drugs and APIs.

Exports and imports of bulk drugs and formulations over four periods encompassing pre- and post-TRIPS agreement are summarised in Figure 4.8. The data show that the implementation of the TRIPS agreement in 2005 was the turning point in the global participation of the Indian pharmaceutical industry,

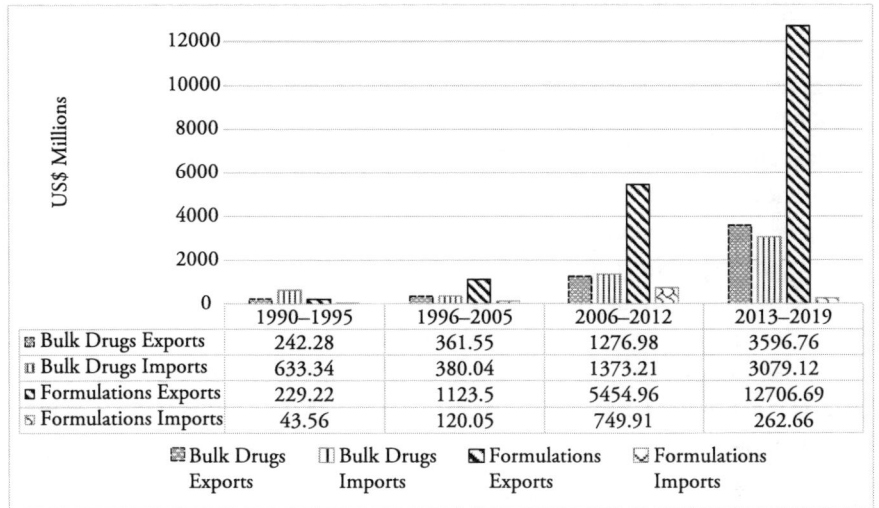

	1990–1995	1996–2005	2006–2012	2013–2019
Bulk Drugs Exports	242.28	361.55	1276.98	3596.76
Bulk Drugs Imports	633.34	380.04	1373.21	3079.12
Formulations Exports	229.22	1123.5	5454.96	12706.69
Formulations Imports	43.56	120.05	749.91	262.66

Figure 4.8 India Pharmaceutical Segment-wise Exports and Imports (Average Per Year during Each Period)

Sources: Computed by authors from the following sources: Pharmaceutical Export Promotion Council, Pharmexcil Annual Reports, 1990–2019, https://pharmexcil.com/annual-report (accessed 15 April 2021); Joseph (2009, 2016); Statista, http://statista.com/statistics (accessed 15 April 2021).

with substantial increases in both the export and import of bulk drugs and formulations. In terms of bulk drugs, India had a trade deficit during the 1990–1995 period, which narrowed in subsequent periods, turning into a surplus during 2013–2019. Some of the bulk drugs to be used as raw materials for formulations manufactured in India need to be imported, while the export of bulk drugs by Indian companies is likely input for branded drugs manufactured by multinational corporations in other markets. The balance in India's export and import of bulk drugs reflects the different roles played by the Indian pharmaceutical industry (that is, producer of finished generic products, contract manufacturer and supplier of both bulk drugs and formulations) (Horner 2014; Greene 2007). The increasing dependence on bulk-drug imports from China (almost two-thirds of total bulk-drug imports in 2019) is being seen as a cause for concern (Khurana and Iqbal 2020) for a number of reasons. First, it reflects India's cost disadvantage in manufacturing vis-à-vis China. Second, the low margins in bulk drugs disincentivise Indian manufacturers from making investments to improve productivity. Third, dependence on a single geographical source for imports of essential materials required for the formulation segment creates uncertainty in both the supply chain and the input costs (IBEF 2019; Joseph 2016; Khurana and Iqbal 2020).

Exports and imports in the formulations segment tell a different story. There has been an exponential growth in the export of formulations from India, increasing from an average of USD 229 million per year during 1990–1995 (pre-TRIPS but after economic liberalisation) to USD 1.12 billion during the transition period (1996–2005) and continuing to grow from 2006 onwards. Most formulation exports are manufactured by Indian pharmaceutical companies, who have since shifted their efforts to the manufacture of generic drugs in anticipation of the product patent regime initiated by the TRIPS agreement (Joseph 2016). Exports in formulations not only allowed India's pharmaceutical industry to expand its market for generics but also allowed it to find markets not subject to onerous price controls as in the domestic market. Formulation imports into India are distributed by foreign multinational companies, and these imports include high-priced branded or patented drugs. The easing of import barriers as well as the reduction in the number of drugs under price control during India's liberalisation era led to an increase in import of high-priced formulations, increasing from an average of USD 43 million during 1990–1995 to USD 120 million during 1996–2005, and picking up pace after the TRIPS agreement was implemented, averaging USD 750 million per year from 2006 to 2012. In his study of the post-TRIPS pharmaceutical industry, Chaudhuri (2012) wondered whether this increase in import of drug formulations would take India back to the era when the Indian pharmaceutical industry was dominated by foreign multinational corporations. As discussed in the previous chapter, these concerns led to the new pricing policy in 2012 (NPPP-12), which changed the criteria for price controls (one based on essentiality and price control of formulations rather than bulk drugs). As shown in Figure 4.8, this new policy stemmed the import of formulations, with average imports declining by three-fourths during the 2012–2018 period.

The segment-wise exports and imports discussed here show a fundamental transformation in the Indian pharmaceutical industry in anticipation of and response to global institutional change. Because of these global changes and national price constraints, the industry changed the product mix (that is, moving into the manufacture of generic drugs where it could continue to exploit its traditional advantages without running afoul of the intellectual property rights [IPR] regime and higher-priced formulations) and diversified the market for its products (thus being less constrained by domestic price controls). In addition, as will be discussed in the following section, the Indian pharmaceutical industry also moved into a higher degree and more involved modes of internationalisation, which created new opportunities for growth in a changed institutional context.

Geographical Diversification of India's Pharmaceutical and Textile Exports

In addition to the importance of product diversification in an industry's exports (in particular, having a greater proportion of high-value end-products), geographical diversification of export markets is also an important indicator of export competitiveness in an industry. More specifically, there is growing evidence that exporting products to foreign markets and interacting with competitors and consumers serve as important learning mechanisms that provide incentives to move up the value curve (Aulakh 2007; Luo and Tung 2007). For instance, it has been suggested that participating in more advanced economies provides better learning opportunities for developing economies.

We evaluated the destinations of textile and pharmaceutical exports from 1990 onwards using various sources.[4] For the sake of convenience, we divided export destinations into developed (OECD countries)[5] and developing (non-OECD) countries and examined the relative share of exports in each industry for the two groups. A number of interesting aspects emerge from this exercise. First, the share of drugs and pharmaceutical exports across the two groups remained consistent during the 1990–2018 period, with approximately 54 per cent of exports going to developed countries and 46 per cent to developing countries. In contrast, there is greater fluctuation in export destinations of textile exports. In 1992, 77 per cent of exports were destined for developed countries, which declined to approximately 70 per cent in 1995. This share persisted over the next ten years (that is, during the global institutional change transition, 1995–2005) but consistently declined after 2005 and stabilised to approximately 55 per cent since 2015. Thus, in both industries, there has been a convergence since 2015, with approximately 55 per cent of the exports going to developed and 45 per cent to developing economies.

Second, for the pharmaceutical industry, the United States (US) has become the major destination (25 per cent of total exports in 2012–2013 to 30 per cent of total exports in 2019–2020). Furthermore, within the developing countries group, Africa has become the major destination, replacing Russia and the erstwhile Soviet bloc as the major regional destination. Third, in terms of import origins, as highlighted earlier, China has become the major supplier to India of bulk drugs, contributing more than 60 per cent of India's imports.

For the Indian textile industry, there is a distinct difference in the destinations between general textile products and apparel/clothing products. For textile products, the top destinations in 1995 were the United States (14 per cent), the United Kingdom (9 per cent) and Germany (9 per cent).

By 2007, while the United States (16 per cent) continued to be the top destination, China (9 per cent) and the United Arab Emirates (5 per cent) replaced the UK (4 per cent) and Germany (4 per cent) among the top three destinations for Indian textile firms' exports (Kannan 2010). In terms of clothing exports, the US accounted for a lion's share (30 per cent) in 1995 and 2007, followed by European countries such as the United Kingdom (UK), Germany and France, with slightly lower shares in 2007 (Balasubramanyam and Wei 2005; Kannan 2010).

International Investments

Foreign investment provides external resources that help to finance the balance of payment deficits without adding to the country's external debt.... [It] also provides critical access to technology and other types of know-how and provides potential linkages to world markets. In a world where trade is increasingly dominated by transnational corporations, it is important to encourage foreign investment as part of the process of modernising our industry and developing linkages with the rest of the world.

—'Component of Development Strategy', in *Ninth Five Year Plan, 1997–2002* (Government of India 1997)

An important component of India's economic liberalisation in 1991 was the shift from the previous policy of curbing the presence of foreign multinational corporations in the domestic market to encouraging them to invest in India, particularly in 'high priority industries, requiring large investments and advanced technology' (Rao and Dhar 2020: 2). In the initial period, specific industrial sectors were identified, and the upper limit for equity participation of foreign companies was increased to 51 per cent. The salience of inward foreign direct investment (FDI) in India's economic development was acknowledged in subsequent policy initiatives, which led to an easing of the approval process for FDI as well as expanding the industrial sectors in which these investments were allowed. Restrictions on the amount of ownership held by foreign firms were also eased, with 100 per cent allowed in most cases by the early 2000s. As articulated in the aforementioned abstract from India's development strategy in the Ninth Five Year Plan of 1997–2002, FDI was seen not only as easing the balance of payment pressures on the economy but also as an important mechanism for accessing advanced technology and know-how. These were considered necessary for establishing global linkages and facilitating export-led growth objectives. For both the textile and pharmaceutical industries,

FDI restrictions were eased as part of the overall policy changes and as discussed in the previous chapter, to increase these industries' competitiveness in light of the global institutional changes.

Inward Foreign Direct Investments into India

Data on India's overall FDI inflows (Figure 4.9) show substantial increases with the various policy changes. From a relatively low level of USD 236 million in 1990, there was a steady increase in yearly amounts: reaching USD 3.6 billion in 2000, USD 27 billion in 2010, and USD 50 billion in 2020 (UNCTAD[6]). The compound annual growth rate in the overall FDI flowing into India was approximately 26 per cent from 1990 to 2010, 22 per cent from 2001 to 2010 and 7 per cent from 2011 to 2018. Figure 4.9 also shows the steady growth in outward FDI from India, starting with USD 6 million in 1990, increasing to USD 514 million in 2000, USD 15.9 billion in 2010 and approximately USD 13 billion in 2019. Overall, India's inward FDI flows were much greater than outward FDI flows, with cumulative outward flows of approximately 32 per cent of the inward flows during the 1990–2018 period. In terms of India's FDI position relative to global FDI flows, cumulative inward flows form approximately 1.77 per cent and outward flows form approximately 0.6 per cent of the respective world totals (UNCTAD[7]).

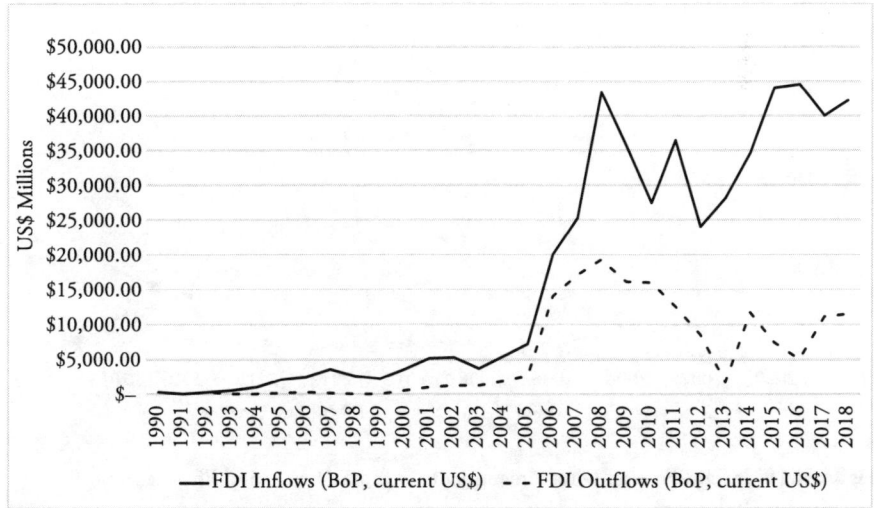

Figure 4.9 Total Inward and Outward Foreign Direct Investments, India

Source: UNCTAD, www.unctadstat.unctad.org (accessed 16 April 2021).

Figure 4.10 summarises inward FDI in India's textile and pharmaceutical industries. Precise sector-specific comparative data are available from 2000 onwards and are reported here. A few noteworthy aspects of these data are that, first, similar to India's overall FDI, there has been a steady increase in inward FDI in both industries (cumulative FDI during the 2001–2005 period: Pharmaceuticals – USD 497 million, Textiles – USD 114 million; 2006–2010: Pharmaceuticals – USD 981 million; Textiles – USD 714 million; 2011–2015: Pharmaceuticals – USD 7,341 million; Textiles – USD 794 million; 2016–2019: Pharmaceuticals – USD 2,887 million; Textiles – USD 1,470 million). Second, most of the increase in FDI growth in both industries occurred after 2005, the period when both global institutional changes were fully in force. Third, in terms of aggregate numbers, it is clear that during the 2000–2019 period, the pharmaceutical industry was able to attract much higher FDI than the textile industry (the cumulative inward FDI in pharmaceuticals was at USD 11.7 billion, while that for the textiles was at USD 3.1 billion).[8] Fourth, while the FDI inflows in textiles have seen steady growth, those for the pharmaceutical sector have been spikier. The primary reason for the spikiness in FDI in the pharmaceutical industry is that it was mostly acquisition-driven, that is, very large investments through acquisition by foreign multinationals of local Indian firms. This is discussed in more detail later. Overall, the pattern of inward FDI in

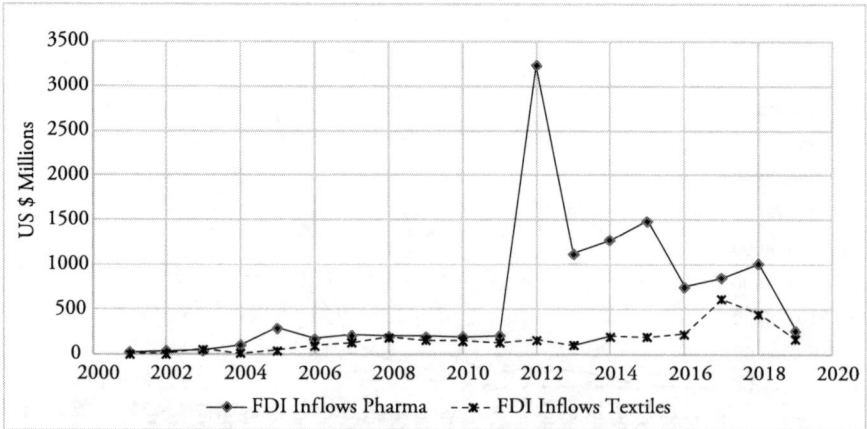

Figure 4.10 Inward Foreign Direct Investments in India's Textile and Pharmaceutical Industries

Sources: Pharma: Annual Reports, Department for Promotion of Industry and Internal Trade, India, https://pharmaceuticals.gov.in/annual-report (accessed 20 April 2021); Textiles: Ministry of Textiles, texmin.nic.in/textile-data (accessed 24 April 2021).

the two industries follows those of the overall flows in India, and the growth rates in these investments also correspond to changing circumstances necessitated by the two global institutional changes.

The nature of inward FDI flows in the two industries warrants further discussion. As mentioned earlier, in addition to the balance of payment benefits of FDI, developing countries see the potential of such investments as contributing 'to increased productivity among local firms by providing them with advanced knowledge and technology, by improving the country's infrastructure for private investment, and by motivating local firms to improve their business practices' (Spencer 2008: 342). Through the 'demonstration effects' of observing the products and processes of multinational corporations, local firms are expected to internalise best practices, which together create positive externalities through various types of spillovers (Spencer 2008). However, studies across various countries and industries have also called into question these purported benefits of inward FDI by bringing out the potential 'crowding out' effect, which 'occurs when the MNE poses competition in local product, labor, or financial markets that is intense enough to disadvantage local enterprises' (Spencer 2008: 341).

Research suggests that when foreign firms have superior technological, product and marketing capabilities, local firms are likely to be crowded out in the new competitive landscape because of limited absorptive capacities (Rao and Dhar 2020). Accordingly, studies have identified various factors that need to be present (for example, types of horizontal and vertical linkages between foreign MNCs and local firms, use of local versus expatriate management, and so on) for domestic industries in developing economies to achieve positive externalities of inward FDI (Spencer 2008). A particularly important factor in the context of the current study is the nature of inward FDI, that is, whether it is a greenfield investment or a brownfield investment, the latter usually taking the form of a merger with or an acquisition of a local firm. It has been suggested that brownfield investments are less conducive to horizontal spillovers in local markets because foreign investors invest in or acquire better local firms, thus further disadvantaging other local firms (Rao and Dhar 2020).

The inward FDI patterns in India's textile and pharmaceutical industries provide interesting contrasts with respect to the aforementioned aspects. In the case of the pharmaceutical industry, the spikes in inward FDI in Figure 4.10 reflect large acquisitions of Indian firms by foreign multinationals. Details of the top equity flows in India's drugs and pharmaceutical sector from 2000 to 2016 show that more than 80 per cent of the inward FDI in the industry is related to approximately fifteen acquisitions of Indian firms, with three Indian acquisitions contributing more than USD 7 billion of the total inward FDI in the sector.[9]

The mode of FDI in the pharmaceutical sector is thus concentrated with large acquisitions of local firms. Although the acquired Indian firms benefit from becoming a part of the acquiring multinational corporations' global production network (Horner 2014), these acquisitions limit horizontal spillovers to the broad industry sector in India (Abrol 2014).

The textile sector has attracted only approximately one-third of the FDI as the Indian pharmaceutical industry, but with more steady growth in investment inflows. A number of characteristics distinguish investments in the textile sector. First, unlike the high-technology sectors (including pharmaceuticals) where almost 86 per cent of the FDI inflows are brownfield in nature (that is, through local acquisitions), the low-technology sectors within which the textile industry falls attract many more greenfield investments (consisting of more than 56 per cent of total) (Rao and Dhar 2020). Second, the average size of the individual FDI projects is much smaller (for example, the largest investment in 2013–2014 was USD 40 million), and investments are spread across different Indian states and geographical clusters (Wazir Advisors 2016). Third, FDI is spread across the different subsegments, with 31 per cent going into the ready-made sector and 12 per cent each into the spinning and weaving sector (Wazir Advisors 2016). Although most of these investment flows are likely going to the organised sector of the textile industry (which is relatively small compared to the unorganised sectors), the distribution of investments is broader across regions and subsegments. Taken together, these factors suggest that the potential for horizontal spillovers in the textile industry was higher than that in the pharmaceutical sector and that it was less likely for local firms to be crowded out.

Outward Foreign Direct Investments

While much of the traditional literature on the relationship between FDI and economic growth in developing countries has focused on inflows from advanced economy multinationals, there is emerging evidence of how developing economies can benefit from outward FDI by their local firms. This phenomenon is relevant in the context of the current study, and before examining the data with respect to the two sectors, we first briefly provide the theoretical context (for details, see Aulakh 2007; Luo and Tung 2007). The traditional models of firm internationalisation were based on two premises: first, firms enter international markets to exploit the advantages developed in their home markets. Second, firms follow an incremental path to internationalisation, starting with low involvement modes of foreign participation such as exporting to institutionally similar markets and increasing escalation of commitments in institutionally distant markets, and followed by high involvement modes that could include equity joint ventures and wholly owned subsidiaries. The international participation of firms from developing economies in these theoretical frameworks was understood to be the exporting of goods where these countries had comparative advantages, and any investment outflows would be directed towards other developing economies. Accordingly, south–south FDI were undertaken by the so-called Third-World multinationals (Lall 1983; Wells 1983). The exporting success of a number of developing economies in the last few decades, with more advanced products and services in which they did not have traditional comparative advantages, and the increase in FDI in developed countries, often through acquisitions of iconic Western brands in a variety of industries (for example, automobiles, computers, white goods and technology), has led to a rethinking of the existing models of internationalisation. First, it is acknowledged that internationalisation motives can incorporate both exploitation of existing sources of advantage and exploration by learning from exposure to foreign customers and competitors. Second, exploration necessitates more involved foreign market participation, which includes acquisitions of foreign firms that may possess different types of capabilities, including technology, know-how and brand equity. Such multinationals from developing or emerging economies are now referred to as 'emerging market multinational corporations (EMNCs)', with common characteristics that include aggressive internationalisation, often through acquisitions, and with objectives of both exploitation of existing resources and exploration of new resources and capabilities (OECD 2006).[10]

The increase in outward FDI from India shown in Figure 4.9 can be understood in terms of the motivations and paths of internationalisation of the country's emerging multinationals who 'seek to access overseas markets, acquire intangible assets like new technologies and skills, ... and, in special cases, secure natural resources...' (Pradhan and Sauvant 2010: 13). The share of India's outward FDI destined for developed countries increased from 23.7 per cent during 1980–1989 to 44.1 per cent during 1990–1999 and further to 49.5 per cent during 2000–2009 before tapering off to approximately 40 per cent in subsequent years (Pradhan 2017).[11] Furthermore, since the early 2000s, acquisitions of foreign firms have been an important mode of overseas investment (for a detailed discussion of the historical trends in outward FDI from India, see Pradhan and Sauvant 2010; Joseph 2019). A number of empirical studies of overseas acquisitions by Indian firms have affirmed their exploration motivations (for example, Buckley et al. 2016; Gubbi 2015) and performance-enhancing benefits of acquisitions, which are especially pronounced when Indian firms acquire targets in advanced countries (for example, Gubbi et al. 2010).

Given the inability to access yearly industry-level outward FDI data from government sources, the period-level data reported in two published studies (Pradhan 2017; Joseph 2019) are summarised in Figure 4.11. As seen from the figure, overseas investments in the two industries picked up the pace after 2000. The textile industry experienced substantial growth from 2000 to 2009, which stabilised in the subsequent period. The pharmaceutical sector has seen consistent growth in outward FDI in the two periods since 2000, and this constitutes approximately 15 per cent of India's total outward FDI in the manufacturing sector. On the other hand, the textile industry's share has declined to slightly more than 2 per cent.

The nature of outward FDI in the two industries differs in terms of the underlying motivations and the modes of investment. Acquisition of foreign firms (mostly in developed economies) is the preferred mode of overseas investments in the pharmaceutical industry, along with a few foreign alliances and joint ventures (Greene 2007).[12] Although there are a few large overseas acquisitions made by Indian pharmaceutical firms (Furtado 2017), similar to the acquisition of Indian firms made by foreign multinational corporations (discussed earlier), a large proportion of the foreign acquisitions are of small- and medium-sized companies (Pradhan 2017).[13] Second, the motivations behind these acquisitions are to 'penetrate overseas markets and widen their global footprint, diversify and enhance their product portfolios, offer their customers a "nearshore-offshore"

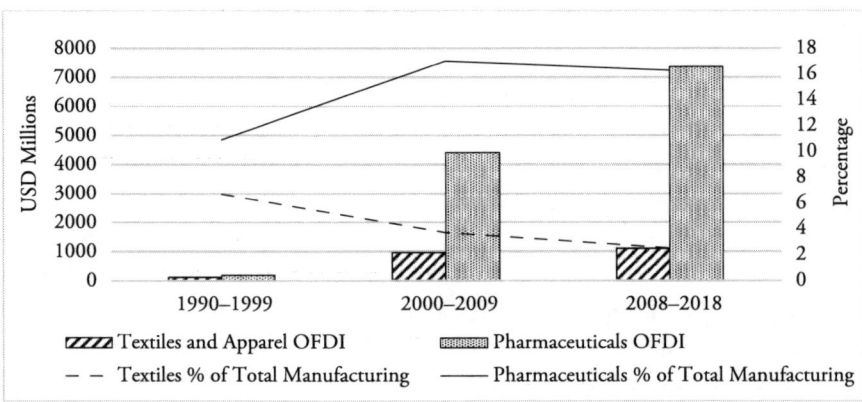

Figure 4.11 Outward Foreign Direct Investments in India's Pharmaceutical and Textile Industries

Sources: Pradhan (2017); Joseph (2019).

Note: There is an overlap in reported data for the latter time periods. This is because of the way the data are reported in the two source studies from which the data are extracted.

option, improve ... R&D capabilities, acquire existing brands, and gain access to the highly regulated markets' (Greene 2007: 8). The outward FDI in the pharmaceutical industry in the post-TRIPS era has followed a dual path of asset exploitation (diversifying into new markets with generic and low-cost products) and asset exploration (acquiring know-how and marketing assets) (Buckley et al. 2016; Pradhan and Alakshendra 2006).

The outward FDI path in the textile industry is different in two aspects. First, according to available data for 2011–2015 (Wazir Advisors 2016), only 11 per cent of the total USD 836 million investments abroad is through acquisitions or joint ventures (6 per cent of the total is through greenfield investment). The vast majority of the outward flows are in holding companies registered in tax-haven countries (Wazir Advisors 2016). Second, while there are a few investments to acquire foreign brands, a large number of greenfield and brownfield investments are in manufacturing plants in other developing countries. In one sense, the outward FDI path followed by the textile industry is closely related to that of the 'Third-World multinationals', while the outward FDI path of the pharmaceutical industry is akin to the 'EMNCs' discussed earlier.

Investments in Assets and Capabilities

[T]he Multi-Fibre Arrangement (MFA) would cease to be in force after 2005. The Indian textile industry would get unrestricted access to the world market but would also face competition in the international market as well as in the domestic market from foreign exporters. It is, therefore, imperative to take urgent steps to bridge the technological gap.... Upgradation [of the sector] needs special attention and large doses of investment [and its] modernization ... would be a major thrust area in the Ninth Plan.

—'Assessment of the Textile Sector', in *Ninth Five Year Plan for 1997–2002* (Government of India 1997)

With the quick phasing out of drugs and introduction of product patenting, the [Indian pharmaceutical] industry is on the verge of losing all its advantages. The challenge for the industry today is a change in attitude towards innovative R&D.

—'Assessment of the Pharmaceutical Sector', in *Tenth Five Year Plan for 2002–2007* (Government of India 2002)

Growth in international trade and investment discussed in the previous sections was seen both as a precursor to and consequence of the investments made in the two industries to upgrade existing assets and capabilities and develop new ones. National policy objectives for these industries, reflected in the extracts from India's five-year plans, included investments to modernise the production capabilities and for R&D in order that production can be shifted towards more value-added products. For the textile industry, the policy initiatives focused on direct intervention through the Technology Upgradation Fund Scheme (TUFS), which provided interest subsidies for investments related to the modernisation of production technology. In the case of the pharmaceutical industry, policy intervention was geared more towards providing a favourable regulatory framework conducive to investments in R&D (Abrol 2016). This section evaluates investments in assets and capabilities in the two industries in the light of these policy initiatives related to global institutional changes. We undertook this analysis using data from the Annual Survey of Industries conducted by India's Ministry of Statistics and the data collected by the Centre for Monitoring of Indian Economy (CMIE) Prowess Database from the companies' annual reports. While the former data source is useful because of its broad coverage of each industry, the latter has the advantage of more fine-grained firm-level data, although the number of firms covered is much smaller than in the Annual Survey of Industries.

Figure 4.12 provides information on fixed-capital (which includes plant and machinery) formation in the organised sector of the textile industry from 1990 to 2017 as well as the number of factories engaged in production. As seen in the figure, the number of factories in the organised sector increased slightly

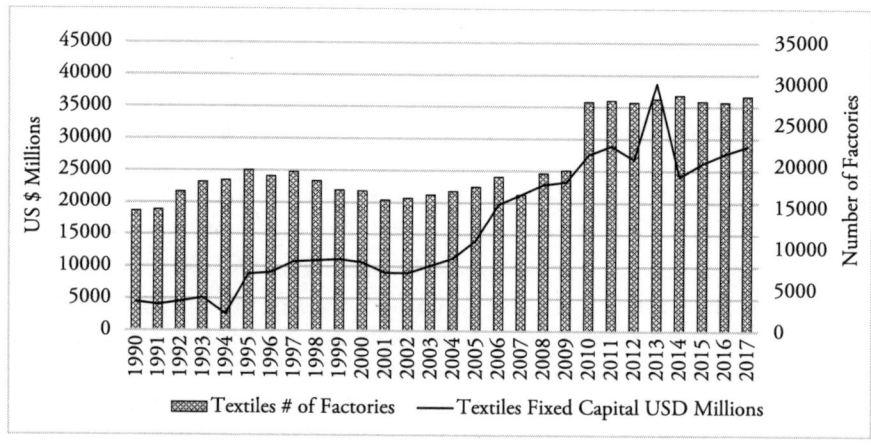

Figure 4.12 Textile Industry Fixed Capital and Number of Factories (Organised Sector)

Source: Ministry of Statistics and Programme Implementation, Government of India, Annual Survey of Industries (ASI), 1990–2017, http://microdata.gov.in/nada43/index.php/catalog/ASI (accessed 1 May 2021); includes both textiles and apparel.

after the 1991 economy-wide economic liberalisation but then declined from 1995 to 2005 (19,500 to 17,500), before seeing a steady increase until 2010 and stabilising since then to approximately 28,000. The trend in total fixed capital shows a relatively flat period from 1997 to 2004 and then a sudden increase in industry fixed capital, more than tripling from 2004 to 2013. In mapping the trend in fixed capital in the textile industry (Figure 4.12) on to the disbursements of TUFS loans in Figure 4.13, it is clear that much of the increase in fixed capital can be attributed to these loans, which were specific to technology upgrading and involved investments in plants and machinery. Although the TUFS programme was initiated in 1999 to prepare the industry for the impending global change to come into effect in 2005, the scheme did not gain much traction until 2004–2005. It was only after 2004 that the number of applications and actual disbursement of subsidised loans to upgrade the production technology increased (NCAER 2009). It should also be noted that the TUFS loans were provided primarily for the organised sector and, as will be discussed later, may have impacted the overall productivity in the various subsegments.

Data for the pharmaceutical data are summarised in Figures 4.14 and 4.15. As shown in Figure 4.14, the number of factories involved in the production of drugs and pharmaceuticals increased steadily from 1,794 in 1990 to 5,051 in 2017, and this growth was much higher than that in the textile sector. In terms of investments in plants and machinery, reflected in fixed capital,

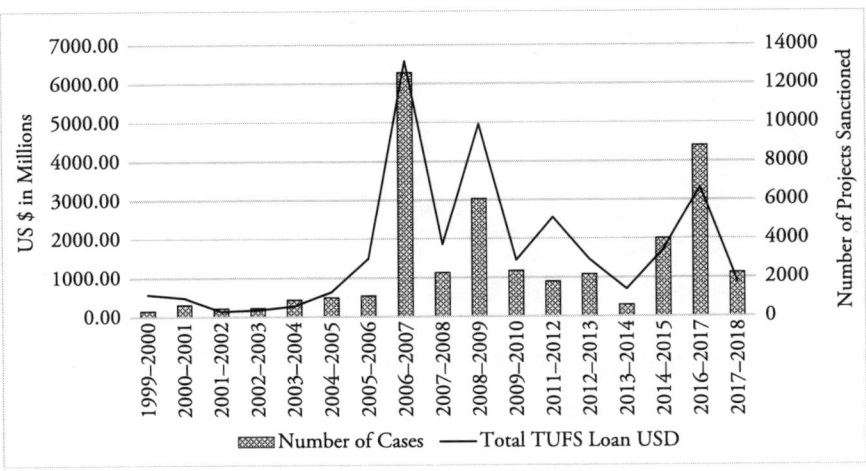

Figure 4.13 Loans Sanctioned in the Textile Sector under TUFS

Source: Computed from Ministry of Textiles, Government of India, Annual Reports, 1999–2018, http://texmin.nic.in/documents/annual-report (accessed 5 May 2021).

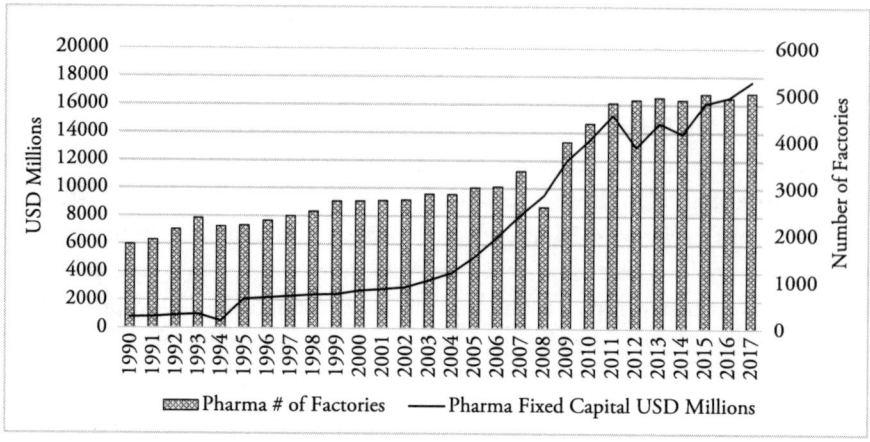

Figure 4.14 Pharmaceutical Industry Fixed Capital and Number of Factories

Source: Ministry of Statistics and Programme Implementation, Government of India, Annual Survey of Industries (ASI), 1990–2017, http://microdata.gov.in/nada43/index.php/catalog/ASI (accessed 1 May 2021). *Note*: There are some missing data for a few years. In those cases, averages of previous and subsequent years have been used.

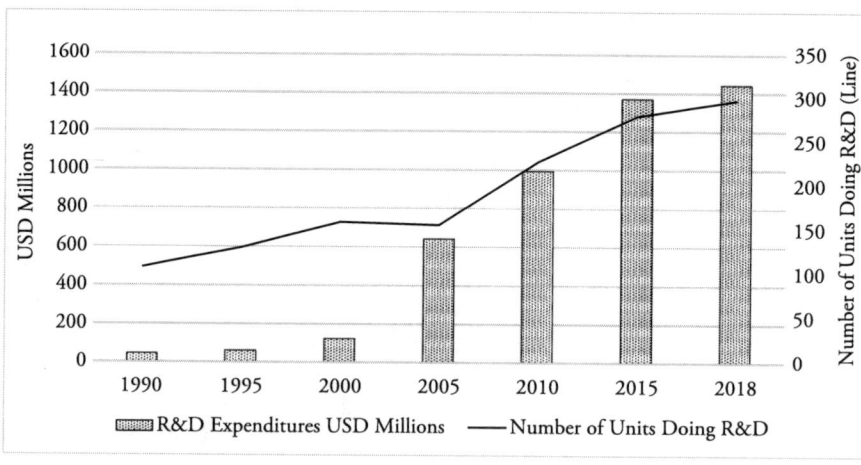

Figure 4.15 Total R&D Expenditures in India's Pharmaceutical Industry

Source: Department of Science and Technology, Government of India, Biannual Reports, R&D Statistics, 1990–2018, http://digitalrepository-nstmis-dst.org/adv_search.php?type_doc=Research%20and%20Development%20Statistics (accessed April–May 2021).

we see that there was not much shift after the adoption of economically extensive liberalisation in 1991, with an increase in investments coinciding with the TRIPS agreement of 1995. During the interim period (1995–2005), fixed capital in the industry increased from USD 2,100 million to 5,115 million. In the following decade (2016–2105), fixed capital almost tripled to USD 16,000 million. Since much of this increase in fixed capital happened through investments by the private sector, it is possible that some of the inward FDI in the industry financed this increase. There is also evidence that a large number of local pharmaceutical firms shifted to contract manufacturing for the large multinational corporations that entered India after the TRIPS agreement, and these firms increased investment in plants and machinery to achieve better productivity, and modernised to meet the manufacturing standards of foreign regulatory bodies (Abrol 2014; Aggarwal 2004; Athreya, Kale and Ramani 2009).

As per Figure 4.15, there was also an increase in R&D activity in the pharmaceutical industry in terms of both the number of firms undertaking R&D and the total investment. Much of the growth in R&D expenditure occurred after 2000, increasing from USD 123 million in 2000 to USD 1,441 million in 2018. Despite this impressive growth in expenditure, there are questions regarding whether these investments are adequate for moving up the value curve, especially in the discovery of new patentable drugs. This aspect is discussed later in the chapter.

Figures 4.16 and 4.17 are based on the firm-level data from the CMIE Prowess database and represent data of the larger firms in each industry. The number of firms in the textile industry within this database increased from 122 in 1990 to the highest level of 615 in 2010, while the number in the pharmaceutical sector increased from 49 in 1990 to the highest level of 443 in 2015. The increase in the number of firms reflects new industry entrants (as well as new inclusion in the database), and the decline can probably be attributed to mergers and acquisitions. These figures provide more specific data on average plant and machinery assets, and the trend lines with the smaller samples are very similar to increases in fixed capital reported in the Annual Surveys of Industries. That is, much of the growth in investments occurred in the period after global institutional changes were implemented in each industry, rather than in the interim period (1995–2005), when the two industries had time to prepare for impending institutional changes. In addition to investments in plants and machinery, the two figures also capture average expenditures in marketing and R&D. In terms of R&D, there is negligible investment in the textile industry (an increase from USD 0.01 million to 0.03 million), while the pharmaceutical industry saw higher growth (increasing from an average of USD 0.05 million in 1990 to

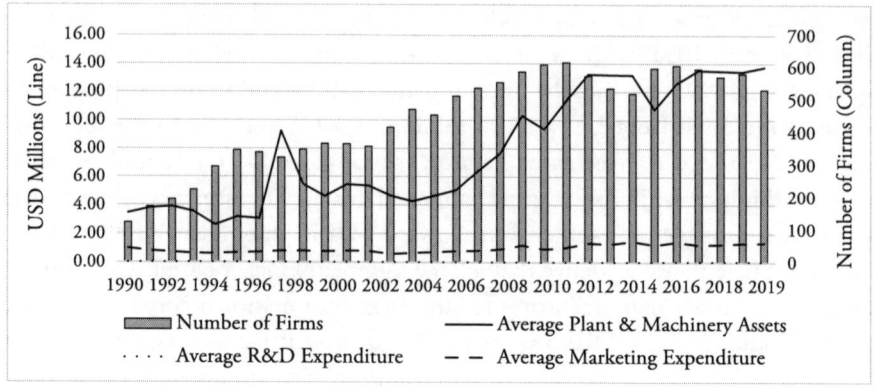

Figure 4.16 Textile Industry: Investments in Plant and Machinery, R&D and Marketing

Source: CMIE Prowess.

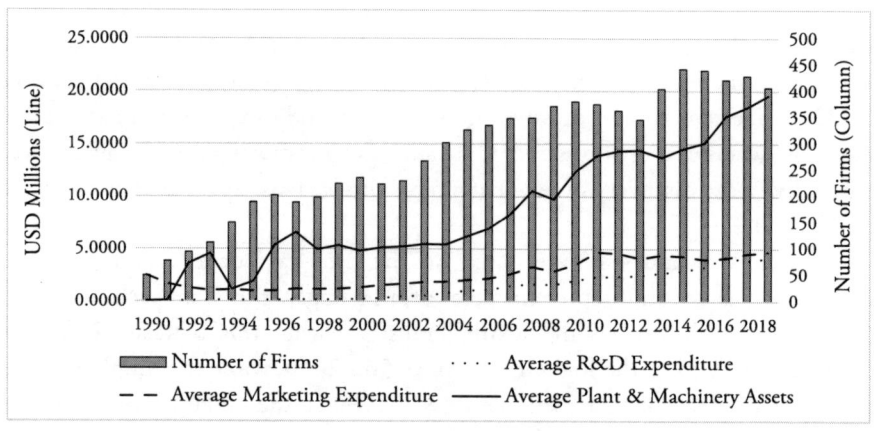

Figure 4.17 Pharmaceutical Industry: Investments in Plant and Machinery, R&D and Marketing

Source: CMIE Prowess.

USD 4 million in 2018). In the pharmaceutical industry, average marketing expenditures declined from 1990 to 2000, but since then, they have increased from an average of USD 1.3 million in 2000 to almost USD 4.7 million in 2018. The textile industry also saw a decline in marketing expenditures during the 1990–2002 period, after which it showed a slow increase (from USD 0.65 million in 2002 to USD 1.35 million in 2018). In comparing the two industries, it seems that while there is a substantial increase in investments in plant and machinery in both industries, the textile industry has lagged behind the pharmaceutical sectors in marketing and R&D investments.

Performance Outcomes in the Two Industries

The previous sections outlined major shifts in various aspects in the Indian textile and pharmaceutical industries within the context of multi-level institutional changes and the associated policy interventions. We have also examined strategic performance outcomes such as export performance, which is critical in the context of both industries. In this section, we evaluate some value-added and financial performance parameters associated with these strategic shifts. We first compare the two industries on common parameters related to productivity relative to each other and to India's overall manufacturing sector, as well as the average profitability of firms in the two industries using data from the CMIE Prowess database. Subsequently, we assess the performance of each industry according to specific parameters relevant to each industry. That is, for textiles, we examine sectoral production in the light of employment considerations, while for the pharmaceutical industry, we focus on R&D-related outcomes.

Figure 4.18 shows the value-added share of the Indian textile and pharmaceutical industries in the country's total manufacturing. Given the historical importance of the textile industry to India's economy, its high share of 15 per cent in 1990 is not surprising, prior to the economy-wide liberalisation of 1991. The Indian pharmaceutical industry, on the other hand, played a small role in 1990, which remained consistent (approximately 2 per cent) until 1995. Since 1995, the industry's contribution has increased steadily, with contributions

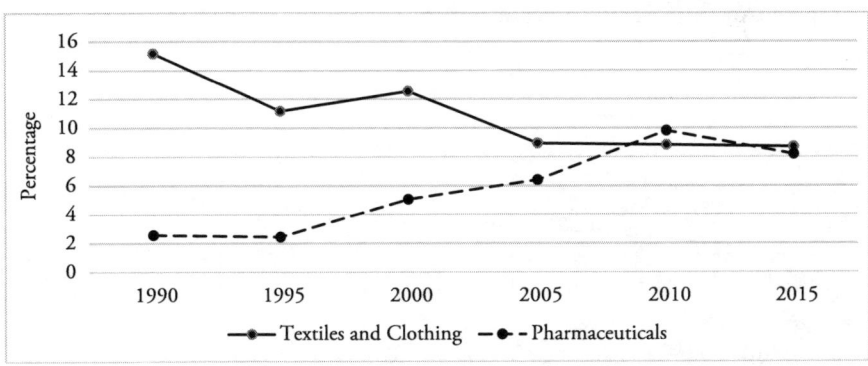

Figure 4.18 Textiles and Pharmaceuticals Value Added to Total Manufacturing in India

Sources: Computed by authors from data.worldbank.org; Reserve Bank of India, *Handbook of Statistics on the Indian Economy*, 1990–2015, https://rbi.org.in (accessed April–May 2021); and Ministry of Statistics and Programme Implementation, Government of India, Annual Survey of Industries (ASI), http://microdata.gov.in/nada43/index.php/catalog/ASI (accessed 1 May 2021).

Note: Value-added is calculated as the sum of gross output less the value of intermediate inputs.

reaching 5 per cent in 2000, 6.3 per cent in 2005 and 10 per cent in 2010. The textile industry's share showed mostly a downward trend, going down to approximately 9 per cent in 2005, a level where it stayed for the following decade. While these numbers may also reflect the general catch-up of other industries (such as pharmaceuticals), including the contribution of new sectors to India's manufacturing, it is clear that the prominence of the textile industry in total manufacturing has declined in the era of economic liberalisation and the post-ATC trade regime.

To further assess the growth in production of the two industries, the index of industrial production published by the Reserve Bank of India is examined over different time periods. This index is a composite indicator measuring changes in the volume of production of a basket of industrial products over a period of time with respect to a chosen base period. The index provides indicators for the prominent industrial sectors in India's economy as well as of total manufacturing. Comparing an industrial sector with overall manufacturing gives a sense of the relative production of the chosen sector. Given the historical weight of the textile and apparel industry, the indices are available for an extended time period. The pharmaceutical industry was included in more recent years. The indices for the textile and apparel industry for the 1994–2016 period are given in Figures 4.19 and 4.20.

With the base year 1993–1994 (index = 100), Figure 4.19 shows that the index for overall manufacturing more than doubled, reaching 214 in 2014–2015. Compared to this overall increase in production, the growth in cotton textiles

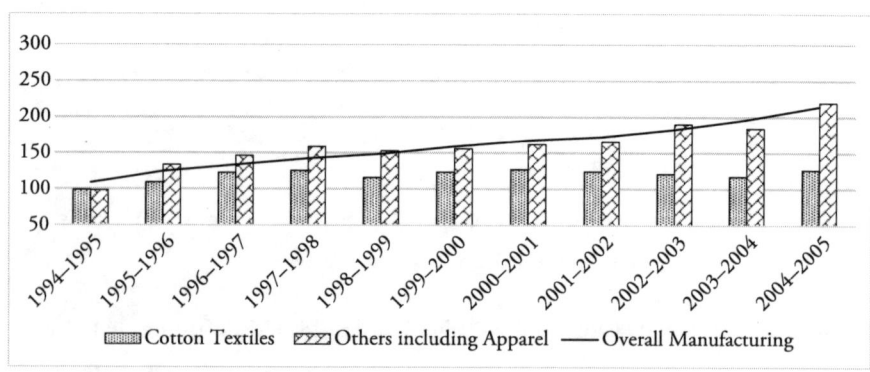

Figure 4.19 Textile Industry: Index of Industrial Production (1994–2005); Base Year: 1993–1994 = 100

Source: Reserve Bank of India, *Handbook of Statistics on the Indian Economy*, 1994–2005, https://rbi.org.in (accessed April–May 2021).

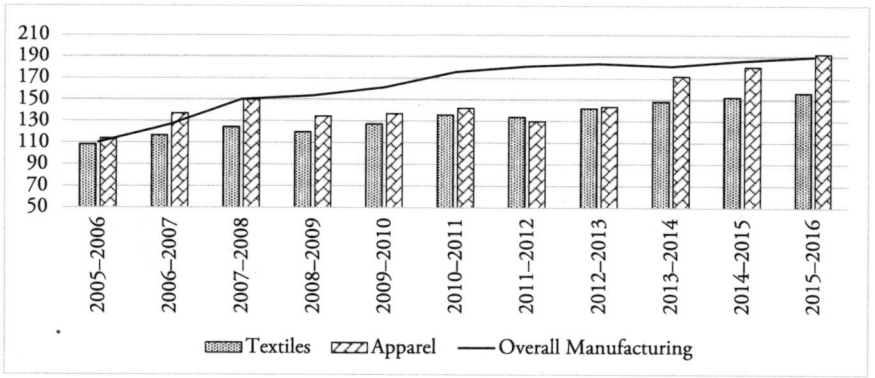

Figure 4.20 Textile Industry: Index of Industrial Production (2005–2016); Base Year: 2004–2005 = 100

Source: Reserve Bank of India, *Handbook of Statistics on the Indian Economy*, 2005–2016, https://rbi.org.in (accessed April–May 2021).

over the ten-year period was 25 per cent, while the apparel sector kept pace with the overall growth in the manufacturing sector (109 in 1994–1995 to 220 in 2004–2005). This trend of underperformance of the textile sector continued in the following decade, as shown in Figure 4.20. With a base year of 2004–2005 (index = 100), the value for overall manufacturing almost doubled (reaching 190 in 2015–2016). The increase in the production of textiles remained below that of overall manufacturing throughout the period (increasing to 156 in 2015–2016), while apparel production exhibited greater fluctuation, outperforming overall manufacturing at the beginning and end of the period and underperforming during the middle period.

Figure 4.21 provides the index of industrial production since 2012, with the base year set at 2010–2011 (index = 100). For this period, drugs and pharmaceuticals were included in the index and, thus, this figure gives a comparison between the two industries of interest as well as their relative production vis-à-vis the overall manufacturing sector. During this time period, the textile sector performed close to that of overall manufacturing, slightly overperforming in the first half and underperforming in the second half. The apparel sector performed better during the period (going from 99 to 155). Relative performance was the highest for the pharmaceutical industry, which went from 108 in 2012–2013 to 215 in 2019–2020, thus outperforming the textile and apparel sectors as well as the index for overall manufacturing. The above data on the index of industrial production show a consistent underperformance gap for the textile sector

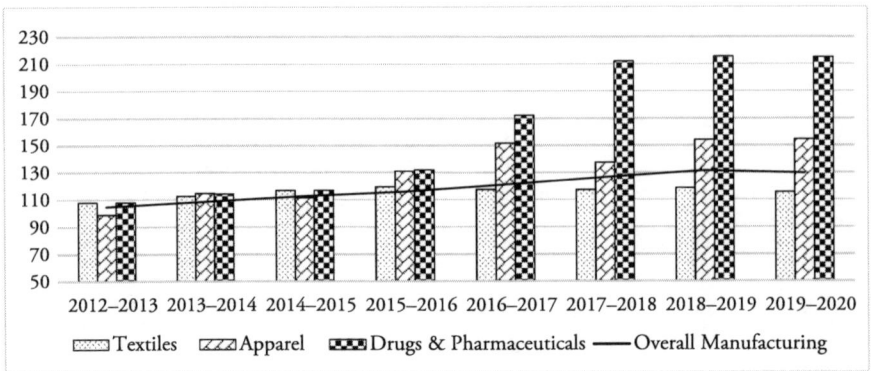

Figure 4.21 Textile and Pharmaceutical Industries: Index of Industrial Production (2012–
          2020); Base Year: 2010–2011 = 100

Source: Reserve Bank of India, *Handbook of Statistics on the Indian Economy*, 2012–2020, https://rbi.org.in
(accessed April–May 2021).

(which comprises the production of cloth in the industry). The following section
probes this further by examining productivity in the three main subsegments
involved in cloth production.

From the broader value-added and production outcome measures discussed
earlier, we now move to more specific firm-level financial performance outcomes
such as profitability. We choose two measures of financial performance:
(*a*) return on assets (ROA) measured as profit before interest and tax divided by
total assets; and (*b*) gross margins measured as profit before depreciation interest
and tax divided by total sales. We consider gross profit measures instead of net
profit measures to discount for the effects of government support incentives such
as subsidies on taxes and borrowings (for example, interest subsidies on loans).
The trends in industry average ROA and gross margins during the
1990–2019 period are captured in Figure 4.22 (textile industry) and Figure 4.23
(pharmaceutical industry). As shown in Figure 4.22, the average ROA and gross
margins in the textile industry decreased from 11–12 per cent in 1990 to 6–8 per
cent (ROA) and 2–4 per cent (gross margins) in 2019. The profitability drop was
quite precipitous between 1990 and 2000 as firms prepared for the upcoming
institutional change and recovered some lost ground in the next decade.
This seems to indicate that Indian textile firms dropped prices and sacrificed
profitability to retain their market share in the globally competitive marketplace
of the new institutional regime. Any further improvement from these profitability
levels could only be achieved through a shift towards more value-added products
and improvements in cost efficiencies.

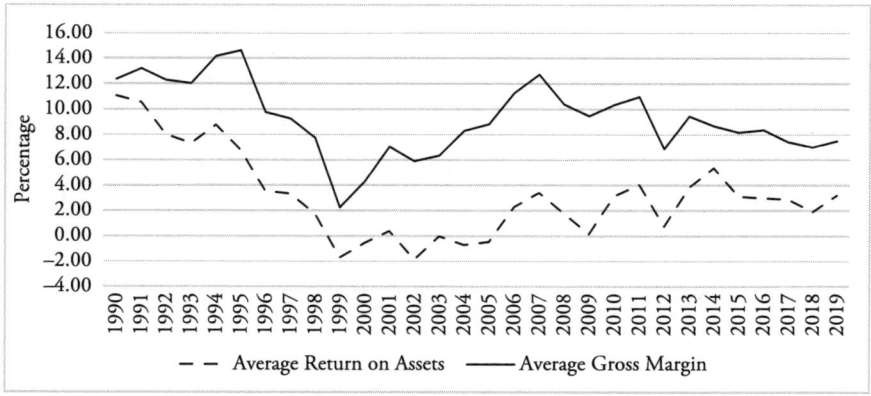

Figure 4.22 Textile Industry Profitability

Source: CMIE Prowess.

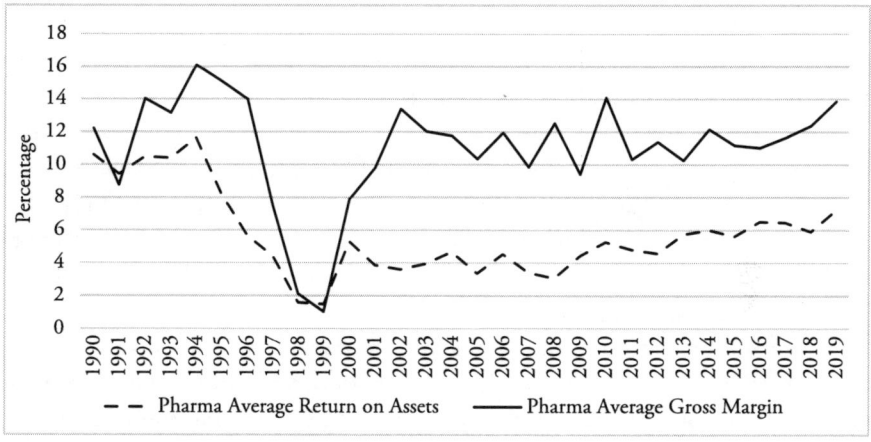

Figure 4.23 Pharmaceutical Industry Profitability

Source: CMIE Prowess.

Interestingly, the average profitability in the pharmaceutical industry in terms of ROA and gross margins was also at the 11–12 per cent level in 1990 and saw a similar steep decline to just approximately 2 per cent by 2000. However, the recovery was also very sharp in the case of the pharmaceutical industry, with the average ROA rising to 12 per cent within two to three years and staying within a healthy range of 12–14 per cent since then. Average gross margins have also shown a similar recovery to approximately 4–5 per cent and have since been rising gradually over the last decade. The healthy financial performance, on average, of the pharmaceutical industry demonstrates its successful strategic response to global institutional change, which is a combination of firm-level, industry-level and institutional-level responses. Specifically, this financial performance has been the result of (*a*) a strategic shift towards more internationalisation—both inward and outward—and (*b*) a strategic focus on generic drugs by building and leveraging core capabilities for this product market.

Segment-wise Production and Employment in the Textile Industry

In assessing the role of India's textile industry in the country's overall economy, successive five-year plans have identified three important roles: contributor to overall industrial output, generator of substantial employment, and foreign exchange earner. Thus, as discussed in the previous chapter, the policy thrust has been to provide the resources and regulatory framework for the industry to continue to achieve these three objectives. However, the nature of the evolving global competition since the quota regime was abolished has led to a paradox whereby simultaneously achieving these three goals is difficult—in particular, balancing an increase in productivity (and export growth in cost-competitive markets) with employment generation. In the following paragraphs, we evaluate production and employment in three subsegments of cloth production (that is, the organised sector, which includes the mill sector and part of the factory apparel or ready-made segment, the power loom sector and the handloom sector) for which longitudinal data are available.[14]

Figure 4.24 summarises the total cloth production in India in various years between 1990 and 2019, which includes fabric from cotton and man-made materials. The total production increased from 22,928 million square metres in 1990–1991 to 71,051 square metres in 2018–2019. However, over the years, there has been a shift in the relative share of different sectors in the production of cloth. The dominant sector is the decentralised power loom sector, which has consistently contributed more than 55 per cent of the total production. The share of the organised mill sector declined from 11.3 per cent in 1990–1991 to 2.9 per cent in 2018–2019. Similarly, the contribution of the handloom sector has declined from almost 19 to 11 per cent. The main beneficiary during this period was the ready-made or apparel sector, whose share in total production increased from 12 to 30 per cent from 1990 to 2019. The implications of these shifting shares are discussed later.

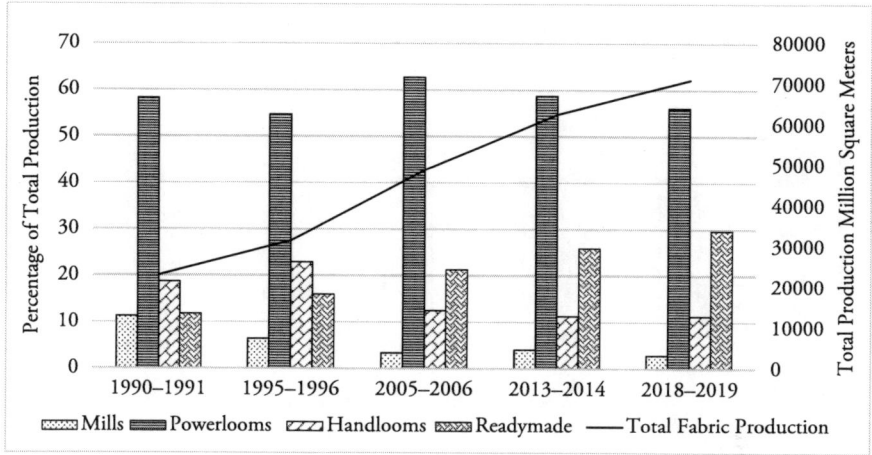

Figure 4.24 Segment-wise Cloth Production

Sources: Ministry of Textile, Government of India, Annual Reports, 1990–2019, http://texmin.nic.in/documents/annual-report (accessed April 2021).

Organised sector

We first examine the organised sector of the textile industry, which consists of all of the mill sector[15] and a small part of the factories making ready-made apparel.[16] The organised sector was the first to avail itself of the TUFS loans to invest in the upgrading of plants and machinery.[17] Employment, production and output data in this sector are provided in Figures 4.25 and 4.26. As seen in Figure 4.25, both the number of factories and total employment declined after 1995, which continued until 2000, and in the next five years, both figures reached the pre-1995 levels. It is only after 2005 (when the quota regime came to an end, and with an increase in TUFS loans [see Figure 4.13]) that we see an increase in employment, going from 1.6 million in 2005 to 2.5 million in 2017. In the same period, there was also an increase in the number of factories involved in production, going from approximately 17,000 in 2005 to 28,000 in 2017.

In addition to the uptick in employment and the number of factories, the organised sector has seen gains in labour productivity since 2000. The Annual Survey of Industries provides output data based on monetary value rather than production. As shown in Figure 4.26, output per worker showed a modest growth from 1993 to 1999 (average output per worker increased from USD 12,000 per year to USD 19,000 in 2000). Since 2001, output per worker has increased from USD 17,000 to USD 42,000 in 2013. While the wage increase did not keep pace with output growth, average wages more than doubled between 2002 and 2017.

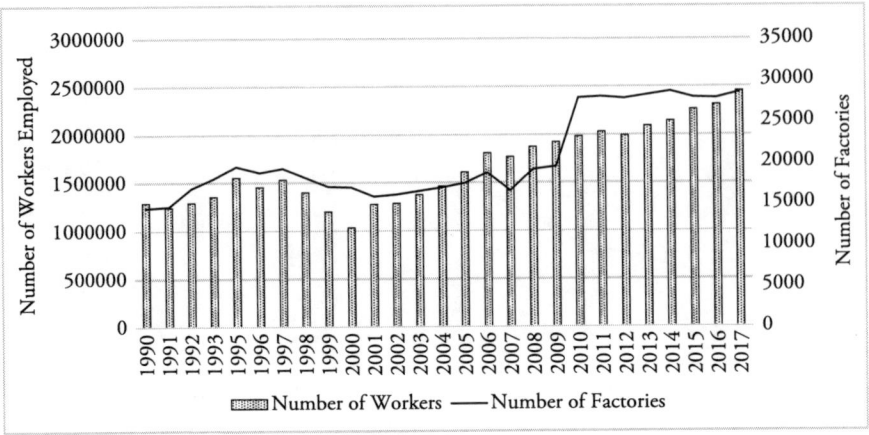

Figure 4.25 Textiles: Organised Sector Factories and Employment

Source: Computed from Ministry of Statistics and Programme Implementation, Government of India, Annual Survey of Industries, 1990–2017, http://microdata.gov.in/nada43/index.php/catalog/ASI (accessed May 2021); includes both textiles and apparel.

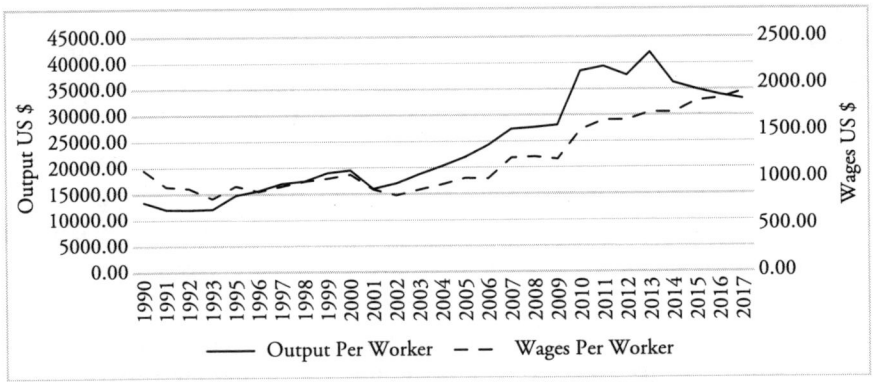

Figure 4.26 Textiles: Organised Sector Average Annual Output and Wages Per Worker

Source: Computed from, Ministry of Statistics and Programme Implementation, Government of India, Annual Surveys of Industry, 1990–2017, http://microdata.gov.in/nada43/index.php/catalog/ASI (accessed May 2021); includes both textiles and apparel.

Overall, one can conclude that the mill sector benefitted from TUFS loans for technology upgrading, which in turn not only increased investments in new factories, leading to an increase in production, but also led to an increase in employee productivity since the onset of the new global institutional context of increased competition in the textile sector.

Unorganised sector

Decentralised production in the textile industry at a small scale has been a priority in various policy regimes since 1947, with this segment protected from competition from the larger scale and more cost-efficient composite mill sector. The decentralised textile sector consists of the *power loom and handloom sub-segments*, and, as described above, the power loom sector is the dominant segment in cloth production (more than 55 per cent share), while the share of handloom has been declining. The following paragraphs discuss the structural changes in these two sub-segments.[18]

Data drawn from the Ministry of Textiles' Annual Reports on the power loom segment are provided in Figures 4.27 and 4.28. Detailed data are available from 2001 onwards. As shown in Figure 4.27, the average number of installed power looms in the Indian textile industry increased during the three periods, going from 1.86 million during the 2001–2005 period to 2.6 million during the 2012–2016 period. Given the increase in production capacity, the overall production of cloth has also seen a corresponding increase. More importantly, and from the policy point of view, there was substantial growth in employment in the sector, increasing from 4.4 million to more than 6 million workers employed on average per year from 2001 to 2016. The productivity of the installed capacity and employed labour in this sector is provided in Figure 4.28. As seen from the figure, the average production per power loom and per worker remained flat across the three periods. Thus, while the power loom sector is dominant in cloth

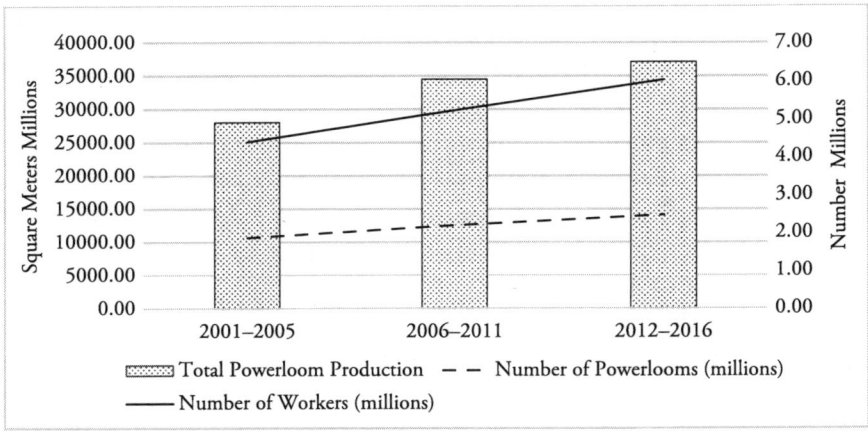

Figure 4.27 Decentralised Power Loom Sector: Production, Units and Employment

Source: Computed from Ministry of Textiles, Government of India, Annual Reports, 2001–2016, http://microdata.gov.in/nada43/index.php/catalog/ASI (accessed April–June 2021).

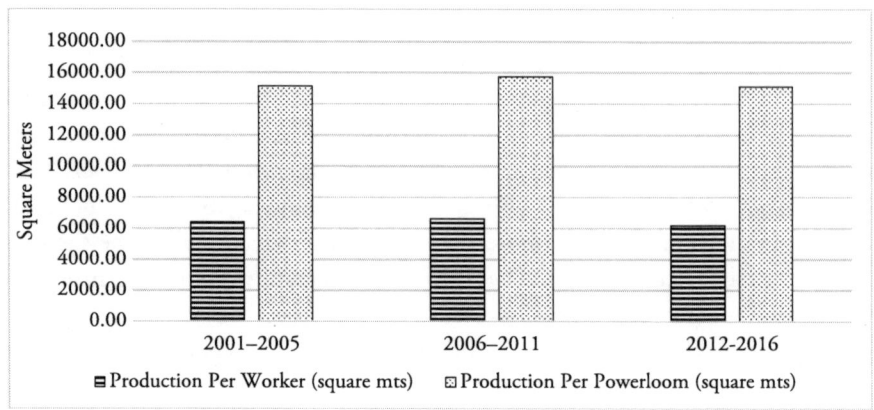

Figure 4.28 Decentralised Power Loom Sector: Per Capita/Per Unit Production (Average Per Year)

Source: Computed from Ministry of Textiles, Government of India, Annual Reports, 2001–2016, http://microdata.gov.in/nada43/index.php/catalog/ASI (accessed May 2021).

production and employment relative to the other sectors, it has not seen any increase in productivity or cost efficiency during the 2001–2016 period, which poses a severe challenge in the post-2005 era of global competition.

The third major segment in the production of cloth is the handloom sector. According to the Ministry of Textiles, the Indian handloom sector meets 95 per cent of the world's handwoven fabric demand because of 'its uniqueness, flexibility of production, openness to innovations, adaptability to the supplier's requirements and the wealth of its tradition'. However, it is also noted that the adoption of modern techniques, 'competition from power loom and mill sectors, availability of cheap imported fabrics, changing consumer preferences and alternative employment opportunities have threatened the vibrancy of the handloom sector' (Government of India, Ministry of Textiles 2011–2012: 115). We use data from four handloom censuses commissioned by India's Ministry of Textiles to see shifts in production and employment in the handloom sector. The data are summarised in Figures 4.29 and 4.30.

Figure 4.29 shows a substantial increase in the production of cloth in this sector between the first two censuses (increasing from 4,000 million square metres in 1987–1988 to 7,000 in 1995–1996) but a slower growth in the subsequent periods (first a decline in production and then a slow increase to approximately 8,000 million square metres in 2019–2020). Furthermore, in line with the earlier-quoted concerns, both the number of installed handlooms and the number of workers employed (including those employed by master weavers

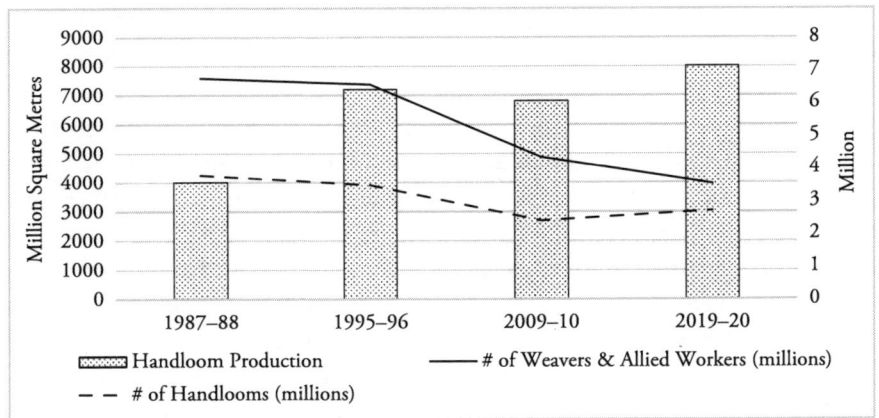

Figure 4.29 Handloom Sector: Production, Units and Employment

Source: Computed by the authors from National Council of Applied Economic Research for Development Commissioner (Handlooms), Ministry of Textiles, Government of India, Handloom Censuses, 1987–2020.

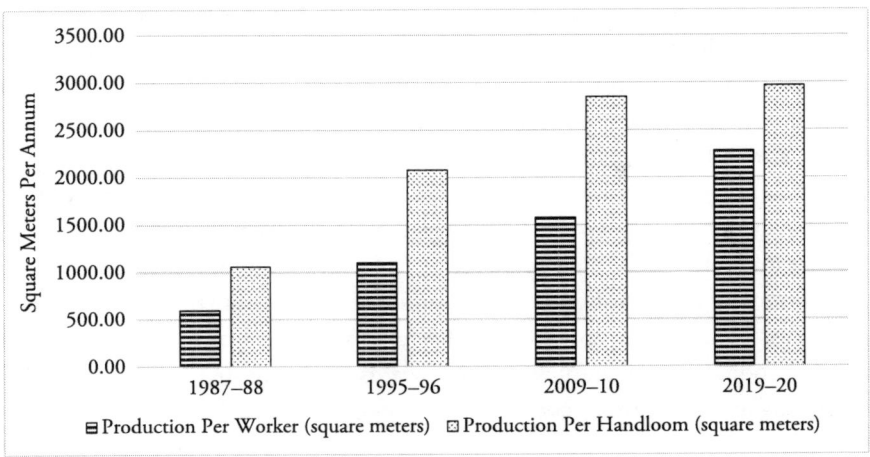

Figure 4.30 Handloom Sector: Per Capita/Per Unit Production

Source: Computed by the authors from National Council of Applied Economic Research for Development Commissioner (Handlooms), Ministry of Textiles, Government of India, Handloom Censuses, 1987–2020.

and the self-employed) have declined significantly. From more than 6.5 million weavers in 1995–1996, the numbers declined to 4.3 million in 2009–2010 and 3.52 million in 2019–2020. The number of installed handlooms also declined from 3.47 million in 1995–1996 to 2.39 million in 2009–2010 and then increased to 2.7 million in 2019–2020.

Productivity data are provided in Figure 4.30. Unlike the power loom sector, where both per-unit and per-person output remained flat during the three periods, the handloom sector saw substantial gains in both parameters. The increase in production per handloom saw the maximum growth from 1987–1988 to 1995–1996, doubling from 1,000 to 2,000 square metres. In the subsequent periods, the growth slowed, increasing to approximately 2,800 square metres in 2009–2019 and 3,000 square metres in 2019–2020. The output per worker has seen more consistent growth over the four periods (that is, from 600 to 2,200 square metres). Although the overall share of handloom sector production in India's total cloth production has declined over the years, and especially since the onset of the global institutional change in 1995, there has been an increase in productivity in this sector, which is surprising given its low-tech, manually intensive nature.

In evaluating employment in the three sectors of the textile industry, the total number of workers remained consistent at approximately 12 million from 2000 to 2018. Thus, structural changes in the industry due to various institutional pressures did not have an adverse impact on employment (at least in the reported figures in the three sectors). However, the intersectoral shift in employment had potential implications for the competitiveness of the industry in the context of more intense global competition. As discussed earlier, an increase in employment in the power loom sector has been at the expense of the handloom sector; however, the power loom sector has not shown any increase in either output per unit or output per worker. Similarly, the organised mill sector has seen an increase in output per worker as well as an increase in employment; however, the contribution of this sector to total cloth production continues to decline. Overall, while employment has not suffered due to institutional changes, the sectoral shift in production and employment is towards the sector that has accomplished hardly any growth in productivity in the post-1995 period.

Innovation Performance Outcomes in the Pharmaceutical Industry

In exhorting the domestic pharmaceutical sector to focus more on new drug discovery, India's Ninth Five Year Plan for 1997–2002, however, noted that the industry would need to invest approximately 12–15 per cent of its sales turnover in R&D to achieve this objective, which was the norm in developed countries.[19] As shown earlier in Figure 4.15, R&D expenditures in the Indian pharmaceutical industry increased from USD 60 million in 1995 to USD 640 million in 2005 and further to USD 1,440 million in 2018. However, these investments have not reached close to 12–15 per cent of sales, with the top ten Indian pharmaceutical firms mustering investments in R&D to just approximately 8.7 per cent of sales (IBEF 2019). This section evaluates the innovative output of the industry in the light of the investments in R&D made in the post-1995 product patent global institutional regime.

Number of patents is an important indicator of innovation performance in technology-oriented industries (Katila 2004). Patents are an output indicator of innovation against input indicators such as the ratio of R&D expenses to sales. Patents are also more appropriate measures than other output indicators in the pharmaceutical industry, such as new chemical entity (NCE) molecules or molecules under clinical trials, which may take several years to produce. We examined data provided by the India Office of the Controller General of Patents for patents filed and granted in India. For international patents, the World Intellectual Property Organization (WIPO) publishes data on patents granted by major patent offices and provides yearly information on the home country and industry of the patentees. We used both sources to understand the innovation performance of India's pharmaceutical industry. The data are summarised in Figures 4.31 and 4.32.

Figure 4.31 maps the patent applications filed and granted in India in the pharmaceutical industry from 1998 to 2017. As shown in the figure, the number of patents filed and granted between 1999 and 2002 was relatively low. This was the period when the intellectual property protection regime in India was

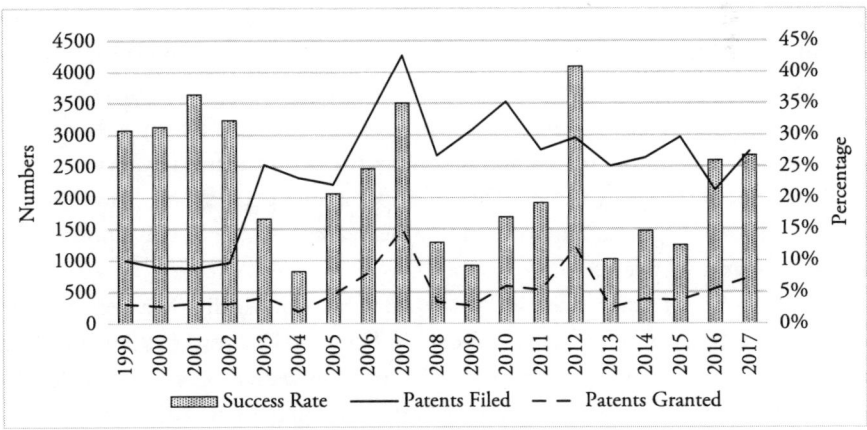

Figure 4.31 Pharmaceutical Patents Filed and Granted in India

Source: Collated from annual reports (1999–2017) of the Government of India, Ministry of Commerce and Industry, Department for the Promotion of Industry and Internal Trade, Office of the Controller General of Patents, Designs & Trade Marks, https://ipindia.gov.in/annual-reports-ipo.htm (accessed May 2021).

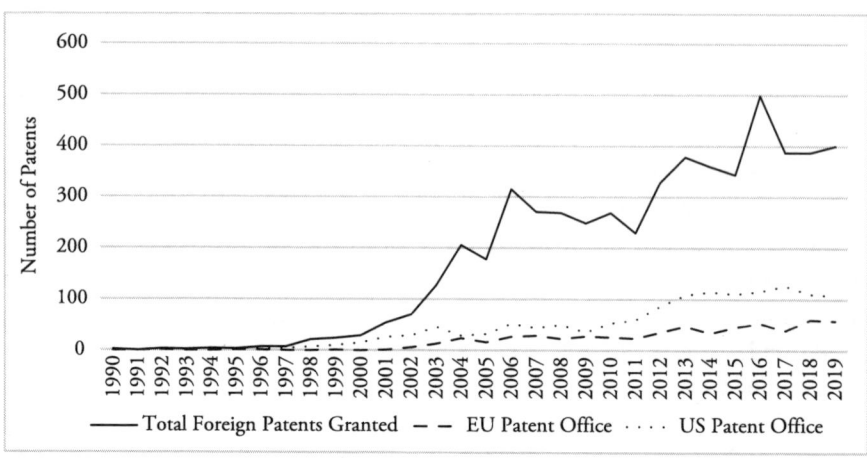

Figure 4.32 India-Origin Pharmaceutical Patents Granted by Foreign Patent Offices

Source: World Intellectual Property Organization (WIPO), https://www3.wipo.int/ipstats/ (accessed May 2021).

in transition, as incremental changes were being institutionalised in preparation for the shift from a process to a product patent regime necessitated by the TRIPS agreement. Approximately 1,000 applications were filed per year in this period, out of which one-third of the applications were successful in the granting of a patent. The number of applications increased substantially in 2003 and 2004 when new rules were put in place in the Patents Amendment Act of 2002, which extended the time period of the patent to twenty years and clarified the items that could be patented. However, the rate of successful patent applications decreased to less than 10 per cent. With the adoption of the full product patent IPR in 2005, the applications for patents in the pharmaceutical industry saw a major increase and, since then, the number of applications per year has stayed above 2,000 but with high fluctuations in the percentage of successful applications (between 9 and 41 per cent).

The number of pharmaceutical-related patents from India that were granted overseas has also been on the rise, as shown in Figure 4.32. From 1990 to 1999, an average of 7 patents per year were granted, which increased to 110 patents for the 2000–2005 period. Since the change in India's IPR regime in 2005, the number of foreign patents granted has shown considerable growth in the post-TRIPS era, going from yearly averages of 274 and 328 to 392 in the successive periods of 2006–2010, 2011–2015 and 2016–2019. The number of patents granted in two prominent foreign offices (that is, the European Union and the US) has also shown significant growth, with more than 35 per cent of total patents granted to applications originating from India from these two offices.

While broad indicators of both input (that is, R&D expenditures) in innovation activities and output from these activities (that is, domestic and international patents) in the Indian pharmaceutical industry have seen growth patterns, especially in the post-TRIPS period, there have been concerns about the depth of these inputs and outputs (for example, Abrol 2014; Abrol et al. 2019; Differding 2017). As alluded to earlier, despite an increase in R&D investments, the levels of these investments fall far short of what are needed for drug discovery (reflected in NCE patents).[20] Abrol (2014) and Abrol et al. (2019) report that out of the over 1,500 patents granted by the US Patent Office from 1992 to 2013 to the Indian pharmaceutical industry, only 19 were NCE patents. A vast majority of approved applications were related to process patents, method of treatment, new drug-delivery systems and new forms of substances.

It is clear from the available data that the Indian pharmaceutical industry has not attained the capabilities in drug discovery to compete with major multinational corporations for blockbuster new drugs. However, its strategic focus has been to occupy a prominent space in the global generic drugs market segment, which has witnessed substantial growth (that is, the share of generics has increased from 72 to 90 per cent of the total prescriptions during the 2008–2017 period (IQVIA 2019). Thus, many of the innovation efforts of the industry have been directed at improving the manufacturing processes and delivery systems of various types of generic drugs. Some of the indicators of the performance parameters on these specific innovation activities show success for India's pharmaceutical industry in the post-2005 period. These include the largest share in the global generics segment, the highest number of abbreviated new drug applications (ANDAs) and drug master files (DMFs) filed and approved by the US Food and Drug Administration (USFDA), and an increase in the number of USFDA and World Health Organization approved manufacturing plants to produce drugs, among others (Athreya et al. 2009; Malerba and Nelson 2011; IQVIA 2019).[21] This evidence, taken together, suggests an increase in the innovation orientation of the Indian pharmaceutical industry, albeit following distinct pathways (or what Lee [2019] calls 'detours') that did not entail radical innovation leading to the discovery of new drugs. Given the large investments needed for new drug discovery (estimated to be over USD 1 billion for bringing a new drug into the market), the need for acquiring a completely new capability set and the high levels of uncertainty and failure associated with the new drug-discovery business model, the decision to focus on the relatively larger-sized global generics segment could very well be a wise strategic choice by Indian pharmaceutical firms (Chittoor et al. 2009).

Conclusions

The purpose of this chapter was to study the evolution of the two industries within the context of global and national institutional changes. Taking 1990 as a starting point (that is, with the onset of economy-wide reforms in India), the chapter traces the changes in the textile and pharmaceutical sectors over the following three decades, which were punctuated by the adoption of industry-specific global agreements in 1995 (TRIPS and ATC in the case of the pharma and textile industries, respectively) and their implementation in 2005. Both institutional changes transformed the parameters of global competition, and, in essence, the policy interventions were geared to maintain and/or enhance the position of India's two important industries in a new competitive landscape. The pertinent questions addressed in this chapter relate to whether the two industries were able to achieve this objective and whether they followed similar or different paths to achieve it.

In terms of the position of India's two industries in their respective global markets, the data show an increase in exports throughout the period, as well as an increase in global market share (see Figure 4.4). Indian national policies to cope with and respond to global institutional changes enabled the two industries to upgrade the production and technological base to effectively compete under the new rules of the game in international markets. On the shift to more value-added products, the data also show movement up the value curve (though with some caveats), with an increased share of the apparel or ready-made garment segment in India's textile exports and formulations contributing to much of the country's pharmaceutical exports.

While both the Indian textile and pharmaceutical industries were able to fulfil national expectations of increased exports, including exports of more value-added products, the two industries took different paths to achieve these objectives. In particular, three contrasting positions stand out from the data. The first contrast relates to the relative integration or participation of the two industries in global production networks and/or global value chains (Seric and Tong 2019; Blazek 2016). The Indian pharmaceutical sector, which developed organically from 1970 onwards because of policy choices related to process patents and price controls, re-established its linkages with major pharmaceutical multinationals in the mid-1990s to cope with the impending global institutional change. Horner (2014) refers to this as the strategic decoupling and recoupling of India's pharmaceutical industry to multinational-corporation-centred global production networks. This recoupling took many forms, including contract R&D and manufacturing for foreign multinationals, alliances and joint ventures, and the ultimate form of coming together, being acquired by a multinational corporation (Kamiike 2020). Concurrently, there were also attempts by a few Indian pharmaceutical firms to develop their own production or value chain networks through the acquisition of foreign firms with capabilities at different stages of the value chain (that is, R&D, marketing, production, and so on). The export growth of the pharmaceutical industry (as well as the composition of imports) reflects the effects of participation in both types of networks.

India's textile industry, in contrast, has adjusted to the post-quota global trade regime through organic structural adjustments rather than significant participation in existing global value chain networks (Gupta 2015). According to Tewari (2006: 2326), 'the vanguard of India's growing global presence are a tier of competitive domestic firms' whose restructuring predates global institutional change but was able to deepen the integration with buyers and suppliers in the light of the changing global competitive dynamics ushered in by the changes at the end of the twentieth century.

Irrespective of the path taken for structural adjustments to global institutional changes, the new competitive context in both industries necessitated a shift to value-added products, which could only be accomplished through investments in the development or acquisition of new capabilities across the value chain (that is, production, R&D, marketing, and so on). It is in both the funding sources for these investments and the value chain activities in which investments were made that we see a second contrast between the two industries. In the case of the pharmaceutical sector, India's policy interventions were targeted towards improving the regulatory context (such as easing imports of technology, FDI regulations) to facilitate investments for the upgrading of the industry's capabilities, rather than providing substantial direct resources. Accordingly, the resources for investments in the industry came from inward FDI and the domestic private sector, and were targeted towards both tangible and intangible assets, such as increasing production capacity, R&D and marketing capabilities. In contrast, the textile industry received much less inward FDI, and, owing to the large unorganised sector with a majority of small- and medium-sized firms, it was not in a position to raise the capital for investments from domestic financial markets. Thus, the main source for investments to upgrade the technology and improve productivity was through institutional resources provided by the TUFS programme initiated by the Indian government in 1999 to prepare the industry for the post-quota era. However, as we saw earlier, given the mechanisms used for such funding (primarily organised-sector banks), institutional resources were accessed primarily by textile firms belonging to the organised sector.

Third, the structural adjustments in the two industries occurred within contrasting constraints related to the welfare aspects of the two industries. According to the expectations of the Indian government, global competitiveness in the pharmaceutical industry had to be achieved without compromising the overall goal of accessibility of affordable drugs for the domestic market. The textile industry, on the other hand, had to ensure that any productivity gains through technological upgrading were not at the expense of domestic employment, especially in the predominant unorganised sector spread throughout the country. The nature of these different constraints had implications for the realm of possibilities in strategic responses in the two industries. In particular, the pharmaceutical industry had multiple paths to move up the value curve and provide affordable drugs in the domestic market, that is, focus on generic products, improve manufacturing capabilities, and optimise differential pricing in domestic and foreign markets, among others. The textile industry's options were much more limited and, as the data showed, led to differential productivity gains in the various sub-segments.

This chapter focused on industry-level analysis and provided aggregate data for the two industries as they evolved during periods of global and national institutional changes. In the following chapter, we shift to a firm-level analysis for each industry to understand and explain the differences in firm responses within the industry. This shift in the level of analysis allows for an understanding of firm-level heterogeneity in adjusting to institutional changes through the development of necessary capabilities for success in global markets. The industry-level analysis of the two industries has also highlighted the different types of resources (for example, financial, know-how, and so on) and their sources (that is, government programmes, inward and outward FDI, inter-firm networks, and) available to and used by firms in the two industries. In the next chapter, we develop a formal model to test the efficacy of these different resources on firm-level capability development and international performance. In addition to institutional resources, firms can tap into network resources that are specific to sectoral and country contexts. In developing our model in the next chapter, we incorporate the role of two such networks, business groups and geographical clusters. The overall model developed and empirically tested in the next chapter assesses the interaction between organisational, institutional and network resources in facilitating success in foreign markets for India's textile and pharmaceutical firms.

Notes

1. This does not form the core focus of our book.

2. The detailed structure of the textile industry is beyond the scope of this chapter. For more information on the various stages of production and structure of the manufacturing processes, see Annual Reports of the Ministry of Textiles (http://texmin.nic.in/documents/annual-report, accessed 23 April 2021). Additional information is available in other reports commissioned by the ministry (for example, Government of India, Ministry of Textiles 2014).

3. Some generic manufacturers try and create brand equity by branding even generics (calling them branded generics).

4. These include the World Trade Organization International Trade Statistics, 1990–2018, https://stats.wto.org/ (accessed 15 April 2021); the Pharmaceutical Export Promotion Council, Ministry of Commerce and Industry, Government of India, http//pharmexcil.com; the Annual Handbook of Statistics on the Indian Economy; and the Reserve Bank of India.

5. The Organization for Economic Co-operation and Development (OECD) is an international organisation that is composed of thirty-eight mostly developed nations from across the globe.

6. See https://unctadstat.unctad.org/wds/ReportFolders/reportFolders.aspx, accessed 16 April 2021.

7. See https://unctadstat.unctad.org/wds/ReportFolders/reportFolders.aspx, accessed 16 April 2021.

8. There is a discrepancy in the reported yearly numbers and cumulative amounts of inward FDI in pharmaceuticals as reported in the Government of India statistics. The cumulative amounts show a higher number than the totals of individual years. We use the yearly data for this chapter. For details, see the Department for the Promotion of Industry and Internal Trade FDI Data (https://dipp.gov.in/publications/fdi-statistics, accessed 16 April 2021).

9. See Government of India, Department for the Promotion of Industry and Internal Trade. Statistics, https://dpiit.gov.in/publications/fdi-statistics (accessed 28 April 2021); Furtado 2017; Rao and Dhar 2020.

10. There is another line of argument in the institutional perspective that emphasises the agency of firms in responding to external institutional conditions. According to this view, EMNCs may use outward FDI as a strategic response to home-country institutional deficiencies or voids. These voids hinder the development of product and factor markets at home, motivating emerging economy firms to escape from such environments by entering developed economies. Madhok and Keyhani (2012) argue that EMNCs use acquisitions in advanced economies to overcome their liabilities of emergingness, which are imprinted onto them by their home-country institutional contexts. The difference in the development of formal institutions between home and

advanced host countries also motivates some EMNEs to engage in 'institutional arbitrage' (Boisot and Meyer 2008) as an effective strategy for overcoming home-country institutional constraints (Cui and Aulakh 2019).

11. The share of developed countries as the destination of outward FDI from India in the high technology sector (which includes pharmaceuticals) during the 2008–2018 period is almost 70 per cent (Joseph 2019).

12. The number of overseas acquisitions in India's pharmaceutical industry represents more than 10 per cent of total overseas acquisitions and is second only to the computer software industry (Gubbi et al. 2010; Gubbi 2015).

13. According to the figures reported in Pradhan (2017), the average per firm outward investment during the 1980–2014 period in the pharmaceutical industry is USD 90 million. The corresponding figure in the textile and apparel sector is USD 20 million.

14. We use a variety of sources, including the Annual Survey of Industries, the four Handloom Census, the Statistical Yearbooks of the Ministry of Statistics and Programme Implementation, and the Ministry of Textiles Annual Reports to put together the production and employment data for the three segments.

15. The mill sector consists of spinning mills that make yarn from all kinds of natural and man-made materials, as well as composite mills that are involved in spinning, weaving and finishing of cloth (Simpson and Shetty 2001).

16. Similar to the power loom and handlooms sectors, the ready-made apparel sector is largely in the decentralised and unorganised sectors. Only a few firms in the industry are vertically integrated (details about the structure of India's textile industry can be found in NCAER 2009; Simpson and Shetty 2001).

17. Ministry of Textiles, Government of India, Annual Reports, 2000–2020, http://texmin.nic.in/documents/annual-report (accessed April 2021).

18. There have been critical debates on the efficacy of policy choices that are favourable to the handloom and power loom sectors, both relative to each other and relative to other segments. For more details on these debates, see Roy (1998a) and Deshpande (2018).

19. Industrial Sector, Drugs and Pharmaceuticals, Five Year Plan, 1997–2002, https://niti.gov.in/planningcommission.gov.in/docs/plans/planrel/fiveyr/index5.html (accessed May 2021).

20. NCE is a chemical molecule developed by an innovator firm in the early drug-discovery stage, which, after undergoing clinical trials, may translate into a drug that could be a cure for some disease (Chittoor et al. 2009).

21. ANDAs are mandatory regulatory filings with the USFDA, whose approval is needed before a firm can launch and market a drug in finished dosage form in the United States. A DMF is a submission that provides detailed information about facilities, processes or articles used in the manufacturing, processing, packaging and storing of one or more human drugs (Greene 2007).

5

Strategic Renewal and Firm-Level Responses

How did organisations in India's textile and pharmaceutical industries respond to institutional changes triggered at the global level? To what extent was their successful response co-determined by firm-level investments in developing new capabilities and the resources provided by the institutional system in which they operated? Continuing with our analysis of the three levels of the institutional system developed in Chapter 2, in this chapter we address these research questions by keeping the organisation as the central focus of attention. We develop a conceptual model that links organisational choices around resources and capabilities in response to global institutional changes with their success in global markets and test the model through analyses of fine-grained firm-level data from the Indian pharmaceutical and textile industries during the thirty-year period of 1990 to 2019. Some prior scholarly work has examined the transformation in the Indian pharmaceutical industry (for example, Pradhan 2003; Joseph 2016; Chittoor, Sarkar, Ray and Aulakh 2009; Chaudhuri 2012), and there is limited work in the context of the Indian textile industry (for example, Dhiman and Sharma 2017); however, to our knowledge, prior work has not compared and contrasted empirical evidence from two strategically important industries of India and developed a unifying theoretical framework as we do in this chapter.

As outlined in earlier chapters, until 2005, the Indian pharmaceutical industry was governed by the Patents Act of 1970, which allowed patenting based on manufacturing processes rather than end products. This regulation enabled Indian pharmaceutical firms to reverse engineer and produce drugs that were product patented in other countries at a fraction of the cost incurred by other multinational corporations. In 1995, soon after signing up with the World Trade Organization (WTO) as a member country, India consented to enforce product patents and to provide legal protection to Trade-Related Intellectual Property Rights (TRIPS) effective 1 January 2005. The implications of adopting the TRIPS framework were particularly severe for Indian pharmaceutical firms. They could no longer manufacture and sell knock-offs of patented drugs in India by exploiting the prevailing process patent regime once the new framework came into effect. In other words, these firms were deprived of not only a traditional core advantage that gave them a competitive edge but also alternate sources of competitive advantage to compete with global competition.

In a parallel development, beginning in 2005, the quota system defining the trade in the global textile and apparel industry came to an end, as agreed to by the members of the WTO a decade earlier. The textile industry was opened to full global competition in 2005, allowing buyers to purchase goods from where they were most efficiently produced rather than from where quotas dictated transactions. Governments of various countries with salient textile industries, including Bangladesh, China, India and Vietnam, launched a series of initiatives around 1995 to prepare their respective incumbent firms to face impending free-market global competition in the post-quota regime. The most prominent of such initiatives by the Indian government was the Technology Upgradation Fund Scheme (TUFS), which was launched in 1999 for the textile industry. Contending that manufacturing capability is the key for Indian textile firms to be globally competitive, the government of India established the TUFS programme to enable firms to upgrade their manufacturing assets, scale and technology. This programme was operationalised by making available cheap credit to firms in the form of a 5 per cent interest subsidy on loans provided by banks for acquiring plant and machinery and other manufacturing assets.

Both pharmaceutical and textile industries played a critical role in the Indian economy for generating employment as well as for generating the much-needed foreign exchange and trade surplus, the shortage of which triggered the post-1991 economic liberalisation programme. How well did the two industries cope with the change in the global institutional regime that was initiated in 1995 and came into effect in 2005? Did their average degree of internationalisation suffer or could Indian textile and pharmaceutical firms keep up with increased global competition? Figure 5.1 captures the trends in the average export intensity[1] (export sales as a proportion of total sales) of internationalised firms in the two industries.[2]

One of the striking aspects revealed by these charts is the emergence of active internationalisation as a key strategic response of the Indian pharmaceutical industry, as individual firms responded to global institutional change (that is, an increase from approximately 10 per cent of total sales through exports in 1990 to almost 45 per cent in 2014). This is interesting because unlike Indian textile firms,

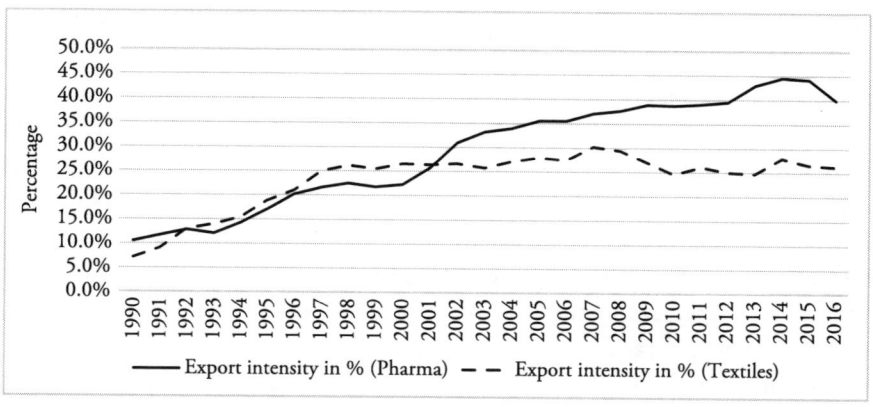

Figure 5.1 Trends in Export Intensity (1990–2016)

Source: Firm-level data from Prowess, Centre for Monitoring Indian Economy (CMIE).

which always had a significant export thrust, pharmaceutical firms in India were more focused on domestic markets before the adoption of the TRIPS framework. As the trend in Figure 5.1 indicates, an average firm in the pharmaceutical industry was able to improve its export intensity steadily throughout the period, including the post-2005 institutional change. The export intensity for an average firm in the textile industry did not improve during the post-2005 period but held more or less steady without any significant drop (that is, between 25 and 30 per cent of total sales in foreign markets). What factors or strategic responses enabled these firms to maintain or improve their position in international markets? What were the determinants of the heterogeneity in the degree of internationalisation witnessed for firms within the pharmaceutical industry and the textile industry as well as between the two industries? In the following sections, we develop a conceptual model and a set of propositions to seek answers to these questions.

Institutions and Resources

Historically, the search for explaining heterogeneity in performance has led to the discipline of strategy in management science. Strategy scholars have studied explanatory factors inside the firm (Penrose 1959; Chandler 1962; Andrews 1971; Wernerfelt 1984; Barney 1991) and outside the firm (Porter 1980, 1985; Gulati 1998; Oliver 1997) back and forth like the swinging of a pendulum (Hoskisson et al. 1999). One important focus of strategy research in the recent past has been on institutional theory to highlight how institutions matter and the important role played by institutional factors in shaping strategy (Powell 1996; Oliver 1997; Lawrence 1999; Peng 2002). The institution-based view of strategy suggests that the institutional environment in which a firm operates can influence its strategic choices directly, for example, through regulatory constraints and incentives, or indirectly by shaping firm resource and through capability development as well as organisational structures (Khanna and Palepu 1997; Peng, Wang and Jiang 2008). In this chapter, we build on this literature and identify theoretical mechanisms of how firms specifically build capabilities and gain advantages in international markets through a combination of internal, quasi-internal and institutional resources as they respond to institutional change and operate in a globally competitive market (for more detailed reviews, see Hoskisson et al., 1999; Ahuja and Yayavaram 2011).

Organisations are embedded in and hence depend critically on their external environment (Pfeffer and Salancik 1978). Instead of viewing firms as autonomous entities, the external perspective views firms as embedded in networks of social, professional and exchange relationships with other entities in the environment (Granovetter 1985; Gulati 1998). Inter-organisational ties such as joint ventures and alliances could have strategic significance and act as sources of rent generation for firms (Kogut 1988; Dyer and Singh 1998). In addition to the strategic role of inter-firm relationships, there has been an increasing interest in how the environmental and social context in which firms are embedded influences and shapes their behaviour and performance (Gulati, Nohria and Zaheer 2000). The different dimensions of the environment that could have an influence on firms' strategies include structural, cognitive, institutional and cultural (Zukin and DiMaggio 1990). Among these, the influence of the new institutional theory (North 1990; Scott 1994) has been the strongest, which posits a significant effect of the institutional environment on the strategies and performance of firms. Formally, the 'institutional framework' has been defined as 'the set of fundamental political, social, and legal ground rules that establishes the basis for production, exchange, and distribution' (Davis and North 1971: 6). Hence, market activity is both constrained and facilitated by the presence and quality of appropriate institutions (Ahuja and Yayavaram 2011).

We use the broad term *institutional resources* to capture the resources provided by the institutional environment to firms. We build on the aforementioned arguments and propose that there are multiple ways in which institutions and institutional environments confer differential advantages on firms and contribute to the heterogeneity in their rent generation capacity. First, firms from different economies and geographies are differently endowed in terms of their institutional environments and therefore the institutional resources available to them. For example, a firm in India will have a disadvantage in terms of access to the quantity and quality of venture capital when compared to firms in the

United States (US) due to underdeveloped capital markets in India. Another example of the opposite type could be that indigenous firms from China could have access to various government incentives and subsidies made available to them in a specific industry, which may not be available to firms in other countries, such as the United Kingdom (UK), in the same industry. In a recent report in the *New York Times* on the solar panel industry, a number of recent bankruptcies of US firms and an upsurge in Chinese firms were attributed to aggressive investments in additional capacity by the Chinese government. In addition to lower labour costs, Chinese firms in the solar panel industry are reported to benefit from a lower cost structure due to cheaper access to capital from the government (Mulkern 2011).[3]

The second source of heterogeneity arises due to the differential ability among firms embedded in the same institutional environment to access and benefit from institutional resources. Some firms develop and possess the capability to access and utilise more institutional resources than other firms. For example, for decades before India became a signatory of the WTO, India followed a regime of process patents, which allowed Indian pharmaceutical firms to produce in India drugs patented in developed countries by simply changing the manufacturing process. Over time, many Indian pharmaceutical firms developed special process-engineering capabilities. Even though the trigger for developing such process-engineering capabilities was the erstwhile patent regime, which was common to all pharmaceutical firms in India, there was still substantial heterogeneity in the process-engineering capabilities of different firms. Furthermore, there is evidence that governments promote certain industries or firms as vehicles for economic development (see Kohli 2004 for an extended discussion of the close interactions between state and private businesses in different economies) and thus provide preferential institutional resources. For example, in developing economies, business groups (BGs)[4] were viewed 'as a device of the state to achieve both political and economic policy objectives' (Yiu et al. 2007: 1557). These included economic development objectives where certain firms were provided resources and incentives to enter industries considered strategic to the country (Kim et al. 2004) or political objectives to secure the support of key entrepreneurs by granting them rent-seeking opportunities (Evans 1979).

Third, and more closely related to our proposed National Institutional System in Chapter 2, is the role of institutional resources in resolving competing logics. We have suggested that global institutional changes require distant or exploratory search in products and markets to effectively compete with international competitors, which competes with the existing templates of incumbent domestic firms based on proximate search or exploitation of existing resources and capabilities. Organisation inertia and/or unwillingness to undertake risky exploratory searches limits firms' ability to pursue the necessary strategic renewal. Here, institutional resources play a potentially important role because access to such resources influences the risk-taking propensity of organisations and helps overcome intra-organisational inertial forces that restrict exploratory search necessitated by changing competitive conditions.

The aforementioned discussion describes how institutional environments in general have an influence on organisational opportunities and constraints. In the following paragraphs, we identify specific mechanisms through which institutional resources play a role in firms attempting to catch up with global competitors and adapt to global institutional changes.

Institutional Resources through Regulatory Reforms and Trade Liberalisation

In the context of the catch-up process of developing economy firms, a broad-natured, but critically important, institutional resource is the benevolent environment for imports facilitated by regulatory reforms. Since the early 1990s, there has been a significant opening up of the economy by the Government of India. This happened after a severe crisis in its balance of payments position triggered a series of major economic liberalisation measures by the Indian government. Starting in 1991, these encompassed (*a*) industrial policy; (*b*) trade policy; and (*c*) foreign direct investment (FDI) (Ahluwalia 2002). Industrial policy was liberalised to allow the private sector to enter all but three industries—defence, atomic energy and railway transport. Industrial licensing was abolished except for a few sensitive industries, and many industries that were reserved for small-scale sectors (including textile garments) were freed up so that they could achieve scale economies that are needed for export competitiveness. There were also significant reforms in India's trade policy that reduced tariffs and import restrictions. Import licensing was abolished for capital goods, raw materials and intermediate goods, which allowed firms in all industries to freely access foreign technology in manufacturing and research and development (R&D). The weighted average import duty declined from 72.5 per cent in 1991–1992 to 24.6 per cent in 1996–1997 but has remained at approximately that level since then (Ahluwalia 2002). Finally, FDI policies were liberalised to include many sectors for 100 per cent foreign ownership and many others with caps at 74 and 51 per cent. The modest export performance of India (when compared to China), despite all these significant reforms, has been attributed to red tape and a slow progress in lowering import duties (Ahluwalia 2002).

Nevertheless, compared to the institutional environment prevailing before 1991, Indian firms from all industries benefitted significantly from the opening up of the economy in 1991, and began to access foreign technology in capital goods and other intermediate products through imports. The stifling pre-1991 import regime is illustrated by a telling observation from N. R. Narayana Murthy, one of the pioneers of information technology (IT) exports from India, that it took three years and approximately fifty trips to the Indian capital city of New Delhi to import a computer! (*Economic Times* 2016).

Government Incentives and Subsidies as Institutional Resources

I see the rest of the world investing in competitiveness. I see the rest of the world wanting to gain share versus the United States.... Every one of my competitors is global and believe me, all of them get Government support ... from the German Government, from the UK Government, from the Chinese Government ... there are many ways we can help build competitiveness in the United States.
—Excerpt from an interview of Jeff Immelt, Chairman and CEO of General Electric, with Fareed Zakaria of CNN

Another category of institutional resources that is increasingly playing a role in the competitiveness of firms in various industries is government support, often through explicit subsidies. Such government support can take one or more of the following forms: (*a*) industry-wise export-oriented units set up to assist exporting firms such as technology parks or special economic zones (SEZs); (*b*) export promotion capital goods (EPCG) regulations that exempt customs duties on imports of capital goods or other goods; (*c*) special credits provided for exporters of specified products or to specified markets that can be utilised to meet tax obligations; and (*d*) tax incentives to set up export-oriented plants. Some of these export subsidy measures by India have been challenged in recent years by the US as WTO-inconsistent (Dhingra and Meyer 2021). In the light of the growing importance of intangible assets compared to tangible assets on a global basis, it should be noted that most of the Indian government's support programmes are aimed at encouraging investments in tangible assets and not directed towards intangible resources such as R&D or marketing.

The pharmaceutical industry did not have industry-specific subsidy programmes, but all the aforementioned types of government support were available to it. Firms in the industry made use of EPCG programmes in particular to invest in plant and machinery and R&D equipment in the 1990s (see Figure 5.2).

On the other hand, given the critical role of the textile industry in employment and in being a leading earner of foreign exchange for India, the Government of India launched a special scheme to help textile firms improve their manufacturing assets and efficiencies. While the Government of India has launched a number of schemes from time to time with the aid of the Indian textile industry, the most prominent among them by far has been the Technology Upgradation Fund Scheme (TUFS). This scheme was introduced after India became a signatory of the WTO and hence needed to prepare itself for the free-market regime to be effective in 2005. The TUFS is a type of subsidy programme sponsored by the central government of India through which concessional loans are provided to Indian textile firms through a network of nodal and co-opted banks. The scheme primarily provides for reimbursement of 5 per cent interest charged by the banks for technology upgrading projects. The scheme was introduced with the objective of encouraging Indian textile firms to upgrade their technology and modernise their production facilities. It was launched in 1999 and continues in a modified form until today. The TUFS is a perfect example of the various subsidy programmes initiated by the national governments of different countries that provide definite advantages to firms as they compete in global markets. While firm-level data on the amount of TUFS loans utilised by each textile firm are not available, the addition of manufacturing assets is a good proxy measure of the utilisation of TUFS funds because the bank loans under this scheme are necessarily secured by manufacturing assets.

Conceptual Model and Proposed Relationships

Upgrading Organisational Capabilities

The pioneering work by Andrews (1971) analysing a firm's strengths, weaknesses (inside of a firm; internal) and opportunities and threats (a firm's environment; external) to obtain competitive advantage forms the foundation for explaining the heterogeneity in firms' performance. In much of the early research, the primary focus was on models to analyse environmental opportunities and threats such as industry structure and strategic positioning (Porter 1980; 1985). In contrast, the resource-based view (RBV)[5] portrays a firm as a bundle of resources (Penrose 1959; Barney 1991) and as a potential creator of value-added capabilities through utilisation and recombination of these resources. The RBV complements the traditional work on industry structure and strategic positioning (Porter 1980) and focuses on the internal organisation of firms as determinants of competitive advantage. Developed with the aim of explaining why firms differ and how firms achieve sustainable competitive advantages, the

RBV focuses on the idea of valuable, rare, inimitable and non-substitutable attributes or resources of the firm to achieve superior performance and competitive advantage (Barney 1991).

A firm's resources consist of all the assets of a firm, tangible and intangible, that are possessed or controlled by a firm (Wernerfelt 1984; Barney 1991). Tangible resources typically consist of assets such as land, plants and machinery, factory or office buildings, laboratories, and so on. On the other hand, intangible resources include and stem from investments in human resources, R&D, patents, information technology, marketing or brands, and improvement in business processes. Intangible resources can also be in the form of 'capabilities', which often manifest as a mix of people and practices such as design capabilities, logistics systems, production planning and control systems. The heterogeneity in firms' resources and capabilities is proffered as a central factor in explaining the heterogeneity of performance among firms. The strategic importance of intangible resources has grown over the years when compared to tangible assets; in a recent book Haskel and Westlake (2018) point out that investments in intangible capital now exceed those in tangible capital in many developed countries, such as the US, Sweden and the UK. Other papers (Corrado and Hulten 2010; Gu and Lev 2017) reinforce this fact using evidence from the US economy and question the prevailing accounting practice of immediately expensing investments in intangible resources such as R&D while their benefits increase over time.

An extension of this enquiry is the question as to how such heterogeneity in terms of firms' resources comes about in the first place. It cannot be entirely attributed to founding conditions. This enquiry led to the concept of a new higher-order capability, the inherent capability of firms for self-renewal or a capacity to seek, develop or acquire new resources and capabilities, termed dynamic capabilities (Teece, Pisano and Shuen 1997). Dynamic capabilities are the organisational routines by which managers alter their resource base—acquire and shed resources, integrate and recombine them—to generate new value-creating strategies. Dynamic capabilities allow the creation of new products and processes, access new markets and enable the company to successfully respond to changing environments. Organisational resources and capabilities tend to be dynamic (Helfat and Peteraf 2003), and as a firm attains critical levels for a given capability, its marginal returns from that capability may decline, and the marginal returns to building other complementary capabilities may increase (Ethiraj et al. 2005).

Such a process of revitalising resources and capabilities and adapting to the changing needs of the markets is often referred to as strategic renewal.

Strategic renewal helps organisations shed their inertia and develop new competencies that protect them from obsolescence during periods of technological and market disruptions (Burgelman 1991; Huff, Huff and Thomas 1992). An evolutionary concept, renewal, emphasises the acquisition of new knowledge-based resources and productive assets as a route to effect a concomitant change in a firm's product-market domains and generate new competencies (Floyd and Lane 2000). By recognising how firms engage in path-dependent adaptation over time, the notion of renewal mirrors the dynamic capabilities argument that changing environments require firms to engage in activities that enable them to reconfigure their resources, product markets and capabilities (Teece, Pisano and Shuen 1997; Eisenhardt and Martin 2000; Danneels 2002). The central idea of this chapter is how Indian pharmaceutical and textile firms undertook strategic renewal by accessing critical resources needed for their survival and success.

The internationalisation of resources and markets constitutes an important driver of the renewal of capabilities for local firms from developing economies. The literature suggests that international markets not only serve as learning laboratories (Hitt, Hoskisson and Kim 1997; Hitt, Li and Worthington 2005) but also as channels through which firms obtain access to diverse, locally embedded ideas and knowledge from across the world (Doz, Santos and Williamson 2001). There are primarily two broad means by which firms can access international knowledge and gain from globalisation and build innovation capabilities. The first is through resource internationalisation, such as technology imports, and the other is through product-market internationalisation, such as exporting and international expansion. A great deal of technological development in emerging economies comprises the import of foreign technology and its adaptation to develop new innovations (Pradhan 2004). In addition, product-market internationalisation through exports results in learning and building capabilities. 'Exporters access diverse knowledge inputs not available in the domestic market. This knowledge spills back to the focal firm and results in increased innovation' (Salomon 2006: 135).

The above discussion on strategic renewal and the need for reconfiguration of firm-level resources from time to time raises the obvious question: in the light of the global institutional changes triggered in 1995 in both the pharmaceutical and textile industries, did their configuration of core resources change, and if yes, how? As both industries are manufacturing intensive, the first core resource that can logically be considered strategically important is a tangible resource, namely manufacturing assets. Given the rising strategic importance of intangible assets in globally competitive markets, we can consider two core intangible resources that are relevant for both industries, namely expenses incurred in R&D and marketing. Investments in plants and machinery allow organisations to improve manufacturing processes and achieve efficiency in their operations (Hitt, Hoskisson and Ireland 1994), which become important when they expand into international markets and compete for cost leadership with firms from other countries having cost advantages (Kotabe, Srinivasan and Aulakh 2002). Investments in R&D and marketing capabilities allow firms to move up the value curve by differentiating their products. Both sets of capabilities are considered critical for short-term outcomes (Sapienza et al. 2006) and long-term internationalisation efforts. Marketing capabilities provide links with customers and channel members and enable exporters to compete by predicting changes in customer preferences and by fostering loyal relationships with customers in overseas markets (Aulakh, Kotabe and Teegen 2000), while R&D capabilities enable firms to develop innovative new products and respond to rapidly changing technological environments. We can summarise the discussion in the form of the following proposition:

Proposition 1: Firm investments in manufacturing, R&D and marketing capabilities as a response to global institutional change will be positively associated with product-market internationalisation.[6]

Figures 5.2 to 5.4 demonstrate the trends in investments in these core capabilities as a percentage of sales for an average firm in the two industries over the period 1990 to 2016. As seen in Figure 5.2, an average firm in both industries steeply increased investments just before and after the trigger year of 1995 when the institutional regime change at the global level became clear, which then stabilised over the years. Figure 5.3 indicates that some of the capital shifted from marketing to manufacturing in the initial years but moved back to marketing and stabilised at approximately 4–6 per cent of sales over the years. Finally, as seen from Figure 5.4, pharmaceutical firms dramatically increased their R&D expenses as a response to the global institutional change in 1995 from approximately less than 0.5 per cent of sales on average to approximately 2 per cent of sales, whereas such a response with regard to R&D investments is conspicuously absent in the case of textile firms.

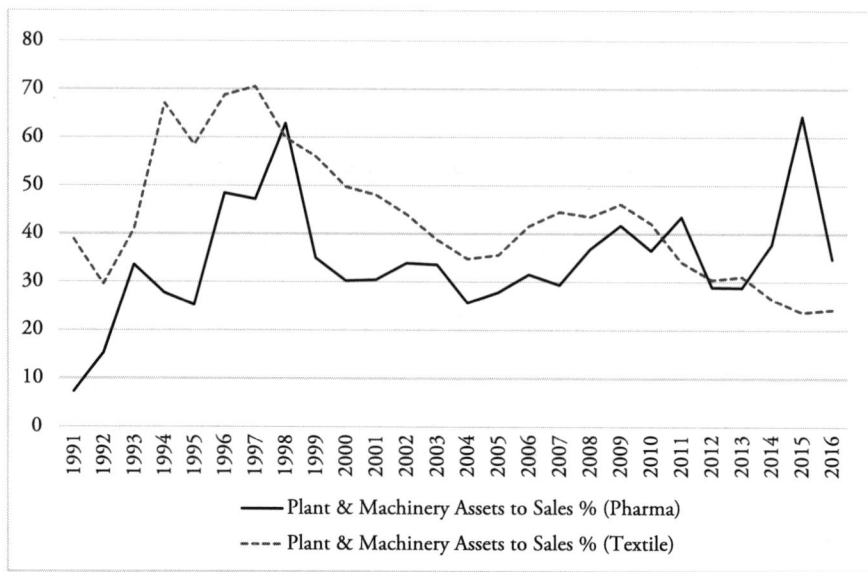

Figure 5.2 Plant and Machinery Assets

Source: Firm-level data from Prowess, Centre for Monitoring Indian Economy (CMIE).

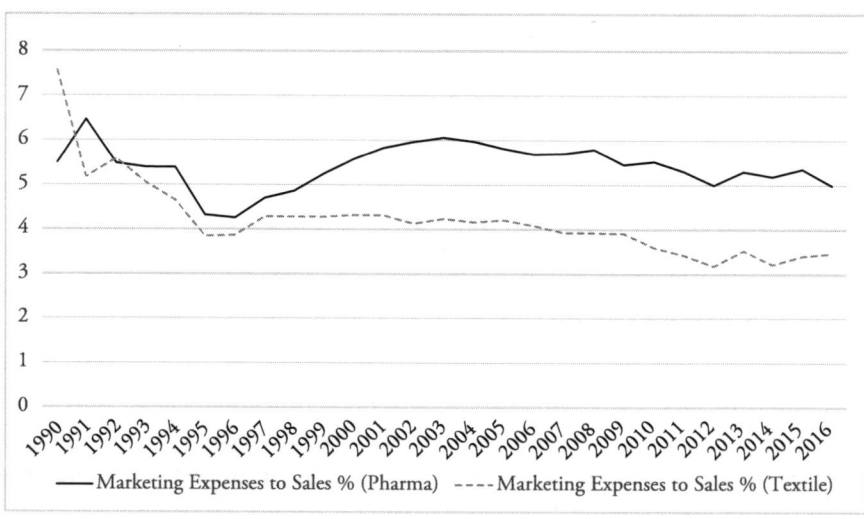

Figure 5.3 Marketing Expenses

Source: Firm-level data from Prowess, Centre for Monitoring Indian Economy (CMIE).

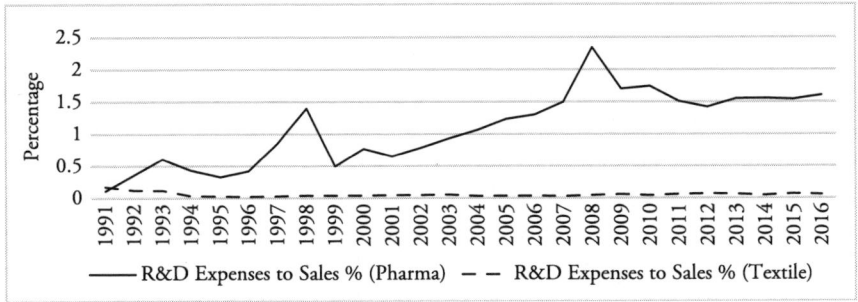

Figure 5.4 R&D Expenses

Source: Firm-level data from Prowess, Centre for Monitoring Indian Economy (CMIE).

International Resources

A fundamental difference underlies the internationalisation process of firms from emerging economies such as India compared to developed economies. The dominant paradigm within which past research on internationalisation has progressed rests on one fundamental assumption typical of Western models of international expansion: that the firm in question already possesses the technology and product-related knowledge it needs to meet the demand of the foreign markets, and the act of internationalisation is undertaken to exploit this stock of existing know-how (Hitt et al. 2006). In the well-known Ownership-Location-Internalisation (O-L-I) paradigm proposed by Dunning (1988), a firm has to have significant 'ownership advantages' (O), which it aims to exploit in foreign markets through internationalisation. Hence, internationalisation is viewed as a process of transferring a firm's unique knowledge, whether it is related to technology, production, marketing or other activities, across borders (Kogut and Zander 1992; Tsang 1999). Another key thesis has been that internationalisation progresses incrementally through a systematic process of learning by doing. This path-dependent model argues that firms accrue internationalisation capabilities to deal with cultural diversities and operational uncertainties of operating in foreign markets through an endogenous process of experiential learning. According to this view, much of the tacit knowledge required to compete in unfamiliar international environments can only be attained through organisational learning, which is largely experiential in nature and occurs in situ (Johanson and Wiedersheim-Paul 1975; Johanson and Vahlne 1977).

However, an alternative exogenous model of internationalisation would suggest that even prior to firms moving into international markets, they would need to upgrade their core resources to be able to offer products that are able to meet the more advanced needs of international markets. Due to underdeveloped strategic factor markets for finance, technology and management, emerging market firms often face difficulties in acquiring resources from their home countries (Hitt et al 2005). Overcoming this initial resource hurdle to be globally competitive is critical for the outward internationalisation process to kick-start. Only after local firms are able to access these resources can they engage in an endogenous (learning by doing) process of learning new capabilities by entering and operating in foreign markets. These critical inputs are unlikely to be available in domestic markets in home countries, as they have been insulated and cut off from international capability or resource pools for decades. For developing or emerging economy firms, therefore, *inward internationalisation* (through import of resources from international markets) is a mode to access new resources and develop capabilities and competitive advantages (Korhonen, Luostarinen and Welch 1996; Mathews 2006). Thus, it appears that these firms need to first internationalise their resource base before they can exploit foreign markets through exports or other modes of *outward* internationalisation. We therefore establish a linkage between resource-seeking inward internationalisation that gives firms the needed resources to subsequently exploit them in foreign markets and succeed in outward internationalisation.

Innovation in the context of developing economy firms includes bringing in technology and learning processes that may have already existed in developed economies for a considerable period of time. Thus, at the base level, investment in capabilities by developing economy firms is facilitated simply through import of technology and know-how (Cusumano and Elenkov 1994; Young, Huang and McDermott 1996; Kumar and Agarwal 2004). This would be akin to the concept of accumulation by economists who argue that economic development is driven by the acquisition of resources through higher investments in capital. Technology forms a critical 'gap' between firms from developing markets and those from developed countries (Khanna and Palepu 2000). Since the quality of technology accessed from domestic sources is often found to be inadequate, technological development in emerging economies often comprises the import of foreign technology and its adaptation to develop new capabilities (Pradhan 2004; Young, Huang and McDermott 1996).

Furthermore, import of technology, know-how and intermediate inputs facilitate continuous interaction with foreign suppliers, which over time could help develop knowledge about foreign markets and the development of a network of valuable contacts (Korhonen, Luostarinen and Welch 1996). UNCTAD (2000) identified backward linkages with suppliers as the ones that had the deepest positive impact on international firms among linkages with suppliers, customers and technology partners. This impact, which it termed 'reverse transfer', was often in the form of exchange of information, technical knowledge and skills. In the specific empirical context of our study, with drastic changes in the domestic environment, Indian pharmaceutical firms lost dual advantages: protection in the domestic market and their core advantage of reverse engineering. Although these firms had access to a pool of scientific manpower, they were isolated from the global technology frontier for decades, and catching up required different types of technological resources. In a liberalised economy, competing with well-entrenched multinational competitors necessitated more advanced manufacturing technology and value-added products. International technology inputs were thus critical to compensate for the lack of domestic technological expertise and provide the impetus to invest in innovations to move up the production function (Kumar and Agarwal 2005). Similarly, one of the challenges for the Indian textile industry was the obsolete manufacturing technology used in the large unorganised sectors (that is, handloom and power loom), and much of the efforts in technology upgradation entailed imports of plants and machinery.

The international trade literature has identified various benefits of imported technologies and intermediate products, especially for developing economies attempting to catch up. According to this view, 'firms benefit from international trade through increased access to previously unavailable inputs.... Access to these imported inputs in turn enables firms to expand their domestic product scope through the introduction of new varieties....' (Goldberg et al. 2010: 1727). Goldberg et al. (2010) use firm-level data from India to show how import liberalisation (that is, through a reduction in import tariffs) during the economic reforms of 1991 led to new product introductions for the domestic market. Similarly, Feng, Li and Swenson (2016) use firm-level data from China to demonstrate that an increase in the import of intermediate inputs led to an expansion of the volume and scope of firms' exports. Mazzi and Foster-McGregor (2021) found complementarities between investments in technological capabilities and imported intermediate goods in enhancing exporting revenues of Brazilian firms.

The above discussion indicates that the freeing up of imports by the government of India through economic liberalisation policies in the early nineties was a *prerequisite* for successful internationalisation. Locally available resources such as plant and machinery, R&D assets and marketing inputs were not sufficient for Indian firms to be successful in more competitive global markets, making imported technology and know-how a prerequisite in the capability upgrading process of India's pharmaceutical and textile industries. Analysis of policy choices in Chapter 2 also showed a further liberalisation of imports and inward FDIs in response to the global institutional changes related to the two industries. Taken together, this suggests that the degree of imports or import intensity of firms would partially or fully *mediate* the relationship between investments in firms' capabilities and export success, the theory we proposed earlier. Accordingly, we propose the following:

Proposition 2: The positive association between a firm's investments in capabilities and product-market internationalisation is contingent on its participation in international resource markets (that is, imports of technology and know-how).

Network Resources

After describing the importance of institutional resources (both domestic and international) in facilitating the development of firm-level capabilities and the associated success in international markets, we now propose a third category of resources that lie at an intermediate level. Such resources are not confined to a single firm, nor are they accessible to all the firms in an industry but are available only to a subgroup of firms in the industry—those that are part of specific networks. We call these network resources. We consider two types of network resources, both of which are relevant in the Indian context and especially to the pharmaceutical and textile industries, namely BGs and geographic clusters.

Business groups (BGs)

A growing body of research has now established that a distinct multi-firm structure—namely the business group (BG)—constitutes a dominant organisational form in many parts of the world (La Porta, Lopez-de-Silanes and Shleifer 1999; Carney et al. 2011; Dau, Morck and Yeung 2021). BGs are broadly defined as 'sets of legally separate firms bound together in persistent formal and/or informal ways' (Granovetter 2005: 429) where the firms in question 'are accustomed to taking coordinated action' (Khanna and Rivkin 2001: 47). BGs have various names in different geographical areas ranging from Japanese *keiretsus*, Korean *chaebols*, Turkish *families*, Latin American and Spanish *grupos* to Indian *business groups*. The strength of ties among BG firms lies somewhere between loose inter-organisational arrangements such as strategic alliances and the close ties among multiple businesses legally consolidated into a single entity in an M-form structure (Granovetter 2005) that arose in the United States. India is home to a large number of BGs.

BGs can be considered a form of closed network, as not all firms are affiliated with BGs and those firms that are affiliated with a BG are conferred some advantages (to be sure, some disadvantages as well). BGs are increasingly seen as providing two types of advantages to member firms (Langlois 2012): 'gap-filling function', whereby in the presence of strategic factor market imperfections (or institutional voids), BGs fill the void by generating their own internal markets for financial capital and managerial talent; and 'coalitional function', whereby BGs 'characterise an economic coordination mechanism in which legally independent companies utilise the collaborative arrangements to enhance their collective economic welfare' (Colpan and Hikino 2010: 17). This includes sharing resources and capabilities and cross-pollination of ideas across group-affiliated firms (*The Economist* 2014).

Firms affiliated with BGs benefit from access to group resources, including capital, technology, human resources and complementary products and services, and hence are in a better position than stand-alone firms in terms of their resource independence on external sources. BGs are characterised by internal markets for products, capital and management talent and hence act as suppliers of such resources to firms affiliated with them. By transferring capital within the group or by leveraging the BG's reputation and underwriting capital issues, BGs are able to alleviate resource deficiencies common to most developing economy firms. For example, there is evidence that internal capital markets operated within *keiretsus* in Japan (Lincoln, Gerlach and Ahmadjian 1996), which in turn allowed BGs to act as de facto venture capitalists and allocate resources to provide the necessary infrastructure for member firms (Mahmood and Mitchell 2004). In addition, due to their superior visibility and reputation benefits, BGs are in a position to attract and retain better talent and develop internal markets for human capital. BGs can thus be viewed as a strategic network providing member firms with access to information, knowledge, resources, markets and technologies (Elango and Pattnaik 2007). Independent firms do not have access to such internal markets and resources and hence are relatively more in need of resources from the government or other external sources.

BG ownership also brings a more long-term orientation to firms. The ties that bind the BG firms together are primarily related to common ownership by a family, particularly in the context of BGs in India. Such BGs consider fostering the values of the group in all the companies within the group an important component of their value addition and actively focus on this (Mahindra, Stewart and Raman 2008). BG owners have long investment horizons, which can mitigate the incentives for myopic investment decisions by managers (Stein 1989; James 1999). For example, projects with a very long gestation period but with superior returns in the long run have a higher likelihood of being conceived and undertaken in a BG-affiliated firm than in a stand-alone firm. For all these reasons, affiliation with a BG serves as an important resource for a firm to begin distant search for products and markets, as well as a repository of various capabilities that can be accessed by group affiliates (Gubbi, Aulakh and Ray 2015).

Geographic clusters[7]

Location in geographic clusters is another important resource for firms. The United Nations Industrial Development Organization (UNIDO) (2020; 18) defines clusters as 'geographical concentrations of inter-connected enterprises and associated institutions that face common challenges and opportunities'.[8]

Firms located in these clusters enjoy a number of advantages such as networking benefits, knowledge sharing, greater institutional support and better access to raw materials and manpower (Bell and Zaheer 2007). Research on regional clusters in developed economies has primarily focused on access to knowledge as the benefit derived from location in a cluster. According to Tallman et al. (2004: 259), 'long-term competitive advantage for ... clusters and their constituent firms must be based on stock of closely held knowledge and mechanisms that limit the dissemination of such knowledge'. However, the benefits of cluster formation in developing economies include not only knowledge flows but also common infrastructure and shared innovation and marketing activities. Small- and medium-sized enterprises that belong to a product specific sector 'can benefit from economies of scale in their engagement in collective actions for the procurement of supplies and the marketing of their products' (UNIDO 2020: 19).

The textile industry in India operates mostly in the form of geographical clusters, most of which formed naturally, and some were created by the government through 'industrial parks' schemes.[9] Examples of natural clusters include Tiruppur in the state of Tamil Nadu in India, which is a leading textile cluster specialising in the manufacture and export of knitted garments. Local availability of raw materials, skilled labour and integration with different activities or units involved in the manufacture of knitted garments such as dyeing, fabric making, knitting, and so on, are among the greatest strengths of this cluster (Ray 2019). Another major knitting cluster, which is also the oldest, exists in Kolkata in West Bengal, although it mostly caters to the domestic market. Similarly, there exists a cluster in Ludhiana in the state of Punjab that specialises in winter wear and another cluster near Delhi (in Okhla industrial estate) that is involved in the manufacturing and export of fashionable garments for women, men and children.

Among the government-sponsored clusters, the Powerloom Cluster Development Scheme of India's Ministry of Textiles envisions geographical clusters developed through private–public partnerships that 'would create world-class infrastructure' and

> integrate the production chain in a manner that caters to the business needs of the local Small and Medium Enterprises (SMEs) to boost production and export.... The broad objective ... would be to enhance the competitiveness of the clusters in terms of increased market share and ensuring increased productivity by higher unit value realisation of the products. (Government of India, Ministry of Textiles, 'Comprehensive Powerloom Cluster Development Scheme', texmin.nic.in)

Similarly, the Comprehensive Handloom Cluster Development Scheme (CHCDS) supports the development of handloom clusters to improve infrastructure and storage facilities and technology and skill upgrading of a large number of small-scale handloom firms, and through shared resources and common marketing activities, these increase the sector's domestic and international competitiveness (www.handlooms.nic.in).

The above discussion suggests that through shared access to knowledge, manufacturing and technological assets and marketing infrastructure, firms located in geographic clusters are in a better position to deal with changes in the external environment than organisations that do not have these benefits. Firms outside the clusters, however, do not have access to network resources and thus require firm-specific investments in capabilities to compete in any changed context. Thus, akin to firms affiliated with BGs that benefit from

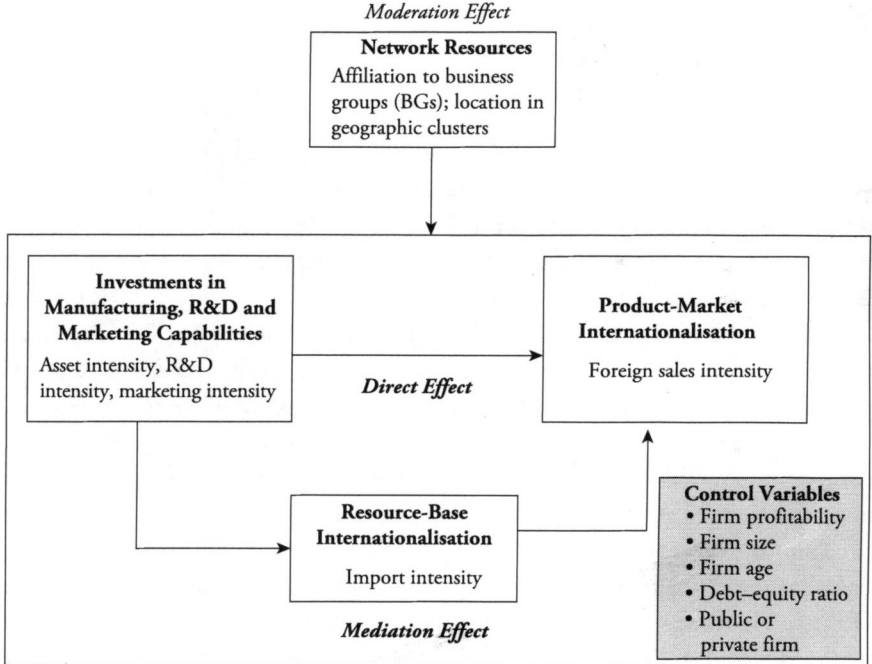

Figure 5.5 Conceptual Model: Resources, Capabilities and Product-Market Internationalisation

Source: This Conceptual Model was developed and tested by the authors in this chapter.

Note: Items in parentheses in this model connote the way each construct was operationalised in the empirical analysis.

'closed networks', firms belonging to geographic clusters can tap into the resources of 'open networks' to reconfigure their capabilities and effectively compete in global markets. Based on these arguments, we offer the following proposition:

Proposition 3: Investments in capabilities and access to international resources to sustain product-market internationalisation are less critical for firms that are part of supra-firm networks (that is, are part of business groups or geographical clusters) than for those firms that are not part of such networks.

In sum, at the organisation-level analysis of strategic response to global institutional change, we explain a firm's product-market internationalisation as a function of its investments in manufacturing, R&D and marketing capabilities, with access to international resources as the mediating mechanism. These relationships are moderated by the network resources available to a firm by virtue of its affiliation with a BG and/or geographic cluster. The overall conceptual model that is empirically tested is captured in a schematic diagram in Figure 5.5.

Data and Measures

Data

We used the Prowess Database from the Centre for Monitoring Indian Economy (CMIE), which is the most frequently used dataset by strategy and international business researchers (for example, Khanna and Palepu 2000, Chacar and Vissa 2005, Chittoor et al. 2009) for large sample studies on India. The CMIE Prowess database contains detailed financial data since 1990 on over 40,000 Indian firms comprising all companies traded on India's major stock exchanges, unlisted public companies and several others, including central public-sector enterprises. The database covers most of the organised industrial activity in India, and the companies covered in Prowess account for over 75 per cent of all corporate taxes and over 95 per cent of excise duty collected by the government of India. We counted 787 companies in CMIE Prowess under the industry classification (two-digit) of drugs and pharmaceuticals, and 1,174 companies under the industry classification of textiles when we considered the full thirty-year time period of 1990 to 2019 for which data were available. We did not include the data for 2020 in our study due to many missing data, probably on account of the disruptions caused by the COVID-19 pandemic. Furthermore, although the number of firms in Prowess is quite comprehensive and includes almost all the firms in the organised sector, nearly 80 per cent of them are unlisted private firms that are not obliged to disclose financial data in the public domain. Our study's focus is on explaining the heterogeneity in the export intensity of domestic Indian firms. Hence, we eliminated subsidiaries of foreign companies, purely domestic firms with no exports for even a single year of the thirty-year period, and firms with missing data on the variables of interest. There were also missing data in Prowess for some of these firms over some of the years. Accordingly, we conducted unbalanced panel analyses with 4,492 observations for the pharmaceutical industry and 5,382 observations for the textile industry.

Measures

Dependent variable: Foreign sales intensity

The foreign sales intensity of a firm was measured as the ratio of export or foreign sales to total sales, the most common measure of internationalisation in the literature (Ramaswamy, Kroeck and Renforth 1996). We chose the ratio of foreign sales to total sales over other possible measures, such as international geographic spread, growth in foreign sales or FDI, for two reasons. First, the validity of any measure needs to be assessed based on its potential explanatory power in the context of the theoretical assumptions on which it is based (Hassel et al. 2003). Given that a majority of firms from developing economies such as India are still in the early stages of the internationalisation process, with export being the dominant mode of international expansion (Aulakh, Kotabe and Teegen 2000), the chosen measure for internationalisation is contextually appropriate compared to more involved measures such as FDI. Second, while the data on foreign sales intensity were available for all the firms, data availability on other variables was limited to a few firms and only for a few years. When we cross-checked the use of the limited available data on alternative measures such as the number of foreign subsidiaries or the countries exported to, we found the correlation between export intensity and other internationalisation measures to be very high. Thus, our measure of export intensity appears contextually appropriate and measures the construct of internationalisation reasonably well.

Independent variables: Investments in capabilities

Manufacturing Asset Intensity As a strategic response to global institutional change, we saw earlier that firms in textile and pharmaceutical industries increased their investments in manufacturing assets. These are reflected as gross plant and machinery assets in the balance sheets of these firms. Hence, we used the percentage of the gross plant and machinery asset values to the total sales of a firm as a proxy for manufacturing asset intensity. Given the differential ability of making such investments depending on the size of the firm in terms of its sales, it is more appropriate to employ a ratio measure such as this instead of an absolute measure.

In the case of firms from the textile industry, this measure also serves as a good proxy for the support received from the government by means of the TUFS. As described earlier, the TUFS was a type of subsidy introduced by the Government of India in 1999 for the benefit of Indian textile firms. It was implemented as concessional loans provided by banks for projects undertaken by firms to upgrade their production facilities or to create new production capacity. The benefit to the firms manifested in the form of a 5 per cent subsidy on the interest to be charged on the TUFS loan provided to the firm. We learned from interviews with various executives from textile industry associations, including the Confederation of India Textile Industries (CITI), that all textile firms took advantage of the TUFS programme by taking bank loans and in turn invested capital in plants and machinery. The firms could not utilise the TUFS for any purpose other than investing in manufacturing assets because such investments were monitored by the banks as security for any additional TUFS loans provided by them. This is reflected in the steep increase in the average gross plant and machinery of textile firms since the launch of the TUFS in 1999. Despite the crude nature of such a measure, this is the best proxy available for the TUFS because the bank loans in the financial statements of the textile firms are not required to be reported separately as TUFS and other loans.

Research and Development (R&D) Intensity   Following Hitt et al. (1997), we used the percentage of annual research and development expenses to total sales, or R&D intensity, as a proxy for a firm's investments in innovation capabilities. While we do recognise the general nature of this measure, it was preferred over more fine-grained measures such as patents for two reasons: availability of data for all the firms for the whole study period, and its very high correlation with other more direct measures of innovation capability. Developing economies present many data-related challenges stemming mainly from poor disclosure requirements (Hoskisson et al 2000). Although output measures such as patents have been used to measure innovation capability in developed economies, it is not as common for many firms to file for patents in developing countries such as India due to less legal protection. Therefore, R&D intensity is a more appropriate measure to capture investments in innovation capabilities for Indian firms.

Marketing Intensity   Similar to R&D intensity, we used the percentage of annual marketing expenses that include advertising and selling expenses to total sales or *marketing intensity* as a proxy for a firm's marketing capability and brand equity. Marketing expenditures are crucial to compete against competitors and win customers, particularly after the global institutional changes that sought to create a level playing field for all firms.

The three measures described here—manufacturing asset intensity, R&D intensity and marketing intensity—constitute three critical firm-level capabilities needed to improve the export intensity of a firm with the first associated with tangible resources and the latter two with intangible resources.

Moderating variables

Business Group Affiliation In line with past research on the performance effects of BG affiliation for Indian firms (Khanna and Palepu 2000a; Chacar and Vissa 2005), we adopt the CMIE's classification of firms into specific BGs to identify whether an individual firm belonged to a business group or if it was a stand-alone firm. The CMIE uses a variety of sources to classify firms into various ownership groups based on continuous monitoring of company shareholding, new announcements and a qualitative understanding of the groupwise behaviour of individual companies. We measure a firm's affiliation with a BG using a simple dummy variable that takes a value '1' if the firm is owned by a BG and '0' if this is not the case.

Location in a Geographic Cluster As described earlier, the Indian textile industry has developed in a few geographical clusters. Some of the well-known textile clusters in India are Ludhiana in Punjab for woollen and synthetic knitwear and Tiruppur in Tamil Nadu for cotton knitwear (SIDBI 2009). We use a dummy variable to measure whether a firm belongs to a cluster and operationalise this based on the address of the registered office of the firm. Following earlier research on textile geographic clusters (Ray 2019), we consider the following major textile clusters to code the cluster dummy: Kolkata, Bangalore, Tiruppur, Ludhiana, Delhi and Maharashtra. The cluster dummy takes a value of '1' if the firm's registered office is located in one of these geographical clusters or else it takes a value of '0'. Thus, a cluster dummy value of '1' indicates that the firm is a part of a strong cluster and '0' if it belongs to a weak cluster or no cluster.

Mediating variable: Import intensity

We proposed in our theoretical model that inward internationalisation as measured by import intensity mediates the relationship between firm-level resources and export intensity. In other words, the resources that are obtained from international markets play a critical role in complementing domestic resources in improving the export intensity of firms in a globally competitive market.

As is typical of closed economies, many government regulations and controls prevail and continue to prevail in India on all transactions involving foreign exchange. Therefore, all Indian companies registered under the Indian Companies Act have to record and disclose data on foreign exchange spending in their annual financial statements. Most firms disclose only what is needed as per the law and do not provide any break-up or details of these expenditures. To maximise the number of observations for our sample, we consider the total forex spending reported in the annual reports to measure import intensity by operationalising it as a ratio of annual forex spending calculated in US dollars to annual total sales also converted into US dollars as per the prevailing exchange rate at the end of the year. CMIE Prowess has the feature of providing these data converted into US dollar equivalents for each year, and we depend on this to calculate the ratio of import intensity for each firm-year. Once again given the lack of availability of more fine-grained data for all the firms in our sample, we resort to using this somewhat general measure to capture inward internationalisation.

Control variables

A comprehensive set of variables was included to control for possible confounds. The size of the firm constitutes a critical control variable, as it can be argued that larger firms are more advantageously positioned to access international resources and to succeed in international markets through exports. *Firm size*, measured as the natural logarithm of total sales, was used to control for size effects. The *age* of each firm since it was founded, in years, was used as a measure of experience. It can be argued that a firm's financial profitability may have an influence on its international expansion. To account for this, we used *firm profitability*, the percentage of profit net of all taxes to total sales of the firm, as a control variable. The capital structure of a firm has an impact on its internationalisation; hence, the *debt-to-equity ratio*, measured as the ratio of total debt to total shareholders' equity (net worth) of a firm for a particular financial year, is included as a control variable. Furthermore, publicly listed firms, compared to private firms, have better access to financial and other resources, and we account for this by including a *listed firm dummy* as a control. However, in the context of India, where firms cannot be easily wound up, there are a significant number of firms that are listed on the stock exchange but are no longer active. Such firms are assigned an inactive ('Z') category by the stock exchange. The *listed firm dummy* takes a value of '1' if a firm is listed in the main stock exchange of India (BSE, or Bombay Stock Exchange) under the categories 'A', 'B' or 'B2', which include firms that are regularly traded on the market (we exclude the 'Z' category) and '0' otherwise. As the entire data set pertains to a single industry, no industry controls are needed for the pharmaceutical industry. However, given that the textile industry has firms focusing on different parts of the value chain, such as yarn, fabric and apparel/garments, we include two industry dummies to indicate whether a firm primarily operates in the *apparel industry* or *fabric industry* (with yarn forming the excluded category). Finally, we included year dummies to control for time effects pertaining to each year of the thirty-year sample period.

Sample description

Table 5.1 indicates the sample characteristics for all the measures used in the study for both industries. While the two industry samples are quite comparable in terms of some measures, such as firm age and manufacturing asset (plant and machinery) intensity, they differ quite significantly in terms of other measures. The export intensity for the average firm in the textile industry (37 per cent) is higher than that of the pharmaceutical industry (approximately 28 per cent), but the average profitability for the textile industry (1.4 per cent) is less than half that of the pharmaceutical industry (3.6 per cent). In another interesting contrast, the textile industry is highly leveraged, with an average debt–equity ratio (2.41) nearly twice that of the pharmaceutical industry (1.26). Such high levels of financial leverage are unusual and can only be a result of a distortion of government incentives such as the TUFS for which firms have to borrow from banks to obtain the interest subsidy. The lower profitability (which is the net of taxes and interest) of the textile sector could be partially driven by the relatively large debt burden of the average firm. In terms of intangible resources, the pharmaceutical industry fares much better with significantly higher investments in R&D and marketing.

As seen from Figures 5.6 and 5.7, the average sales and exports of the pharmaceutical industry are nearly double those of the textile industry, indicating the more fragmented nature of the textile industry. We can also see that the average imports continued to rise in the pharmaceutical industry even after 2005, whereas the average firm imports in the textile industry reached a plateau after 2005.

Table 5.1 Sample Characteristics: Pharmaceutical and Textile Firms

Measure	Pharmaceutical Industry		Textile Industry	
	Mean	Standard Deviation	Mean	Standard Deviation
Firm age (in years)	24.3	16.7	27.1	21.5
Firm profitability (net margin in %)	3.6	23.0	1.4	13.0
Foreign sales intensity (in %)	31.2	27.8	37.0	32.0
Import intensity (in %)	16.0	18.3	11.8	18.9
Manufacturing asset (plant & machinery) intensity (in %)	41.6	326.0	43.0	132.8
R&D intensity (in %)	1.27	4.18	0.05	0.24
Marketing intensity (in %)	5.33	4.89	3.78	3.16
Debt to equity ratio	1.26	2.16	2.41	4.26
Listed firms (% of sample)	30		21	
Business group firms (% of sample)	26		34	
Cluster firms (% of sample)			50	

Source: Firm-level data from Prowess, Centre for Monitoring Indian Economy (CMIE).

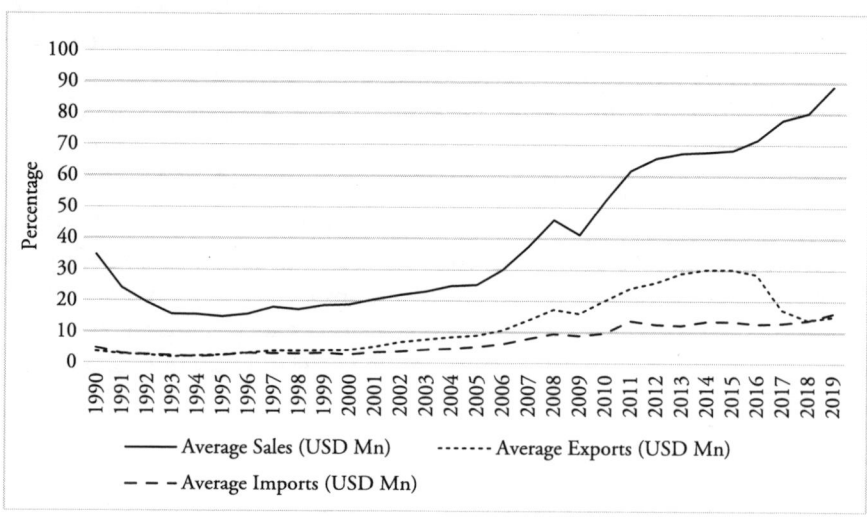

Figure 5.6 Pharma Industry: Average Sales, Exports and Imports Per Firm

Source: Firm-level data from Prowess, Centre for Monitoring Indian Economy (CMIE).

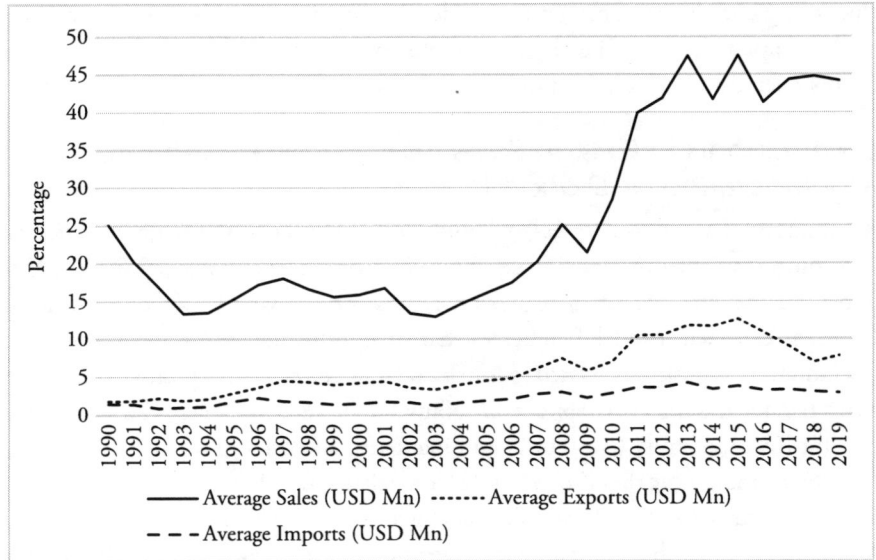

Figure 5.7 Textile Industry: Average Sales, Exports and Imports Per Firm

Source: Firm-level data from Prowess, Centre for Monitoring Indian Economy (CMIE).

Estimation and Key Findings

As we include a near census of substantial firms in the organised sector (that include both private and publicly listed firms) in both industries, we believe that the likelihood of sample selection bias is minimal. We estimate our models using random effects generalised least squares panel regression procedures. We choose a random effects procedure because we have important time-invariant predictor variables (BG affiliation and location in geographic clusters) that fixed effects models cannot incorporate. The panel design offers some advantages. First, since it includes both cross-sectional and time series data, it increases the available degrees of freedom to improve estimation efficiency. Second, panel estimation procedures allow us to control for unobserved heterogeneity (the possibility that estimated results are due to unobserved factors or omitted variables) and thereby reduce the possibility of biased parameter estimates and spurious results (Greene 2002). We report p-values based on heteroscedasticity-consistent White's (1980) robust standard errors as an additional measure of reliability. Before estimating the regressions, we check the data for normality of the residuals, heteroscedasticity and existence of collinearity, if any. Multicollinearity was not found to be an issue, as none of the variance inflation factor (VIF) values was more than 2, much within the normally accepted levels. The complete regression results (including correlation tables) are provided in Appendices 5A.1–5A.6 at the end of the chapter. In the following paragraphs, we summarise and discuss only the results related to the proposed model.

Determinants of Foreign Sales Intensity: Investments in Manufacturing, R&D and Marketing[10]

A summary of the panel regression results for the effect of the main explanatory and control variables on foreign sales intensity is provided in Table 5.2. Model 1 in Table 5.2 captures the panel regression results for the sample of pharmaceutical firms. As expected, Model 1 indicates that manufacturing (plant and machinery) asset intensity is positively related to foreign sales intensity (with a positive coefficient and a p-value less than 0.10) after controlling for all other variables. The same is the case for R&D intensity (p < 0.001) and marketing intensity (p = 0.016). However, it is important to note that the size of the coefficients, which indicate the effect sizes, are much larger for R&D intensity (coefficient = 0.45) and marketing intensity (coefficient = 0.52) than for manufacturing asset intensity (coefficient = 0.002). This clearly reinforces the core thesis of Gu and Lev (2017) about the relatively higher importance of intangible assets compared to tangible assets in current competitive markets. Model 1 also reveals that larger firms have some inherent advantages and are more likely to succeed in international markets (coefficient of firm size = 3.74; p-value = 0.001). On the other hand, older firms are probably less agile in responding to institutional changes and hence are less successful in foreign markets (coefficient of firm size = −0.362; p-value < 0.001). The effect of firm size and firm age reinforces the thesis that path dependencies play an important role in succeeding in internationalisation (Johanson and Vahlne 2009).

Remarkably, the findings using the textile industry sample are quite similar (Model 2 in Table 5.2). As correctly estimated by policymakers and the government about the importance of boosting manufacturing capabilities, the coefficient of plant and machinery asset intensity is positive and statistically significant (coefficient = 0.011 with a p-value < 0.001) after controlling for all other variables. However, surprisingly, even in the case of textile firms, both R&D intensity (coefficient = 2.91; p-value = 0.05) and marketing intensity (coefficient = 2.05; p-value < 0.001) yield positive coefficients that are highly significant. In other words, even though the government did not identify and explicitly support the creation of intangible assets such as R&D and marketing in the textile industry, firms that have strategically invested in these capabilities have achieved a higher degree of internationalisation. Similar to the pharmaceutical industry, firm size confers benefits in terms of increased foreign sales, and firm age creates some inertial effects in responding to institutional changes.

Table 5.2 Panel Estimation Results: Direct Effects of Investments in Capabilities on Foreign-Sales Intensity[a]

DV = Foreign Sales Intensity	Pharmaceuticals		Textiles	
	Model 1		Model 2	
Asset (plant and machinery) intensity	0.002	(0.081)	0.011	(0.000)
R&D intensity	0.454	(0.000)	2.912	(0.054)
Marketing intensity	0.525	(0.016)	2.053	(0.000)
Firm size[b]	3.740	(0.001)	2.635	(0.010)
Firm age	−0.362	(0.000)	−0.274	(0.000)
Control variables[c]	Included		Included	
Number of observations[d]	4,492		5,382	

Notes: [a] Unstandardised regression coefficients; robust p-values in parentheses; two-tailed tests.

   [b] Natural logarithm of firm sales.

   [c] See appendices for a full list of control variables.

   [d] Firm years for the thirty-year period 1990 to 2019. For full results, see Appendices 5A.2 and 5A.5 at the end of the chapter.

Determinants of Foreign Sales Intensity: Mediation Effect of Inward Internationalisation[11]

Our second proposition was that resources obtained from outside the country boundaries (that is, resource base internationalisation) are critical for firms in developing economies in facilitating outward product-market internationalisation. In other words, we propose a mediation effect of import intensity on the relationship between investments in manufacturing, R&D and marketing capabilities and foreign sales intensity. That is, investments in capabilities through the use of international technology and know-how are expected to be more beneficial than relying on locally available resources. We test this mediation hypothesis separately using the samples of pharmaceutical and textile firms. Table 5.3 captures our test of the mediation effect in the pharmaceutical industry sample, and Table 5.4 provides the mediation results for the sample of textile firms.

We first describe the findings using the pharmaceutical industry sample. Mediation analysis involves three steps (Baron and Kenny 1986; Kenny, Kashy and Bolger 1998; Shaver 2005). The first step is to establish that the independent variables (that is, assets, R&D and marketing intensities) influence the mediating variable (that is, the import intensity). This step was tested and was supported as shown in Model 1 in Table 5.3 with import intensity as the dependent variable.

In Model 1, the coefficients for asset (plant and machinery) intensity (coefficient = 0.010, p-value < 0.001) and R&D intensity (coefficient = 0.287, p-value = 0.102) are positive and significant, while the coefficient for marketing intensity is not significant at conventional p-value levels. The second step is to demonstrate that the independent variables influence the dependent variable (that is, foreign sales intensity). We have already checked this before, and we know that they do, but for the sake of completeness, we reproduce this step in Model 2 of Table 5.3. Finally, it must be established that the mediator (that is, import intensity) influences the dependent variable (that is, foreign sales intensity) with the independent variables controlled or included in the model. If the effects of the independent variables are no longer significant when the mediator is included in the model, then full mediation is indicated (Baron and Kenny 1986; Shaver 2005); otherwise, the mediation can be said to be partial. As shown in Model 3 (Table 5.3), where foreign sales intensity is the dependent variable, the coefficient for import intensity is positive and statistically significant (coefficient = 0.182, p-value < 0.001), indicating its effect on foreign sales intensity. Furthermore, with import intensity in the model, the coefficient for asset (plant and machinery) intensity is no longer statistically significant (coefficient = 0.000, p-value = 0.857). This supports a full mediation effect of import intensity on the relationship between asset intensity and foreign sales intensity. However, R&D intensity (coefficient = 0.41, p-value = 0.003) remains statistically significant in Model 3, thereby indicating partial mediation by import intensity for R&D intensity. To summarise these results, import

Table 5.3 Panel Estimation Results: Pharmaceutical Industry Mediating Effect of Imports[a]

	DV = Import Intensity		DV = Foreign Sales Intensity			
	Model 1		Model 2		Model 3	
Import intensity					0.182	(0.000)
Asset (plant and machinery) intensity	0.010	(0.000)	0.002	(0.081)	0.000	(0.857)
R&D intensity	0.287	(0.102)	0.454	(0.000)	0.408	(0.003)
Marketing intensity	−0.102	(0.254)	0.525	(0.016)	0.524	(0.015)
Control variables[b]	Included		Included		Included	
Number of observations[c]	4,492		4,492		4,492	

Notes: [a] Unstandardised regression coefficients; robust p-values in parentheses; two-tailed tests.

[b] See appendices for a full list of control variables.

[c] Firm years for the thirty-year period 1990 to 2019.

intensity fully mediates the relationship between asset intensity and foreign sales intensity, partially mediates between R&D intensity and foreign sales intensity, and does not mediate marketing intensity. Thus, overall, the results for the pharmaceutical industry suggest that international resources play a more important role in complementing manufacturing and R&D capabilities than in marketing capabilities.

We now turn to the findings of the mediation effect in the sample of textile firms. Once again, we follow the three steps of testing for mediation (Baron and Kenny 1986), which are captured in Table 5.4. The first step was tested in Model 1 in Table 5.4 with import intensity as the dependent variable. As in the sample of pharmaceutical firms, we find the coefficients for asset (plant and machinery) intensity (coefficient = 0.059, p-value < 0.001) and R&D intensity (coefficient = 2.492, p-value = 0.099) to be positive and statistically significant, while the coefficient for marketing intensity is not significant. The second step is to check whether investments in capabilities are directly related to the main dependent variable, namely foreign sales intensity, and as we have seen earlier, this is indeed true, as captured in Model 2 of Table 5.4. Finally, we test in Model 3 (Table 5.4) whether the mediator variable (import intensity) is related to the dependent variable (foreign sales intensity) with the independent variables also included in the model.

We can see in Model 3 (Table 5.4) that the coefficient for imports intensity is positive and statistically significant (coefficient = 0.078, p-value = 0.024), whereas the coefficient for asset (plant and machinery) intensity continues to be statistically significant (coefficient = 0.006, p-value = 0.105) even though it is much smaller and has a higher p-value compared to Model 2. This supports a partial mediation effect of import intensity on the relationship between asset intensity and foreign sales intensity in the case of textile firms. To summarise, while the sample of pharmaceutical firms showed a full mediation effect of import intensity, the mediation was partial in the textile industry sample. However, just as we have seen in the case of the pharmaceutical industry sample, R&D intensity (coefficient = 2.80, p-value = 0.054) continues to be statistically significant in Model 3, once again indicating a partial mediation by import intensity for the relationship between R&D intensity and foreign sales intensity. The overall mediation effects hold for the textile industry, the only difference from the pharmaceutical industry being a partial mediation for asset intensity in the case of textile firms and full mediation for pharmaceutical firms.

Table 5.4 Panel Estimation Results: Textile Industry Mediating Effects of Imports[a]

	DV = Import Intensity		DV = Foreign Sales Intensity			
	Model 1		Model 2		Model 3	
Import intensity					0.078	(0.024)
Asset (plant & machinery) intensity	0.059	(0.000)	0.011	(0.000)	0.006	(0.105)
R&D intensity	2.492	(0.099)	2.912	(0.054)	2.799	(0.054)
Marketing intensity	0.013	(0.928)	2.053	(0.000)	2.046	(0.000)
Control variables[b]	Included		Included		Included	
Number of observations[c]	5,382		5,382		5,382	

Notes: [a] Unstandardised regression coefficients; robust p-values in parentheses; two-tailed tests.

[b] See appendices for a full list of control variables.

[c] Firm years for the thirty-year period 1990 to 2019.

Determinants of Foreign Sales Intensity: Moderating Effects of Firms' Business Group Affiliation or Location in a Geographic Cluster[12]

We proposed earlier that networks such as business groups (BGs) and geographic clusters have a moderating effect on the relationship between investments in capabilities and foreign sales intensity. The underlying argument is that firms derive certain benefits from membership in these networks, which allow them to respond to global institutional changes without extensive dependence on institutional resources and new investments in capabilities. The imperative for augmentation of resources and capabilities is much stronger for firms outside these networks. We test these propositions in the context of pharmaceutical and textile industries in the following way. BGs are more predominant in the case of pharmaceutical firms than textile firms; on the other hand, the phenomenon of geographic clusters is predominant in the case of textile firms. Therefore, we test the moderating effect of BGs by dividing the sample of pharma firms into two subsamples of (*a*) firms affiliated with BGs and (*b*) stand-alone firms that are not affiliated with any BG. We then check whether the mediating model differs significantly when we run the panel regressions using the two subsamples of the pharma industry. We follow a similar procedure in the case of textile firms by dividing the full sample into two subsamples of (*a*) firms located in key textile clusters and (*b*) firms that are not located in any major textile cluster.

The moderating effects of BG affiliation in the pharmaceutical industry are summarised in Table 5.5. As shown in the table, approximately one-third of the observations are firms affiliated with BGs and two-thirds are non-affiliated firms. As predicted, the proposed model better captures the relationships for firms not affiliated with BGs. Model 7 shows the positive and significant effects of asset intensity (coefficient = 0.013; p-value = 0.000) and R&D intensity (coefficient = 0.529; p-value = 0.017) on import intensity. Furthermore, the coefficient for import intensity is positive and significant (0.214; p-value = 0.000) in Model 9, which, along with non-significant coefficients for asset and R&D intensities, connotes a full mediation of import intensity between the two capabilities and

Table 5.5 Panel Estimation Results: Determinants of Foreign-Sales Intensity—Moderating Effect of Business Groups in the Pharmaceutical Industry

	Business-Group Firms		Non-Business-Group Firms	
	DV = Import Intensity	DV = Foreign Sales Intensity	DV = Import Intensity	DV = Foreign Sales Intensity
	Model 4	Model 6	Model 7	Model 9
Import intensity		0.108 (0.186)		0.214 (0.000)
Asset (plant and machinery) intensity	0.005 (0.205)	0.000 (0.917)	0.013 (0.000)	–0.000 (0.785)
R&D intensity	0.108 (0.247)	0.580 (0.000)	0.529 (0.017)	0.063 (0.750)
Marketing intensity	–0.248 (0.318)	0.736 (0.013)	–0.067 (0.409)	0.402 (0.115)
Firm size[b]	0.889 (0.487)	5.846 (0.005)	1.164 (0.142)	2.522 (0.025)
Firm age	–0.176 (0.008)	–0.439 (0.000)	–0.138 (0.023)	–0.291 (0.004)
Control variables[c]	Included	Included	Included	Included
Number of observations[d]	1,173	1,173	3,319	3,319

Note: This is a summary of results from Appendix 5A.3.

  [a] Unstandardised regression coefficients; robust p-values in parentheses; two-tailed tests.

  [b] Natural logarithm of firm sales.

  [c] See appendices for a full list of control variables.

  [d] Firm years for the thirty-year period 1990 to 2019.

foreign export intensity. The coefficients for marketing intensity in Models 7 and 9, although positive, are not statistically significant.

The results are markedly different for the sample of firms affiliated with BGs. As shown in Model 4 of Table 5.5, the coefficients for investments in the three capabilities are statistically non-significant when import intensity is the dependent variable. Furthermore, Model 6 shows that the coefficient for import intensity is non-significant (0.108; p-value = 0.186), while the direct effects of R&D intensity (coefficient = 0.580; p-value = 0.000) and marketing intensity (coefficient = 0.736; p-value = 0.013) on foreign sales intensity are positive and statistically significant. All the coefficients for asset intensity remain insignificant in the different models. Taken together, the results show that investments in manufacturing assets play a more salient role for non-BG firms in enhancing foreign market competitiveness, and this is accomplished through an integration of foreign technology and know-how (that is, increased import intensity). Investments in R&D facilitate an increase in foreign sales intensity for both sets of firms; however, the mechanism is different for the two groups: the relationship is mediated by imports for non-BG firms, while the effect is more direct for BG firms. Similarly, investments in marketing capabilities seem to play a more salient role for BG firms than non-BG firms.

Next, we check-test the mediation model with respect to network effects related to geographical clusters in the textile industry. These results are summarised in Table 5.6. The two subsamples of textile firms are roughly equally divided. We can see from Models 6 and 9 that mediation effects are present for just the subgroup of firms that are part of geographical clusters. The coefficient for import intensity in this group is 0.135, which is significant at p = 0.017, while it is not significant for non-cluster firms (coefficient = 0.034; p = 0.432). A further probe of the mediation model for firms in geographical clusters (Models 4 and 6) shows that the effect of investments in manufacturing assets on foreign-sales intensity is partially mediated by import intensity (that is, the coefficient of asset intensity in Model 4 [where DV = import intensity] is 0.051; p = 0.000) and is 0.008; p = 0.012 in Model 6 [where DV = foreign sales intensity]. Import intensity does not act as a mediator for R&D and marketing investments (both coefficients in Model 4 are statistically non-significant), although we find a direct positive effect of marketing intensity on foreign sales intensity (coefficient = 1.428; p = 0.000).

For firms not part of any geographical cluster, Model 9 shows direct and significant positive effects of both R&D intensity (coefficient = 7.262; p = 0.012) and marketing intensity (coefficient = 2.084; p = 0.000) on foreign export intensity. Surprisingly, investments in manufacturing assets have no

Table 5.6 Panel Estimation Results: Determinants of Foreign Sales Intensity—Moderating Effect of Geographic Clusters in the Textile Industry

	Firms in Geographical Clusters		Non-cluster Firms	
	DV = Import Intensity	DV = Foreign Sales Intensity	DV = Import Intensity	DV = Foreign Sales Intensity
	Model 4	Model 6	Model 7	Model 9
Import intensity		0.135 (0.017)		0.034 (0.432)
Asset (plant & machinery) intensity	0.051 (0.000)	0.008 (0.012)	0.067 (0.000)	0.003 (0.454)
R&D intensity	0.944 (0.629)	1.725 (0.227)	5.090 (0.026)	7.262 (0.012)
Marketing intensity	0.171 (0.249)	1.428 (0.000)	−0.177 (0.499)	3.084 (0.000)
Firm size[b]	−1.440 (0.021)	3.970 (0.001)	−2.006 (0.029)	1.418 (0.382)
Firm age	−0.102 (0.000)	−0.303 (0.000)	−0.011 (0.783)	−0.223 (0.014)
Control variables[c]	Included	Included	Included	Included
Number of observations[d]	2,684	2,684	2,698	2,698

Notes: This is a summary of results from Appendix 5A.6.

 [a] Unstandardised regression coefficients; robust p-values in parentheses; two-tailed tests.

 [b] Natural logarithm of firm sales.

 [c] See appendices for a full list of control variables.

 [d] Firm years for the thirty-year period 1990 to 2019.

significant effects in enhancing firms' foreign sales intensity. Given that investments in manufacturing assets are facilitated by institutional resources provided by the TUFS programme, it is plausible that firms not part of geographical clusters use these funds for asset augmentation primarily for the domestic market. However, the results show that for these firms, investments in R&D and marketing pay-offs improve foreign sales.

Overall, the moderation results seem to be stronger for the BG effects in the pharmaceutical industry than the geographic cluster effects in the textile industry. A plausible reason for the results regarding clusters could be that our analysis does not fully account for heterogeneity in the different types of clusters present in India's textile industry. There is evidence that some clusters developed organically over a long period of time, while others were encouraged and supported by government policies as a response to global institutional changes. Some of the clusters in this latter group are still in the early stages of development and may not fully provide benefits to member firms. In addition, unlike BGs, which are closed networks with common ownership ties, geographical clusters are open networks with firms competing for access to common resources (Ter Wal et al. 2016). Because of these factors, the network benefits to member firms may be more straightforward in BGs than in geographical clusters. These aspects need further probing as our findings may be preliminary.

Additional Analyses

Scale effects

As there is a significant effect of firm size in most of the empirical models discussed in the previous sections, we conduct some additional analysis to probe the extent to which scale matters in the two industries. This is an important issue because small- and medium-scale enterprises have always received special attention and protection from the Indian government due to their importance in employment generation. There is an exclusive ministry at the federal government level in India for micro, small and medium enterprises (MSMEs). However, as some of the schemes by the government (such as the TUFS) indicate, there is a need for increasing scale in the two industries to improve cost efficiencies and to be globally competitive. We check if there is any significant difference between small and large firms in the two industries in their average profile of strategic variables such as investments, tangible and intangible assets, extent of imports and foreign sales intensity. As our sample includes only observations with non-zero international sales, this analysis focuses on the scale effect in international firms and excludes firms that may focus exclusively on domestic markets. To capture the scale effect, we divide the sample firms into two simple subgroups—firms with sales less than or equal to mean sales (small firms) and those with sales greater than mean sales (large firms). The comparison between these two categories of firms for the two industries is captured in Table 5.7 and reveals interesting insights.

As seen in Table 5.7, there are substantial differences in the two categories of firms in both industries (and the scale effects are much starker in the pharmaceutical industry than in the textile industry). First, large firms constitute only 895 out of the total sample of 4,492 observations (approximately 20 per cent) in the pharmaceutical industry, whereas in the textile industry, they constitute 2,103 observations (approximately 39 per cent of total observations, nearly twice that of the pharma industry). In other words, a few firms in the pharmaceutical

Table 5.7 Scale Effect for International Firms in the Pharmaceutical and Textile Industries

Firm Average Values	Pharmaceutical Industry		Textile Industry	
	Small Firms (Firms with sales less than or equal to mean sales)	**Large Firms** (Firms with sales greater than mean sales)	**Small Firms** (Firms with sales less than or equal to mean sales)	**Large Firms** (Firms with sales greater than mean sales)
Firm age (in years)	22.7	30.8	23.6	32.5
Firm profitability (net margin in %)	1.8	10.6	0.6	2.7
Foreign sales intensity (%)	29.4	38.2	38.4	34.8
Asset (plant and machinery) intensity (%)	45.7	24.8	50.3	31.6
R&D intensity (%)	0.85	2.94	0.05	0.05
Marketing intensity (%)	5.1	6.3	3.9	3.6
Imports intensity (%)	15.0	20.0	12.6	10.6
Proportion of BG firms (%)	20.4	49.0		
Proportion of firms in geographic clusters (%)			47.1	54.2
Number of observations	3,597	895	3,279	2,103

Source: Firm-level data from Prowess, Centre for Monitoring Indian Economy (CMIE).

industry were able to achieve a much higher scale when compared to the textile sector. In both industries, large firms tend to be approximately ten years older, indicating some degree of path dependency. Reflecting enormous scale benefits of cost efficiencies on the financial bottom line, the firm profitability for large firms in both industries is approximately five times that of small firms. Interestingly, we do not see scale effects on foreign sales intensity in textile firms, although the scale benefits translate to higher foreign sales for pharmaceutical firms.

Manufacturing asset intensity is approximately one-third lower for large firms in both industries, which reflects an improvement in asset turnover or operating leverage for large firms. The R&D intensity in large firms in the pharmaceutical industry is approximately three times that of small firms, which clearly indicates that a larger size and higher profitability allow firms to invest more in R&D. However, we do not see this effect in the textile industry, in which the R&D intensity is negligibly small and is exactly the same for both small and large firms. As our earlier findings clearly showed the importance of R&D in both industries, textile firms probably need an external policy stimulus (such as the TUFS) to sensitise them to the importance of R&D. With regard to the other intangible resource, namely marketing intensity, we see some scale effects in the pharmaceutical industry but none in the textile firms. Furthermore, large firms in the pharma industry have approximately 30 per cent higher import intensity than small firms, but there are no such scale effects in the textile industry. Finally, among pharmaceutical firms, those affiliated with BGs have a much larger proportion of large firms than stand-alone firms, thus confirming the additional network advantages conferred by BGs. In the textile industry, too, we can see that clusters provide additional advantages, as they tend to have a higher proportion of large firms. In summary, this comparison of key firm-level attributes between large and small firms clearly points to multiple advantages of a larger scale both for profitability and for internationalisation.

Segment analysis of the textile industry

We are able to further subsegment the textile firms into yarn, fabric and apparel segments based on the predominant product category in a firm's product portfolio.[13] The three subsegments of yarn, fabric and apparel reflect an increasing degree of value addition in textile products. We tabulate the mean values of the key variables in these three subsegments of the textile industry in Table 5.8.

Table 5.8 reveals that a majority of the Indian textile firms operate in lower value-added segments of yarn (2,284 firms) and fabric (1,885 firms), with apparel (804 firms) forming the smallest segment. The average apparel firm is also much smaller in age (approximately 19 years) and size (sales of USD 39 million) than firms in the yarn and fabric segments (approximately 29 years with sales of approximately USD 50 million). This indicates that Indian textile firms in higher value-added segments, such as apparel, have yet to achieve scale economies needed to compete in global markets. This is reflected in the lower average profitability in the apparel segment (0.75 per cent), which is only approximately half that of the average firm in the yarn and fabric segments. On the other hand, apparel firms seem to be much more focused on international markets, with an average foreign sales intensity of over 56 per cent, while yarn (30 per cent foreign sales) and fabric (39 per cent foreign sales) firms derive the majority of their sales from domestic markets. Hence, it is also probable that the lower profitability of

Table 5.8 Segment-wise Data Summary of the Textile Industry

Firm Average Values	Yarn Segment	Fabric Segment	Apparel Segment
Firm sales (USD million)	47.4	50.8	38.8
Firm age (in years)	28.8	29.5	19.1
Firm profitability (net margin in %)	1.7	1.5	0.75
Foreign sales intensity (%)	29.8	39.5	56.4
Asset (plant and machinery) intensity (%)	45.8	44.0	25.0
R&D intensity (%)	0.03	0.08	0.04
Marketing intensity (%)	3.0	4.2	5.6
Imports intensity (%)	9.4	14.5	11.7
Proportion of firms in geographic clusters (%)	41.0	52.6	66.9
Number of observations	2,284	1,885	804

Source: Firm-level data from Prowess, Centre for Monitoring Indian Economy (CMIE).

apparel firms could also be due to higher competition in international markets (majority of their sales) compared to domestic markets.

When we compare the three segments in terms of investments in key tangible and intangible assets, it becomes clear that as firms increase in value addition, asset intensity decreases, whereas the intensity of intangible assets increases. The asset (plant and machinery) intensity in the apparel segment is only 25 per cent compared to approximately 45 per cent in the fabric and yarn segments. Marketing intensity is the lowest in the yarn segment at 3 per cent, followed by fabric at 4.2 per cent and is the highest in the apparel segment (5.6 per cent). Firms in all three segments invest negligible amounts in R&D, thus reinforcing the earlier conclusion that a policy stimulus or catalyst is needed to nudge the textile industry to invest more in R&D. The intensity of imports also seems to be a function of value addition in products with fabric (14.5 per cent) and apparel (11.7 per cent) segments showing higher percentages of import intensity when compared to yarn (9.4 per cent). Finally, a vast majority of apparel firms (67 per cent) are located in geographic clusters when compared to yarn (41 per cent) and fabric (52.6 per cent) firms.

Conclusions

In this chapter, we proposed and tested a conceptual model to explain the firm-level heterogeneity in foreign sales intensity as international firms try to strategically respond to global institutional changes to maintain their competitiveness in the global marketplace. Our framework underlines the need for a multi-pronged analysis that incorporates not only firm-level choices regarding capability enhancement but also the resources available from networks in which firms may be embedded (that is, support from BGs and geographic clusters) as well as institutional resources provided by national policies either directly through subsidies or indirectly through regulatory changes that facilitate access to global resource markets. More specifically, we proposed that firm-level investments in tangible (manufacturing) and intangible (R&D and marketing) assets are positively related to foreign sales intensity. Next, we argued that since developing economies such as India have been insulated from world markets for decades and resource poor, firms need to access international resource markets to catch up before they can succeed in product-market internationalisation. Accordingly, we proposed that inward internationalisation (for example, import intensity) mediates the relationship between firm-level tangible and intangible resources and foreign sales intensity. Finally, we suggested that these relationships between firm-level resources and foreign sales intensity, mediated by import intensity, are moderated by the extent of support received by firms through network resources from BG and/or geographic cluster affiliation.

We tested our theoretical framework using a comprehensive sample of firms from the pharmaceutical and textile industries in India. Our longitudinal panel research design covers a thirty-year period (1990–2019) spanning fifteen years before and fifteen years after the said institutional change. Rigorous analysis using random effects panel regression procedures provides strong support for the overall conceptual model proposed in this chapter.[14] We find that the impact of intangible resources such as R&D and marketing intensity on foreign sales intensity is substantially higher than that of tangible resources even though government support for firms (for example, the TUFS) has primarily focused on facilitating investments in tangible assets. Network resources through BGs and geographic clusters are found to act as substitutes in providing resource support to firms associated with them, thus reducing the need for firms to make their own individual investments.

The liberalisation of imports that started as part of the overall economic reforms initiated in 1991 by the Indian government and continued to be expanded upon in response to the global institutional changes in the two industries proved to be timely, as they enabled firms to access critical resources from international markets. Import intensity is found to mediate the relationship fully or partially between investments in manufacturing and R&D and foreign sales intensity in the two industries. Further analyses revealed the importance of scale economies to succeed in international markets for both pharmaceutical and textile firms.

These findings suggest a need to revisit the higher priority given to the small-scale sector in the textile industry by the Government of India (with employment generation as a goal), at least in the case of firms competing in global markets. Finally, subsegment analysis and a comparison of yarn, fabric and apparel segments in the textile industry reveal significant differences between low value-added and higher value-added segments in their international orientation and in the mix of tangible and intangible resources needed. These findings suggest that government policy support needs to critically assess the differential need for resources in the various subsegments of an industry and be carefully tailored to address these differential needs.

A final note regarding firm choices in the two industries in response to global institutional changes. The results discussed earlier as part of testing the proposed relationships and the correlation of key constructs reported in Appendices 5A.1 and 5A.4 together suggest heterogeneity in firm choices regarding investments in capabilities, accessing international resources and participation in global markets; that is, firms made trade-offs regarding their search activities, which were probably determined by their attempts to deal with institutional complexity arising from shifts in global norms of competition and the associated need to balance the emergence of conflicting logics. In the concluding chapter, we elaborate on these and link the findings from this chapter based on organisational-level responses to those from the previous chapters, which focused on policy- and industry-level analyses.

Appendix 5A.1 Means, Standard Deviations and Correlations for the Pharmaceutical Industry Sample

		Mean	s.d.	1	2	3	4	5	6	7	8	9	10
1	Foreign sales intensity	31.17	27.84	1.00									
2	Import intensity	16.01	18.30	0.31	1.00								
3	Asset intensity	41.56	326.07	0.06	0.26	1.00							
4	R&D intensity	1.27	4.18	0.09	0.14	0.04	1.00						
5	Marketing intensity	5.33	4.89	-0.11	-0.19	-0.03	0.03	1.00					
6	Business group dummy	0.26	0.44	-0.09	0.05	0.03	0.11	0.06	1.00				
7	Profitability	0.036	0.23	0.01	-0.17	-0.45	-0.13	0.04	-0.02	1.00			
8	Firm size[a]	3.03	1.46	0.13	0.11	-0.10	0.18	0.13	0.31	0.26	1.00		
9	Firm age	24.34	16.73	-0.12	-0.06	-0.06	0.02	0.23	0.19	0.08	0.32	1.00	
10	Debt–equity ratio	1.26	2.16	-0.06	0.03	0.05	-0.02	-0.03	0.03	-0.23	-0.08	-0.11	1.00
11	Listed firm dummy	0.30	0.46	0.08	0.08	0.00	0.12	0.09	0.43	0.10	0.41	0.25	-0.07

Notes: p < .01 for values of 0.04 and more; [a] Natural logarithm; two-tailed significance levels.

Appendix 5A.2 Panel Estimation Results: Determinants of Foreign Sales Intensity—Pharmaceutical Industry[a]

	DV = Imports Intensity	DV = Foreign Sales Intensity	
	Model 1	Model 2	Model 3
Import intensity			0.182 (0.000)
Asset (plant and machinery) intensity	0.010 (0.000)	0.002 (0.081)	0.000 (0.857)
R&D intensity	0.287 (0.102)	0.454 (0.000)	0.408 (0.003)
Marketing intensity	−0.102 (0.254)	0.525 (0.016)	0.524 (0.015)
Business group affiliation (0: non-group; 1: group)	2.818 (0.190)	−3.854 (0.209)	−4.481 (0.125)
Profitability	−2.711 (0.453)	−0.382 (0.905)	−0.060 (0.985)
Firm size[b]	1.084 (0.105)	3.740 (0.001)	3.551 (0.001)
Firm age	−0.155 (0.001)	−0.362 (0.000)	−0.330 (0.000)
Debt–equity ratio	−0.072 (0.678)	−0.314 (0.182)	−0.294 (0.198)
Listed firm dummy	3.816 (0.058)	5.396 (0.111)	4.684 (0.163)
Constant	17.152 (0.000)	11.143 (0.142)	8.117 (0.327)
Year dummies	Included	Included	Included
Model Indices			
R-square	0.1095 (0.000)	0.0849 (0.000)	0.1334 (0.000)
Number of observations[c]	4,492	4,492	4,492

Notes: [a] Unstandardised regression coefficients reported; robust p-values in parentheses; two-tailed tests. [b] Natural logarithm of firm sales. [c] Firm years for the thirty-year period 1990 to 2019.

Appendix 5A.3 Panel Estimation Results: Determinants of Foreign Sales Intensity—Pharmaceutical Industry across Business Group Affiliated and Non-Affiliated Firms[a]

	Business-Group Affiliated Firms			Non-Business-Group Affiliated firms		
	Import Intensity Model 4	Foreign Sales Intensity Model 5	Foreign Sales Intensity Model 6	Import Intensity Model 7	Foreign Sales Intensity Model 8	Foreign Sales Intensity Model 9
Import intensity			0.108 (0.186)			0.214 (0.000)
Asset (plant and machinery) intensity	0.005 (0.205)	0.000 (0.935)	0.000 (0.917)	0.013 (0.000)	0.002 (0.005)	−0.000 (0.785)
R&D intensity	0.108 (0.247)	0.596 (0.000)	0.580 (0.000)	0.529 (0.017)	0.162 (0.336)	0.063 (0.750)
Marketing intensity	−0.248 (0.318)	0.745 (0.011)	0.736 (0.013)	−0.067 (0.409)	0.404 (0.118)	0.402 (0.115)
Profitability	−5.278 (0.394)	0.085 (0.983)	0.553 (0.882)	−2.002 (0.538)	−1.824 (0.674)	−1.565 (0.729)
Firm size[b]	0.889 (0.487)	6.120 (0.004)	5.846 (0.005)	1.164 (0.142)	2.732 (0.019)	2.522 (0.025)
Firm age	−0.176 (0.008)	−0.471 (0.000)	−0.439 (0.000)	−0.138 (0.023)	−0.324 (0.002)	−0.291 (0.004)
Debt–equity ratio	−0.174 (0.640)	0.384 (0.197)	0.416 (0.141)	−0.036 (0.860)	−0.641 (0.028)	−0.629 (0.027)
Listed firm dummy	3.238 (0.339)	0.247 (0.963)	0.338 (0.948)	3.762 (0.076)	9.203 (0.029)	8.277 (0.047)
Constant	27.509 (0.002)	−7.573 (0.358)	−10.330 (0.257)	9.908 (0.000)	28.775 (0.001)	26.666 (0.001)
Year dummies	Included	Included	Included	Included	Included	Included
R-square	0.1591 (0.000)	0.2078 (0.000)	0.2385 (0.000)	0.1024 (0.000)	0.0648 (0.000)	0.1236 (0.000)
Number of observations[c]	1,173	1,173	1,173	3,319	3,319	3,319

Notes: [a] Unstandardised regression coefficients reported; robust p-values in parentheses; two-tailed tests.

[b] Natural logarithm of firm sales.

[c] Firm years for the thirty-year period 1990 to 2019.

Appendix 5A.4 Means, Standard Deviations and Correlations for Textile Industry Samples

	Mean	s.d.	1	2	3	4	5	6	7	8	9	10	11	12	13
1 Foreign sales intensity	37.02	32.01	1.00												
2 Import intensity	11.81	18.88	0.24	1.00											
3 Asset (plant and machinery) intensity	42.97	132.8	0.08	0.44	1.00										
4 Cluster dummy	0.50	0.50	0.04	−0.01	−0.04	1.00									
5 R&D intensity	0.05	0.24	0.04	0.10	−0.01	0.04	1.00								
6 Marketing intensity	3.78	3.16	0.26	0.08	0.04	0.07	0.04	1.00							
7 Profitability	0.014	0.13	−0.01	−0.04	−0.25	−0.01	0.05	−0.03	1.00						
8 Firm size	3.07	1.22	−0.12	−0.10	−0.16	0.02	0.03	−0.06	0.18	1.00					
9 Firm age	27.10	21.52	−0.17	−0.09	−0.09	−0.01	0.05	−0.02	0.03	0.24	1.00				
10 Debt–equity ratio	2.41	4.26	−0.06	−0.02	0.04	−0.04	−0.05	−0.08	−0.23	0.01	−0.00	1.00			
11 Listed firm dummy	0.21	0.41	0.08	0.08	−0.00	0.05	0.04	0.16	0.09	0.36	0.03	−0.05	1.00		
12 Business group dummy	0.34	0.47	−0.03	0.04	0.02	−0.02	0.03	0.07	0.03	0.30	0.23	0.06	0.32	1.00	
13 Apparel industry dummy	0.15	0.36	0.25	−0.00	−0.06	−0.03	0.24	0.14	−0.02	−0.07	−0.15	−0.04	0.07	−0.16	1.00
14 Fabric industry dummy	0.35	0.48	0.06	0.10	0.01	0.09	0.09	0.04	0.01	−0.08	.08	−0.08	−0.07	−0.03	−0.31

Notes: $p < .01$ for mod values of 0.04 and more;

[a] Natural logarithm; two-tailed significance levels.

Appendix 5A.5 Panel Estimation Results: Determinants of Foreign Sales Intensity—Textile Industry[a]

	DV = Imports Intensity	DV = Foreign Sales Intensity	
	Model 1	Model 2	Model 3
Import intensity			0.078 (0.024)
Asset (plant and machinery) intensity	0.059 (0.000)	0.011 (0.000)	0.006 (0.105)
R&D intensity	2.492 (0.099)	2.912 (0.054)	2.799 (0.054)
Marketing intensity	0.013 (0.928)	2.053 (0.000)	2.046 (0.000)
Cluster dummy (0-non-cluster; 1-cluster)	0.062 (0.954)	-1.471 (0.514)	-1.481 (0.507)
Profitability	3.776 (0.486)	5.410 (0.098)	5.112 (0.103)
Firm size[b]	-1.732 (0.002)	2.635 (0.010)	2.777 (0.006)
Firm age	-0.056 (0.016)	-0.274 (0.000)	-0.270 (0.000)
Debt–equity ratio	-0.119 (0.076)	-0.256 (0.041)	-0.246 (0.048)
Listed firm dummy	4.386 (0.009)	-1.673 (0.712)	-2.003 (0.655)
Business group dummy	3.520 (0.024)	0.320 (0.911)	0.024 (0.933)
Apparel industry dummy	2.994 (0.060)	25.524 (0.000)	25.249 (0.000)
Fabric industry dummy	5.512 (0.000)	13.729 (0.000)	13.273 (0.000)
Constant	8.914 (0.002)	0.601 (0.950)	0.053 (0.996)
Year dummies	Included	Included	Included
Model Indices			
R-square	0.2377 (0.000)	0.1309 (0.000)	0.1416 (0.000)
Number of observations[c]	5,382	5,382	5,382

Notes: [a] Unstandardised regression coefficients reported; robust p-values in parentheses; two-tailed tests.

[b] Natural logarithm of firm sales.

[c] Firm years for the thirty-year period 1990 to 2019.

Appendix 5A.6 Panel Estimation Results: Determinants of Foreign Sales Intensity—Textile Industry[a] across Geographic Clusters and Non-Cluster Firms

	Firms in Geographic Clusters				Non-cluster Firms	
	Imports Intensity Model 4	Foreign Sales Intensity Model 5	Foreign Sales Intensity Model 6	Imports Intensity Model 7	Foreign Sales Intensity Model 8	Foreign Sales Intensity Model 9
Import intensity			0.135 (0.017)	0.067 (0.000)	0.005 (0.150)	0.034 (0.432)
Manufacturing (plant and machinery) intensity	0.051 (0.000)	0.015 (0.000)	0.008 (0.012)			0.003 (0.454)
R&D intensity	0.944 (0.629)	1.627 (0.282)	1.725 (0.227)	5.090 (0.026)	7.479 (0.018)	7.262 (0.012)
Marketing intensity	0.171 (0.249)	1.460 (0.000)	1.428 (0.000)	-0.177 (0.499)	3.082 (0.000)	3.084 (0.000)
Profitability	2.424 (0.550)	3.558 (0.340)	3.177 (0.381)	6.004 (0.649)	7.932 (0.220)	7.766 (0.213)
Firm size[b]	-1.440 (0.021)	3.835 (0.002)	3.970 (0.001)	-2.006 (0.029)	1.329 (0.419)	1.418 (0.382)
Firm age	-0.102 (0.000)	-0.317 (0.000)	-0.303 (0.000)	-0.011 (0.783)	-0.224 (0.014)	-0.223 (0.014)
Debt–equity ratio	-0.136 (0.157)	-0.114 (0.525)	-0.099 (0.572)	-0.101 (0.377)	-0.353 (0.029)	-0.348 (0.030)
Listed firm dummy	4.408 (0.072)	-4.147 (0.535)	-4.650 (0.477)	5.319 (0.019)	2.993 (0.568)	2.809 (0.591)
Business group dummy	3.097 (0.169)	0.098 (0.980)	-0.323 (0.931)	3.367 (0.146)	-0.144 (0.972)	-0.275 (0.947)
Apparel industry dummy	1.270 (0.450)	28.913 (0.000)	28.597 (0.000)	6.754 (0.055)	20.269 (0.012)	20.059 (0.012)
Fabric industry dummy	7.368 (0.000)	18.633 (0.000)	17.548 (0.000)	3.206 (0.050)	7.024 (0.090)	6.919 (0.096)
Constant	13.772 (0.000)	13.996 (0.098)	12.474 (0.134)	7.030 (0.027)	-16.790 (0.168)	-17.016 (0.164)
Year dummies	Included	Included	Included	Included	Included	Included
R-square	0.2091 (0.000)	0.1281 (0.000)	0.1511 (0.000)	0.2991 (0.000)	0.1591 (0.000)	0.1622 (0.000)
Number of observations[c]	2,684	2,684	2,684	2,698	2,698	2,698

Notes: [a] Unstandardised regression coefficients reported; robust p-values in parentheses; two-tailed tests.

[b] Natural logarithm of firm sales.

[c] Firm years for the thirty-year period 1990 to 2019.

Notes

1. Export intensity is the most appropriate and commonly used measure of internationalisation in developing economies, given that a majority of firms are still in the early stages of the internationalisation process with exports being the dominant mode of international expansion (Aulakh, Kotabe and Teegen 2000). In this chapter, we use a closely related construct, foreign sales intensity, which is operationalised as sales in foreign markets as a percentage of total sales of a firm, and likely incorporates any foreign sales of products that may have been manufactured by a firm's subsidiaries abroad.

2. Given the strategic importance of exports for the two industries, it is more appropriate to track the trends in foreign sales rather than profitability, as the exporting firms are likely to make all efforts to maintain or improve their position in the international markets in the post-regime scenario even at the cost of short-run profitability.

3. As discussed in the previous chapter, some attribute the active involvement of the state in facilitating market-oriented activities as a form of 'state capitalism' (see Hu, Cui and Aulakh 2019).

4. An extended discussion on business groups is provided in the following sections.

5. We use the term 'RBV' in a broad sense here and mean it to include not only the RBV as originally proposed (Penrose 1959; Wernerfelt 1984; Barney 1991) but also all its extensions such as the concept of dynamic capabilities (Teece, Pisano and Shuen 1997) and dynamic resource-based view (Helfat and Peteraf 2003).

6. We do not hypothesise a priori any hierarchy in the relative importance of these three capabilities for strategic renewal and association with product-market internationalisation of firms in the two industries. However, in our empirical analysis, we are able to assess investments in which of these capabilities are associated with better international performance.

7. Different terminologies have been used for this concept. For example, 'industrial clusters', 'industrial parks', 'industrial zones', among others (Stein 2020). We believe that the underlying dynamics of these are very similar, and thus use the 'geographic cluster' term in the chapter, although we derive the arguments from the broader literature.

8. This definition of clusters is akin to the one used in the management literature. For instance, Porter (2000: 16) defines a regional cluster as 'geographically proximate group of interconnected companies and associated institutions in a particular field, linked by commonalities and complementarities'.

9. See various Annual Reports by the Ministry of Textiles, Government of India, https://www.india.gov.in/annual-reports-ministry-textiles (accessed April 2021); Stein 2020. As discussed in Chapter 3, the Government of India has also

initiated schemes to develop technology parks in the pharmaceutical industry in the last few years in order to diversify the product base of the industry (for example, to focus more on the production of medical devices) as well as to support competitiveness of medium-sized firms by providing common manufacturing and supporting infrastructure (www.pharmexcil.com). Since this is a relatively new initiative in the pharmaceutical industry, our focus is on the role of clusters mainly in the textile industry.

10. See Model 2 in Appendices 5A.2 and 5A.5 for complete results.

11. See Models 1 and 3 of Appendices 5A.2 and 5A.5 for complete results.

12. For complete results, see Appendices 5A.3 and 5A.6. Only Models 6 and 9 of the two appendices are summarised in Tables 5.5 and 5.6.

13. Unfortunately, our data do not allow us to divide the pharmaceutical firms into similar subsegments.

14. Even though we use comprehensive longitudinal samples and rigorous econometric analyses, we wish to be conservative in our claims about the study's conclusions. Given the single geographic context from which we draw our empirical evidence, we wish to claim strong associative relationships supporting our hypotheses and refrain from making claims of definitive causality. Another caution which we would like to highlight is related to the sample of firms included in the Prowess database, especially for textile firms. As discussed in the previous chapters, the textile industry in India remains largely unorganised. The data captured by Prowess probably relates to a very small subsample of firms in the textile industry. The firms included may either be the larger firms or those in the organised sector, which publicly report their financial information.

6

Conclusion

Implications for Theory and Policy

The Indian textile industry ... is the 2nd largest manufacturer and exporter in the world, ... contributes 7% of industry output in value terms, 2% of India's GDP and 12% of India's export earnings. The textile industry is one of the largest sources of employment generation in the country with 45 million people employed directly....
The sector has perfect alignment with Government's key initiatives....
— Government of India, Ministry of Textiles (2019–2020: 1)

The Indian pharmaceutical industry is the world's third largest by volume and 14th largest in terms of value. India has the second-highest number of US FDA approved plants outside the US ... [and] is the largest provider of generic drugs globally.... Because of the low price and high quality, Indian medicines are preferred worldwide, thereby rightly making the country the "Pharmacy of the World". Pharma sector ... contributes to around 1.72% of the country's GDP.
— Government of India, Ministry of Chemicals and Fertilizers,
Department of Pharmaceuticals (2020–2021: 3)

The global institutional changes implemented under the auspices of the World Trade Organization (WTO) in 2005 were expected to challenge the existing sources of competitive advantage in the Indian pharmaceutical and textile industries and thus India's trade position in international markets. These challenges acquired strategic significance at the national level given the historical importance of the two industries to India's attainment of various socio-economic objectives. The above-quoted extracts from the annual reports of the respective ministries of the Government of India fifteen years later suggest that each industry adequately adapted to the global institutional change and was able to maintain or increase its share in global trade, while fulfilling the social goals, that is, employment generation in the textile industry and supply of affordable drugs in the pharmaceutical industry.[1] How were these two industries able to adapt to and cope with externally imposed changes that amounted to tectonic shifts in the rules of the game? Studying similarities and differences in the strategic trajectories of these two very different industries in response to global changes was the primary objective of the current book.

The main argument of this book is that coping with such momentous changes triggered at the global level required a multi-level strategic response. Global institutional change necessitated the search for new organisational capabilities by Indian firms to catch up with global competitors and successfully compete in international markets. This upgrading or strategic renewal warranted reconfiguration of existing and acquisition of new resources. However, a combination of firm-specific resource constraints, organisational inertia and presence of competing logics potentially limited the ability of individual organisations to undertake strategic renewal through the required distant or exploratory search in products and markets to cope with new competitive conditions. Overcoming these hurdles warranted support from external sources to facilitate investments in the development of new capabilities. Accordingly, in Chapter 2, we developed a national institutional system framework consisting of the state, the sector or industry, and organisations within that industry, and suggested that coordination across the three levels in facilitating access to and/or allocation of requisite resources was the key factor to effectively cope with the respective global institutional change. In the subsequent three chapters, we discussed how external change introduced competing institutional logics at state, industry and organisational levels, and how these influenced resource allocations and strategic or policy choices.

The objective of this concluding chapter is two-fold. First, we revisit the empirical observations of the previous chapters and integrate them to understand cross-level influences and interactions to deal with competing logics within the broader national institutional system. We do this by comparing and contrasting the adaptation of India's textile and pharmaceutical industries to global institutional change along multiple dimensions. Second, we use insights from these contextual comparisons to discuss theoretical and public policy implications. We pay special attention to policy implications by contrasting the choices made in India in supporting the two industries with those of its main developing economy competitors.

Comparing Indian Textile and Pharmaceutical Industries' Responses to Global Change

The main findings from the previous chapters are summarised in Table 6.1. These are discussed in the following paragraphs. The new Agreement on Textiles and Clothing (ATC) abolished the quota-based international trade, while the

Agreement on Trade-Related Aspects of Intellectual Property Rights (TRIPS), with its emphasis on product patents, impacted the global pharmaceutical industry. In both industries, the new rules of the game altered the global competitive conditions for India's textile and pharmaceutical industries. The former needed to achieve greater manufacturing efficiency and/or produce more value-added products to compete with other textile-producing countries with similar

Table 6.1 Comparing National Institutional Systems of India's Textile and Pharmaceutical Industries

	Textile Industry	*Pharmaceutical Industry*
Initial conditions	Quota-based exports	Process patents under weak global IPR regime
New conditions	Market-based global competition	Product patents under strong global IPR regime
Organisational renewal[a]	Manufacturing (+++); R&D (+); Marketing (++)	Manufacturing (+); R&D (+++); Marketing (++)
Institutional resources	Direct: TUFS loans; clusters and parks Indirect: Regulations conducive to imports of intermediate products and inputs	Direct: Industrial parks Indirect: Regulations conducive to imports of technology and intermediates; facilitation of FDI (inward and outward)
International resources (import of intermediate inputs)	Fully mediates the relationship between investments in manufacturing and international sales, and partially mediates for R&D	Fully mediates the relationship between investments in manufacturing and international sales, and partially mediates for R&D
Network resources	Cluster resources complement international resources in the mediation model	Business-group resources substitute international resources in the mediation model
Sector-level isomorphism	Organic growth	Inorganic growth (domestic and international mergers and acquisitions, or M&As); multinational corporations' production networks
Meeting welfare expectations	Cross-segment adjustments in employment	Cross-national arbitrage in pricing of drugs

Notes: [a] The plus signs reflect the relative importance of investments in each of the three renewal activities in facilitating international sales. Investments in all of them were found to significantly impact foreign sales intensities in both industries, although the relative importance differed for each industry.

traditional advantages (that is, production of raw materials and labour costs), while the pharma industry had to forego its existing approach of manufacturing patented products through the modification of the manufacturing processes and move towards developing product patents for its products in order to compete with multinational corporations from advanced economies.

Increasing production efficiency and moving up the value curve required investments in various activities along the value chain, including in manufacturing, research and development (R&D) and marketing, and we had proposed that investments in these three activities were the key to organisation-level strategic renewal. In Chapter 4 (Figures 4.16 and 4.17), we showed that average firm-level investments in plant and machinery saw substantial growth after 1995 in both industries. Similarly, average investments in R&D increased, more so in the pharmaceutical than in the textile industry. Investments in marketing also saw an upward trend during the period after the implementation of the two changes in 2005.[2] While investments in these three value-chain activities increased during the period of this study, we see important contrasts in terms of their association with firms' product-market internationalisation across the two industries.

As shown in Table 6.1 (based on the detailed empirical results discussed in Chapter 5), investments in each of the three activities had a significant and positive effect on enhancing foreign sales for firms in the two industries. In the case of investments in marketing activities, we saw a similar effect in textile and pharmaceuticals. However, investments in manufacturing played a much stronger role in increasing international sales for textile firms than for the pharmaceutical firms, while investments in R&D were much more important in the pharmaceutical than the textile industry. While the contrast in the relative importance of investments in manufacturing and R&D in the two industries is along predictable lines given the nature of the two industries and their underlying sources of competitive advantage, the key insight from these findings is that investments in all three activities played a significant role in enhancing global competitiveness in both industries. In essence, the nature of global competition necessitates not only production efficiencies but also moving up the value curve by producing innovative products, and investing in marketing to convey the greater value of differentiated products.

One of the challenges for firms from developing economies in their pursuit of catching up with global competitors is the constraints in resources required to achieve this objective. Accordingly, these firms require external resources to either augment the resource gap or act as an incentive to pursue the riskier exploratory search. We examined the influence of institutional resources (provided through the efforts of the state or the industry associations) and network resources (through affiliations with business groups and/or geographic clusters). Empirical results on the role of these external resources show interesting contrasts across the two industries.

In terms of institutional resources, Chapters 3 and 5 identified various policy interventions in the two industries in response to global institutional changes. Some of the policy choices were geared to ensure that each industry maintained its historical social functions (that is, employment generation in the textile and availability of affordable drugs in the pharmaceutical industry). Many of the policy interventions were geared towards increasing the global competitiveness of the two industries. There were three broad mechanisms through which this was accomplished. First, through direct support to organisations primarily in the textile industry. The Technology Upgradation Funds Scheme (TUFS) provided direct interest subsidies to textile firms for investments in plant and machinery to upgrade their manufacturing capabilities, and the effect of these incentives is probably reflected in the increase in manufacturing assets in the textile industry.[3] Second, the state provided direct investments in the development of clusters and industrial parks through public–private partnership models, with cluster formation primarily in the textile industry, while investments in industrial parks were initiated in both industries.[4] The cluster approach by the government hoped to complement the pre-existing geographic clusters that had developed organically over a longer period of time by providing shared infrastructure and facilitating knowledge flows between firms located in a particular cluster.[5]

The third, and probably equally if not more important, institutional resource included the regulatory changes initiated through lobbying efforts of industry associations (as well as part of the overall economic liberalisation model put in place in 1991). Regulatory interventions facilitated both access to international resources (that is, via easing of import tariffs for intermediate inputs and allowing infusion of foreign capital through inward foreign direct investment [FDI]), as well as participation in international markets (that is, through the support of industry export promotion councils and allowing outward FDI by Indian firms). Our industry-level analysis in Chapter 4 demonstrated that easing of FDI regulations played a much stronger role in the pharmaceutical industry, evidenced by higher inward and outward FDI activity in this industry relative to the textile industry. However, our firm-level analysis in Chapter 5 showed that import of intermediate inputs, which was facilitated because of the lowering of import tariffs and easing of foreign exchange regulations during the post-1995 period, played an important role in realising the benefits of investments in manufacturing and R&D capabilities. Data show that import intensity fully mediated the relationship between investments in plant and machinery and foreign sales intensity in both industries, and partially mediated this relationship for investments in R&D.

The implication of these findings is that access to international resources (both tangible and intangible) was critical to Indian firms' strategic renewal through the development of new capabilities and maintaining or increasing their foreign sales. Investments in marketing capabilities, on the other hand, had direct effects on foreign sales intensity, and without the influence of imports. The aforementioned results point towards the importance of institutional resources in facilitating capability development both through direct support and through regulatory changes that ease the participation of indigenous firms in global resource and product markets.

Besides institutional resources provided directly or indirectly by the state, our empirical model also examined whether resources available to individual firms through affiliations with two types of supra-firm networks (namely business groups [BGs] and geographic clusters) played any role in investments in capabilities and realisation of internationalisation goals.[6] Past research has shown the benefits of both types of networks to firms in the form of providing access to network-level resources, both tangible and intangible. For the pharmaceutical industry, we found that for firms affiliated to a BG, available group-level resources substitute for international resources. That is, we did not observe any mediation of import intensity between investments in capabilities and product-market internationalisation. The importance of international resources was much more salient for independent firms in the pharma industry that did not have access to group-level resources. Surprisingly, in the textile industry, we found stronger support for the import intensity mediated model for firms that were part of a geographical cluster than for firms not part of any cluster. In essence, we found a substitutive effect of BG affiliation in the pharmaceutical industry and a complementary effect of cluster affiliation in the textile industry.

Two other noteworthy aspects summarised in Table 6.1 relate to sector- or industry-level organisational isomorphism in response to shifts in the external environment. Isomorphism is a 'process that forces one unit [within an organisational field] to resemble other units that face the same set of environmental conditions' (DiMaggio and Powell 1983: 149).[7] The literature has identified coercive (that is, arising from power relationships and resource dependence relationships such as that from organisation–state interactions), mimetic (that is, under uncertainty, organisations imitate peers to be acceptable) and normative (that is, adopting an accepted 'proper' or 'moral' course of action)

(Bohenbaum and Jonsson 2017) pressures that explain homogeneity in organisational responses to external contingencies. All three types of isomorphic pressures were in play for India's textile and pharmaceutical industries as they responded to global institutional change. In Chapter 4, we identified a number of aspects on which the responses in the two industries converged (for example, export orientation, investments in capabilities, moving towards value-added products), which taken together were aligned with the expectations of the state. However, on two aspects, there was isomorphism within each industry, but which varied across the two industries. One was the dominant pathway of industry adaptation. In the textile industry, much of the adaptation was through organic growth, which entailed investments by Indian textile firms in upgrading capabilities, with reliance on institutional resources either directly provided by the state (that is, TUFS loans) or indirectly facilitated through regulatory changes (that is, import of intermediate products). The pharmaceutical industry, on the other hand, while taking advantage of import liberalisation, followed a different path of inorganic growth. This entailed both domestic and international mergers and acquisitions with foreign pharmaceutical companies, as well as becoming part of existing production networks of established multinational corporations and undertaking contract manufacturing and/or contract research for these corporations. Existing research has identified the pros and cons of these contrasting approaches of developing economy firms, which we discuss in the following sections.

The second contrast relates to the industry-level responses to the state's expectations about meeting social or welfare goals while adapting to changing global competitive conditions. As discussed in previous chapters, besides the common contributions of both industries in helping India's trade position, the textile industry was an important sector for employment, while the pharmaceutical industry played a critical role in providing affordable drugs in the domestic market. How did each industry accommodate the new market-based competitive conditions while maintaining its traditional contributions to social welfare?

Our analysis in Chapter 4 showed that the pharmaceutical industry was better able to reconcile the conflicting demands, that is, producing more value-added drugs and ensuring affordability of the drugs for local consumers. It should be reiterated that the price control policies in the industry were initially relaxed as part of economic liberalisation but were subsequently tightened again under the National Pharmaceuticals Pricing Policy, 2012 (NPPP-12) (see Chapter 3). Thus, the pharmaceutical industry was subject to price controls in the domestic market. The industry was able to meet the affordable pricing goals while producing more value-added products (especially formulations) because of two reasons. One, empirical studies have shown that investments in manufacturing facilities and R&D by Indian pharmaceutical firms in response to the TRIPS agreement and the entry of foreign multinational corporations in the Indian market as part of the government's regulatory reforms during the 1990s led to productivity gains in the manufacture of drugs in India (Saranga and Banker 2010). These productivity gains allowed firms to achieve price competitiveness, and, accordingly, strategic choices by firms and their outcomes were compatible with policy goals of increasing industry competitiveness while ensuring affordability of drugs. Second, the diversification of the industry's exports into country markets with different levels of regulatory hurdles around pricing helped Indian pharmaceutical firms to use cross-national price differentials to adhere to pricing controls in the domestic market (Lichtenberg 2010).[8]

New competitive conditions for India's textile industry in the post-quota regime necessitated an increase in productivity and movement up the production value curve. As discussed in previous chapters, these were accomplished through investments in various firm-level capabilities, facilitated by subsidised TUFS loans provided by the state. However, the simultaneous achievement of the dual objectives of increased productivity through technology upgrading while maintaining or increasing employment in the industry proved to be a challenge. Though the overall industry was able to maintain its important employment-generation role in India's economy, this was accomplished through heterogenous gains in productivity and employment across the three major segments of the industry. In particular, the handloom sector was able to achieve greater productivity per worker and per handloom during the post-1995 period (see Figures 4.29 and 4.30), but at the expense of decreased employment in the sector (reduction from 6 million workers in 1995–1996 to less than 4 million in 2019–2020). The smaller organised mill sector (which was the main beneficiary of the TUFS loans) was able to increase productivity because of technology upgrades and economies of scale while increasing employment as well as improving labour productivity (see Figures 4.25 and 4.26). However, the largest power loom segment of the industry, which produces more than 50 per cent of India's cloth, was not able to make productivity gains, although it increased its contributions to the total employment in the overall textile industry (see Figures 4.27 and 4.28).[9]

In terms of accommodating competing logics for the two industries at the policy level, the discussion here shows a greater ability of the pharmaceutical industry to do so through differential pricing ability across country markets, while the textile industry was able to achieve the state's employment goals only through cross-segment adjustments whereby some segments sacrificed productivity to maintain employment while others sacrificed employment to increase productivity. From an overall industry competitiveness point of view, the segment that sacrificed productivity was also the largest in the industry.

Theoretical Implications

Institutional System and Catch-up of Developing Economy Firms

Catch-up, defined as the narrowing of a country's gap in productivity, income or technology vis-à-vis a leading country (Lee 2013), has been of continuing interest amongst scholars and policymakers. Much of this work used macro-growth models to study catch-up between different sets of national economies (for example, western Europe relative to the United States [US] [Abramovitz 1986; Gerschenkron 1962]; East Asian economies relative to developed economies [Kim and Lau 1994]; developing economies relative to advanced economies [Nayyar 2013]). Investments in physical and human capital, primarily through state support, were the main mechanisms that allowed countries to move up the production function. These macro-growth models have been questioned on the grounds that they do not incorporate firm-level heterogeneity in their analysis, arguing that economic growth is driven by entrepreneurship, innovation and learning, which varies across firms (Nelson and Pack 1999; Nelson et al. 2018). Accordingly, more recent research has looked at catch-up at the firm level (that is, catch-up is the narrowing of the gap between focal firms and the leading firms globally in the industry [Lee and Malerba 2018]), and has identified the mechanisms or paths through which developing economy firms catch up with leading global players. In contrast to the traditional approaches to catch-up based specifically on investments in physical assets, the emerging approach sees catch-up as

> a dynamic evolutionary process which is not deterministic and cannot be planned in details because it faces uncertainty and continuous change; is associated with a variety of exogenous events (windows of opportunity) and is the result of the idiosyncratic behavior of heterogenous actors characterized by different understanding, views and experiences. (Malerba and Lee 2021: 986)

Two important features of this approach to studying catch-up of developing economy firms relevant to our study are: the possibility of multiple paths to catch up, and the systems approach whereby various institutional actors play complementary roles in facilitating the catch-up goals (Lee and Malerba 2018; Lee 2019).

Our study contributes to this emerging stream of research in a number of ways. First, while much of the existing empirical work deals with cross-national comparisons of firm- or sector-level catch-up, based on the characteristics of national institutional systems (for example, Lee 2013, 2019; Fatas-Villafranca, Sanchez-Choliz and Jarne 2007; Malerba and Nelson 2011), this book examines two different systems within the same country, each comprising three institutional levels: the state, industry and organisations. Our findings show both convergence and divergence in the adaptive responses to global institutional change across the two sectoral institutional systems. New competitive conditions heralded by sector-specific global change warrant strategic renewal at the organisational level through the development of new capabilities in both industries. However, the specific mechanisms through which renewal is undertaken vary across the two industries because of idiosyncratic sources of advantage specific to the industry and the constraints of meeting national socio-economic goals.

Second, while the emerging literature on firm-level catch-up has identified firms, the sector and the country as three anchors of the institutional system, the different possibilities of inter-level coordination in the catch-up process are conceptually and empirically underdeveloped in the existing literature. Our study provides evidence of the ways in which an interconnected system facilitates, and sometimes hinders, the processes and pathways for organisational catch-up. We show how various types of institutional resources help organisations in their quest for renewal and catch-up in response to externally imposed changes. These include direct resources provided to the textile industry for technology upgrading as well as for developing clusters and industrial parks in both textile and pharmaceutical industries through public–private partnerships. Equally important were the regulatory changes initiated in each industry through negotiations and consultations between the state and industry associations that facilitated organisational access to international resource and product markets.[10] Our findings foreground the importance of imports in achieving international competitiveness through investments in manufacturing and R&D capabilities by Indian firms in both industries. Furthermore, industry-level evidence for the pharmaceutical industry shows how easing of FDI controls led to both investments by established multinationals in various value-chain activities in India (which increased the potential of positive knowledge spillovers for local firms) as well as outward FDIs by Indian pharmaceutical firms in foreign markets to gain access to technology, know-how and marketing infrastructure needed to compete in the changed global institutional environment. However, our results show a contrast between the two industries, as a similar easing of FDIs did not see substantial inward and outward foreign investments in the textile industry.

These differences in the role of FDI are partially attributable to the structure of the textile industry, which consisted primarily of small firms operating in the unorganised sector, but also to the continuing regulatory hurdles in the domestic market (for example, labour regulations, cross-segment competition, foreign retailers and so on [Ganesh 2002; Kabir, Singh and Ferrantino 2019; Narayanan G. 2005; Simpson and Shetty 2001]).

We also considered the effect of network resources available to firms in the two industries through their affiliation with BGs and geographical clusters, both of which play a prominent role in India and are encouraged and/or supported by the state (Kohli 2004; Chittoor and Aulakh 2015). Our study shows that firms affiliated to BGs tap into group resources for strategic renewal and catch-up while independent firms are more reliant on accessing externally acquired international resources.[11] Geographic clusters on the other hand complement firm-level resources in the textile industry as location in a cluster by itself does not provide the full array of benefits required for capability development and improving product-market internationalisation.

The aforementioned workings of the national institutional systems in the two industries support the arguments made in the emerging catch-up literature about the need to examine synergies across different levels within the system that provide the incentives and resources for organisations to undertake investments in capability development. In addition to the system approach, the literature also identifies different product pathways for developing economy firms to catch up. This aspect also resonates with another literature stream that is anchored around the participation of developing economy firms in existing global networks to move up the value chain and increase their presence in global markets.[12] We elaborate on these product and global network pathways and discuss how the experience of India's pharmaceutical and textile industries contributes to these literature streams by examining the efficacy of different catch-up pathways.

Lee (2019: 9) considers economic catch-up by developing economy firms 'as not only a matter of building capabilities but also a matter of choice of specialization in certain technologies, sectors, or activities to find niches for entry and survival'. Laggard firms (that is, from developing economies) need to carve their own paths or 'detours' to upgrade their competitive advantages rather than blindly imitating the paths taken by leading firms from advanced countries. These detours include imitative innovations, focus on short-cycle products and promotion of domestic value-added rather than reliance on existing global value chains (Lee 2019; Lee and Malerba 2018). The pathways taken by the Indian pharmaceutical industry in its attempts to upgrade its capabilities under the post-1995 global intellectual property rights (IPR) regime provide evidence of different detours for catch-up. First, since Indian firms neither had the resources nor the experience or capabilities to carry out radically new product innovations (that is, new drug discovery), their pathway for growth in global markets was through off-patented innovations in producing generics (Guennif and Ramani 2012). The second pathway was through continued focus on discovering new methods of production and 'officially claiming ownership rights to processes developed during the earlier re-engineering regime' (Chattopadhyay and Bercovitz 2020: 1001). Third, Indian pharmaceutical firms invested in production capabilities to manufacture formulations and bulk drugs (although as discussed in previous chapters, the industry was not effective in producing active pharmaceutical ingredients [APIs]) and became a major contract manufacturer for international multinational corporations. These capabilities are reflected in India having the largest number of Food and Drug Administration (FDA) approved factories for the production of drugs. Fourth, a few Indian firms forayed into gaining experience for new product innovations by performing contract work in the drug discovery process. Along with these detours, some of which involved participating in existing global production networks with advanced country multinational corporations as lead firms, the Indian pharmaceutical industry also developed South–South networks whereby new production networks with Indian firms as the lead firms were initiated and which comprised manufacturers, distributors and traders from other developing economies (Horner and Murphy 2018). This evidence from the Indian pharmaceutical industry affirms the importance of alternative pathways and new global networks relevant for developing economy firms in their quest for global competitiveness.

The Indian textile industry's catch-up pathways present an interesting contrast from the pharmaceutical industry. Part of this difference can be explained by the nature of the two industries, whereby innovation as understood in terms of radically new products is not as relevant in the textile industry, and upgrading involves either improvements in production efficiency or moving into product segments with higher value and possibilities for product differentiation. The dominant paths of upgrading in the global textile industry, especially during the post-quota trading regime, were through the global value chain or production networks of advanced economy lead firms which included giant retailers, marketers controlling major apparel brands and brand name manufacturers (Gereffi 2010; Frederick and Gereffi 2011). In these networks, developing economy firms move up the value chain by starting as a supplier (assembler), and slowing upgrading to original equipment manufacturing (OEM), original brand name manufacturing (OBM) and finally performing original design manufacturing (ODM) (Gereffi 2010). As discussed in previous chapters, the Indian textile industry has largely operated outside these global production networks (see also Gupta 2015; Tewari 2006, 2008). Instead, the industry increased its global presence through the use of domestically available resources for upgrading manufacturing capabilities (for example, the TUFS scheme), exploitation of regulatory regimes since the mid-1980s (that is, regulations that provided incentives for modernisation while keeping the domestic market relatively closed forced firms to use locally made inputs and restricted inter-segment competition), and selective acquisition of small distributors and design centres in advanced markets (Tewari 2008). In addition, the higher-valued apparel segment of the Indian textile industry has increased its share of total industry exports (see Figure 4.6), and this segment invests higher amounts in marketing activities than the yarn and fabric segments (see Table 5.8).

Our findings point to different pathways of catch-up and international success for developing economy firms. The Indian pharmaceutical industry's experience demonstrates the use of multiple pathways (that is, knowledge spillovers and resource access through FDI, following niche product strategies, becoming part of global production networks (GPNs), and so on), while the textile industry demonstrates more organic growth but with specific strategic choices to move up the value curve and use of the domestic market and regulatory conditions to accomplish this task. Despite these differences, as argued by Lee (2019), the experience of these two industries to effectively deal with global institutional changes points towards the necessity of finding creative 'detours' by developing economy firms rather than following path-dependent deterministic approaches that may have worked in other geographical and temporal contexts.

Managing Competing Logics in the Institutional System

The core argument of the book is that global institutional change necessitates organisation-level reconfiguration of resources and capabilities, which is accomplished through coordinated efforts between different levels of the system (that is, organisations, industry and state). The catch-up literature discussed in the preceding paragraphs assumes that coordination is a function of resource availability and prioritisation within the system, which in turn impacts the paths taken for strategic renewal to cope with external changes. However, we argue that external changes also create institutional complexity at each level within the system, which manifests itself through competing logics (Greenwood et al. 2011). The presence of competing logics often constrains effective adaptation to external contingencies, and this problem is aggravated in the presence of various competing logics operating at the different levels of the system (Thornton, Ocasio and Lounsbury 2012). In the context of this study, in developing our organising framework, we identified economic efficiency–social welfare, organic–inorganic mechanisms for growth, and proximate–distant search as the possible competing logics operating at the state, industry and organisational levels, respectively. Our analysis of the institutional system across the two industries provides some implications for the literature on competing logics.

Our findings show numerous cross-level effects in managing competing logics in the inter-institutional system. First, the interactions between the state and the organisations within an industry. One of the challenges for state objectives for the textile industry in India was finding ways to balance the need for increased efficiency of the industry in the light of global market-based competition while continuing the sector's historical role in generating employment, especially for marginalised sections of society and in underdeveloped geographical regions. At the organisational level, given the preponderance of small- and medium-sized firms operating in an unorganised sector, there was both inertia and resource constraints to making the riskier strategic choices of investing in capabilities for international growth. Thus, both institutional levels had to deal with competing logics brought in by global change. The policy interventions by the state through the TUFS scheme initiated in 1999 and subsequently amended a few times in the post-2005 period allowed the accommodation of competing logics for the state while facilitating the overcoming of constraints at the organisational level to invest in new capabilities. More specifically, variants of the TUFS scheme provided direct resources for upgrading technology to achieve production efficiency in the textile industry, and also financially rewarded firms if they increased employment along with technological improvements.[13] Furthermore, to achieve the dual objectives of technology upgrading and employment, the state initiated various schemes for skills development in the industry (Kuzhiparambil, 2020).

Second, our analysis provides evidence of state–industry interactions to manage competing logics. In the textile industry, we found evidence of segment-level differences in adapting to global change, that is, while the organised mill and handloom segments achieved productivity gains with some sacrifice of employment gains, the power loom sector sacrificed some productivity in the interest of increased employment. These are examples of 'structurally differentiated' hybrids where different segments of the industry were compartmentalised and tasked with achieving different goals in the national institutional system. While prior research has shown the presence of structural separation to achieve competing objectives within an organisation (Greenwood et. al. 2011; Gupta, Smith and Shalley 2006), our findings provide evidence of the efficacy of this approach at the field or industry level, and more importantly through cooperative efforts between the state and the industry.

Third, the TRIPS agreement introduced competing logics at the different levels of its national institutional system, for example, how to balance the stronger IPR regime, with emphasis on higher-priced product-patented drugs, with affordability and accessibility of these drugs in the domestic market at the state level, and sustaining the existing advantages of reverse-engineering processes with developing new capabilities in product innovation and new drug discovery at the organisational level. Our analysis supplements evidence from a few other studies of both intra- and inter-level approaches to managing these competing logics. At the organisational level, some firms followed a 'blended' hybrid approach whereby the competing logics, such as exploration and exploitation, were synthesised within the firm (Greenwood et. al. 2011). That is, sub-unit tasks were differentiated along activities that required refinement of existing capabilities and others that necessitated distant search (for details, see Abraham and Kumar 2020; Chaturvedi, Chataway and Wield 2007). This approach of pursuing both exploration and exploitation by Indian pharmaceutical firms was facilitated by the regulatory reforms negotiated between the state and the industry in allowing both inward and outward FDI in the sector. Inward FDI helped Indian firms to embed themselves in existing production networks of multinational corporations and overcome the resource and inertial hurdles of shifting their innovation orientation, while outward FDI and acquisitions of firms in advanced markets facilitated initial structural separation, which could then be integrated with the overall intra-organisational system. Furthermore, Chittoor and Ray (2007) report the emergence of five distinct strategic groups in the Indian pharmaceutical industry, differentiated by exploration and exploitation around products and international markets. This approach is akin to the one in the textile industry mentioned earlier, that is, structurally differentiated groups, each balancing competing logics in different ways. The separation of the industry into structurally different groups, some exploiting the existing advantages in process innovations while others moving into the higher-priced product innovations, was also compatible with the state's objectives of the continued availability of affordable drugs for the domestic consumers.

Public Policy Implications

Before we outline some implications for public policy that can be drawn from our study, we would like to briefly contrast the strategic response of India's national institutional system to global institutional change with that of a few other developing economies that were similarly impacted in one or both industries of interest. As our study's primary focus is on India, this comparison with other countries is not extensive, but the purpose is to identify some broad similarities and differences that may have policy implications.

Comparing Country Pathways in Coping with Global Institutional Change

Along with India, China was an important player in the global markets in both textile and pharmaceutical industries before the onset of WTO-initiated global institutional changes. Like their Indian counterparts, Chinese firms have successfully coped with the institutional changes and were not only able to sustain but also improve their position in global markets. In terms of national-level institutional changes ushered in China, once again we see interesting parallels to India. As suggested by Hsueh (2012: 32), the two countries' approaches have

> departed from East Asian developmental states, which have restricted foreign direct investment (FDI) to protect domestic industry, and the liberal FDI strategy of Latin America during a similar stage of development as they have eschewed dependent development. Instead [China and India] … have taken a 'liberalization two-step,' which follows liberalization with regulation that varies across industrial sectors.[14]

Economy-wide or country-wide reforms in China preceded industry-specific policy changes, though they were initiated over a decade before India's economic liberalisation. The economy-wide reform process in China began around 1978 but the turning point of the reform process is usually attributed to Deng Xiaoping's 'southern tour' in 1992 which helped jettison any remaining concerns or opposition to reforms (Vogel 2011). The economy-wide reforms allowed entry of foreign firms and imports of foreign machinery and technology, setting up of special enterprise zones to facilitate duty-free imports for export firms, closure of smaller, inefficient state-owned enterprises, ushering in private and foreign competition and relaxing migration constraints, which allowed free movement of labour within the country (Hanson 2020). These reforms coupled with the country's comparative advantages facilitated China's rise as 'the world's factory' with its global share in exports growing from 2.8 per cent in 1990 to 6.8 per cent in 2000 and to almost 18.5 per cent in 2015 (Brandt and Morrow 2017; Hanson 2020).

China's overall export success was replicated in the textile and pharmaceutical industries. The global share in value of Chinese textile firms grew from about 7 per cent in 1985 to 12 per cent in 2002 whereas in the apparel segment it grew from about 5 per cent in 1985 to nearly 22 per cent in 2002, making China the world's largest textile exporter in the world (Balasubramanyam and Wei 2005).

China's global market share after 2005 continued to improve but stabilised from 2010 onwards with the focus shifting to more value-added and branded products to counteract the disadvantage stemming from increasing labour costs (Zhang, Kong and Ramu 2016; Hanson 2020). Industry-specific policy support was extended to the textile segment that consisted of horizontal technological upgrading (training of manpower, process improvements and upgrading of machinery) as well as vertical capability upgrading (support for packaging, logistics, design, product development, brand building, and so on) (Rasiah, Miao and Xin Xin 2013). Policy reforms also shifted the concentration of the industry from the inefficient and small state-owned enterprises to more efficient and larger-sized private sector firms. Much of China's success in the textile industry came by means of tapping into global value chains and producing or subcontracting for foreign multinational companies (Hanson 2020). Most of the well-known clothing brands from Nike and Adidas to Levi Strauss & Co and Calvin Klein get their apparel made in China. Special enterprise zones, an initiative pioneered by Deng Xiaoping, facilitated such exports by creating superior infrastructure for manufacturing and simplifying procedures for imports and exports (Vogel 2011). Recent five-year plans reveal China's goals of making the industry shift its focus more towards domestic markets, becoming 'greener' and more environmentally friendly as well as balancing production capacities from the east coast to the west for more equitable geographical growth (Lu and Dickson 2015).

Chinese pharmaceutical industry consists of both Western-type chemical pharmaceutical products and a significant share of Chinese traditional medical products. For the sake of comparison, we focus our discussion only on the former, which is comparable to the Indian pharmaceutical industry. Once again, there are interesting parallels between the two countries. Akin to the Indian industry, the primary focus of the Chinese pharmaceutical firms was on (*a*) meeting the needs of the domestic markets, (*b*) with products focused on generic drugs (*c*) to make affordable drugs available to the local healthcare sector. China's global share of exports in 2008 was 1.8 per cent, almost comparable to India's share of 1.5 per cent in the same year (Zhang et al. 2011). Internationalisation of Chinese firms was achieved by developing and leveraging low-cost process manufacturing capabilities with a focus on bulk drug intermediate products (as against formulations in the case of Indian pharmaceutical firms). As in India, price controls have always existed in China (except from 1992 to 1996 when market-driven pricing was introduced and later withdrawn), leading to a focus on production costs instead of innovation (Sun et al. 2008). The average Chinese pharmaceutical firm is much smaller compared to the Indian counterparts and the average R&D intensity in China is only about 2 per cent whereas larger Indian pharma firms have increased their R&D intensity since 2005 to about 6–8 per cent. Recent initiatives by the Chinese government are aimed at increasing R&D investments and improving innovation capacity and quality (Sun et al. 2008). Following 2005, the share of foreign multinational pharmaceutical companies (mostly existing as joint ventures) has been gradually increasing, with an estimated market share of more than a third of the Chinese chemical pharma market (Chen et al. 2019). In implementing the product patent regime as required by TRIPS, it has been observed that China did not incorporate any safety or protection clauses (for example, against evergreening) as done by India.

Overall, the Chinese national institutional system has produced larger firms with scale economies, value-added products and a high degree of internationalisation in the case of the textile industry, but a fragmented pharmaceutical industry with low innovation levels—which is just the other way around, ironically, in the context of India. Furthermore, while China's textile industry has responded to global institutional change through greater participation in global value chains, India's textile industry has followed more of an organic growth model. In the pharmaceutical industry, on the other hand, Indian firms have used the global production networks to move up the value chain. A group of specialist contract manufacturers focusing on specific pharmaceutical products emerged in India as the country became home to the largest number of FDA certified manufacturing facilities. For example, the Serum Institute of India emerged as the world's largest vaccine manufacturer by number of doses produced (more than 1.5 billion doses annually).

Besides insights from comparing the trajectories of the textile and pharmaceutical industries in the two largest developing economies, China and India, another useful comparison is with some smaller countries that successfully navigated the new global institutional regimes. In the textile industry, these include Bangladesh and Vietnam, which, despite their relatively small size, have overtaken India in apparel and clothing exports. Both these countries followed the global value-chain model, with Bangladesh more closely aligned with value chains of the European Union (EU), and Vietnam with the US (for details, see Alam, Sevatnthan and Selvantahn 2017; Curran and Nadvi 2015; Goto, Natsuda and Thoburn 2011). The coupling of the two countries' textile industries with the respective global value chain was facilitated by the bilateral trade agreements negotiated by their governments. The initial impetus to the growth of the textile industry in each country came during the quota regime. However, the potential impact of the abolition of quotas for Bangladesh was cushioned by the preferential access granted by the EU through two agreements in 2001 and 2011.[15] The textile industry in Vietnam was able to withstand the end of the quota regime because of the bilateral free trade agreement with the US initiated in 2001. In addition to the preferential access to the biggest and more affluent markets because of bilateral trade agreements and participation in global value chains (Frederick and Cassill 2009), policy instruments in both countries were put in place to upgrade the production capabilities in their respective industries. These initiatives included liberalisation of the imports of technology and intermediates, and encouragement of product and geographical diversification (Frederick and Gereffi 2011).

A few studies have also compared the trajectories of the post-TRIPS pharmaceutical industries of Brazil and India through the lens of the 'national system of innovation' framework (for example, Guennif and Ramani 2012; Malerba and Nelson 2011). The pharma industry in both countries followed similar paths of operating in regulated environments and developing advantages in drug-manufacturing processes in the pre-TRIPS eras. However, the responses to global change diverged, leading to India's pharmaceutical industry gaining a more prominent global position than Brazil's industry. These included a greater role of the private sector in India, participation in global production networks, and more aggressive internationalisation of both resources and products by Indian pharmaceutical firms.

Policy Dilemmas

The different pathways to coping with global institutional changes across different countries, along with the previously discussed findings from the Indian textile and pharmaceutical industries at multiple levels of analysis, point towards certain dilemmas faced by policymakers as they balance the upgrading of their respective industries to make them competitive in global markets with broader socio-economic goals. In the following paragraphs, we discuss the implications of our findings to three such dilemmas related to realising economies of scale and firm size, value of local and global value chain networks, and efficacy of trade policies.

Economies of scale: Large number of small firms versus small number of large firms

A distinctive characteristic of developing economies when compared to developed countries is the fragmented structure of industries and the presence of a large number of small firms and entrepreneurs. Such small firms account for the lion's share of employment as in the case of the Indian textile industry. However, small firms face the disadvantage of low economies of scale and a low capacity to invest in innovation. These disadvantages translate into enormous challenges and threats when they have to suddenly compete with large global players both in the home markets and in international markets, an inevitable consequence triggered by global institutional changes.[16]

Economic policymakers in India have been conducting a balancing act between protecting the employment capacity of the industry and the need to create scale and operational efficiencies. This is particularly evident in the case of the textile industry, which employs the second-largest number of people in India after agriculture, but less so in the case of the pharmaceutical industry. As can be seen fifteen years after the global institutional changes came into effect, both the industries fared reasonably well, but the pharmaceutical industry with a few global-scale players did much better in terms of growth, profitability as well as employment. It seems that the Indian policymakers too are moving away from the position of balance and tilting towards the creation of a few global-scale enterprises, which they believe could serve their core objective of employment generation better. The Economic Survey of India, an enormous exercise in economy-wide data collection and analysis, prepared by the chief economic advisor to the Government of India and presented before the annual budget, states the following in its report for 2018–2019 (Government of India, Ministry of Finance 2019):

> A startling fact is how the bane of dwarfs, which are defined as small firms that never grow beyond their small size, dominates the Indian economy and holds back job creation and productivity.... Our policies protect and foster *dwarfs* rather than *infants* ... while infant firms are small and young, dwarfs are small but old.... [O]ur policies create a 'perverse' incentive for firms to remain small.... The lack of productivity and growth inhibits the ability of the dwarfs to create jobs.

When we consider the choices based on the findings of our study of the two industries, it becomes clear that policy prescriptions need to be adapted to each industry, as well as to the subsegments within an industry. For the pharmaceutical industry, we draw from our findings based on the Indian industry and the challenges that our preliminary analysis revealed in the case of China. Both the low-end segment of the industry (such as the bulk drug intermediates) and the high-end value-added segments (such as generic drug formulations and innovative drugs) benefit from scale economies and operational efficiencies whether it is in manufacturing or R&D. The Indian pharmaceutical industry benefitted from a trend towards higher industry concentration without suffering any setbacks in the form of significant loss of jobs, whereas the fragmented nature of the industry acted as a drawback for the Chinese pharmaceutical industry. Similarly, even though both India and China shared the same concerns and goals of ensuring affordable prices of pharmaceutical products, Indian firms fared better on this objective as they were able to achieve operational and scale efficiencies that reduced production costs. In other words, scale and size complemented instead of compromising the low-price objectives set by the policymakers. Therefore, the policy prescription of the Economic Survey of India for more consolidation towards creating larger, more productive and globally competitive companies seems quite appropriate for different segments of a process industry like the pharmaceutical industry.

However, such a one-size-fits-all approach may not be appropriate for the Indian textile industry, given its legacy and path dependence. Even though the Chinese textile industry benefitted from consolidation and successfully moved up the value chain by following this approach, as we described in Chapter 3, the Indian textile industry is structurally very distinctive due to the significant presence of the unorganised power loom and handloom sectors, and their associated socio-political implications. Therefore, a two-pronged approach targeted at different segments of the textile industry may be more appropriate in the context of India. Unlike in China, the Indian textile industry has not generated large players that enjoy scale economies and are globally competitive (with a handful of exceptions such as Arvind Limited). This explains the low average level of investments in intangible capabilities such as R&D and marketing. Therefore, policy interventions that nudge the industry towards more consolidation and creation of scale economies are needed in the subsegments of the textile industry that clearly benefit from scale such as the yarn and apparel or ready-made garments.

On the other hand, innovative and creative solutions need to be evolved for the vast employment generating segments such as power looms, handlooms, handicrafts (for example, carpets) and even some specialised subsegments of the ready-made garments sector. An example of a much-needed creative approach can be found in the Indian garment sector, led by a private retailer through the development and nurturing of a domestic network. Fabindia is one of post-independence India's oldest and most successful apparel retailers with over 340 physical stores spread across the country and some international locations, which sources from 55,000 small artisans a wide range of fabrics and apparel representing the rich tradition and cultural diversity of India's textiles.[17] It was established in 1960 by John Bissell, an American working for the Ford Foundation in New Delhi, but its successful business model and retail expansion can be attributed to his son, William Bissell, who took over the leadership of the organisation in 1998. Fabindia follows modern management practices and has been able to create a strong brand equity with significant online presence as well as domestic and international reach, with over fourteen international stores as of 2020. The company adopted a unique ownership structure and business model whereby it sources a wide range of products from across India through a large number of community-owned companies in which a certain proportion of shares (normally 26 per cent) is collectively owned by artisans and crafts persons. All the employees of the company also hold shares in the company and the company's management attempts to balance the interests of multiple stakeholders (producers such as artisans, employees and customers) as well as create a balance between economic objectives and the social ethos of the company. Fabindia represents just one of the many possible business models that can combine value-addition potential and scale economies while protecting the employment of the millions of workers engaged with the textile industry in India.

Another way of overcoming scale challenges without sacrificing socio-economic goals is through industry-level cooperatives. A cooperative business model is not new and there are already a large number of textile and agricultural cooperatives operating in India and around the world. A cooperative is an excellent mechanism by which scale economies and operational efficiencies can be achieved without sacrificing the employment capacity of an industry. Recognising the promise of this model, the Government of India set up a public sector organisation, the National Cooperative Development Corporation, to assist cooperatives in India either directly or through the various state governments. However, the textile cooperatives in India are highly fragmented along product lines and divided across the many states and districts of India (with dozens of cooperatives existing even in a single state). Due to the fragmentation, their intended objectives of scale and branding are not achieved. States that have a consolidated textile cooperative agency with scale and professional management have had reasonable success while most other textile cooperatives languish due to their small size. For example, the Tamil Nadu Handloom Weavers' Cooperative Society Ltd has created a popular brand called Co-optex. With the help of professional management and modern management practices, it has set up a network of over 200 retail stores all over India with an annual sales turnover of INR 1,000 crores (about USD 150 million).[18]

Participation in global value chains

One of the important differences in adaptation to global changes between the Indian pharmaceutical and textile industries is their participation in existing global production and/or value chain networks. While one of the pathways of catch-up by Indian pharmaceutical firms is through embedding themselves in multinational corporation led production networks, the Indian textile firms have diverged from the catch-up model of their peers from other developing countries by avoiding active participation in existing global value chains, which was the dominant mode of other major textile- and apparel-producing developing countries. In fact, the recent report from the Indian government's Economic Survey recommends the adoption of the global value chain model to improve the country's export performance in certain industries:

> China's remarkable export performance vis-à-vis India is driven primarily by deliberate specialization at large scale in labour-intensive activities, especially 'network products', where production occurs across Global Value Chains (GVCs) operated by multi-national corporations. Laser-like focus must be placed on enabling assembling operations at mammoth scale in network products. (Government of India, Ministry of Finance 2020: 100)

We evaluate the appropriateness of global value chain (GVC)/ global production network (GPN) approaches to industry upgrading, given the stage of India's textile and pharmaceutical industries fifteen years after global institutional change was implemented in the respective industry, and the emerging insights in this literature (for example, De Marchi and Alford 2021; Horner 2017; Ponte, Gereffi and Raj-Reichert 2019). One of the concerns about over-reliance on existing global networks by developing economies is the ability to extract private benefits when the locus of governance of these networks lies with lead firms from advanced economies. As suggested by Ponte, Gereffi and Raj-Reichert (2019: 2),

> GVCs have opened up new opportunities for developing countries to participate in the global economy, but have also heightened the related risks and uncertainty of doing so. GVC participation *per se* does not lead to inclusive development outcomes unless increasing shares of value added are created and captured domestically and are fairly distributed among different social groups.

It has been suggested that governments in developing economies need to play more active roles to maximise the catch-up possibilities through global networks as well as to ensure diffusion of these benefits to various societal stakeholders. The traditional role of the national governments in the global value chains was primarily seen as a facilitator whereby states sought 'to promote, attract, and retain private investment, ... as well as to promote local actors in order to participate in these chains and networks (Horner 2017: 7). The more active role would require that the state also regulate the global networks, whereby it governed the activities of the foreign multinational-corporation-centred networks within its national boundaries to protect the interests of its businesses, consumers, workers and citizens. Such regulations could include restricting the monopoly power of multinational corporations, improving product quality standards and labour practices, and addressing environmental concerns, among others (Horner 2017).

Besides deriving more economic and social value from traditional networks developed around lead firms from advanced economies, there is growing evidence that state policies in developing economies can also help in establishing global networks centred around lead firms from developing economies. For example, Haakonsson (2009: 75) argues that institutional change heralded by the TRIPS agreement led to the emergence of different value-chain strands in the global pharmaceutical industry, which included a 'producer-driven strand for branded products' and 'buyer-driven strand for quality generics'. While the advanced country multinationals continue to play the lead firm roles in production networks related to branded products, there is an opportunity for developing economy firms (such as from India) to act as lead firms for buyer-driven generic products and develop their own global production networks (Haakonsson 2019). To this end, Horner and Murphy (2018) show the gradual emergence of South–South production networks led by Indian pharmaceutical firms focusing on generic and low-cost drugs, and these networks complement the North–South production networks for firms with aspirations to move into branded products.[19]

The experiences of various developing economies across different sectors in GPNs/GVCs over the past three decades have highlighted the pros and cons of participation in multinational-corporation-centred networks. Furthermore, the different levels of catch-up achieved by developing economy industries or firms mean that they may have already reached the limits in the benefits that can be derived from such networks. Accordingly, the policy conundrum for the state is to evolve its involvement in these global networks, either by playing a more active role in both facilitating and regulating local firm participation or by supporting the development of new networks built around local firms.

Institutional resources, trade policies and capability development

Our study's findings clearly indicate that institutional support from the government and from supra-organisational networks such as BGs and geographical clusters have a significant influence on firms' ability to successfully respond to global institutional change. Indian policymakers have designed and implemented specific interventions such as the TUFS to help firms cope with the post-2005 institutional change. However, such policy interventions have primarily focused on building tangible assets such as plants and machinery whereas not much direct support was provided for developing intangible capabilities such as R&D and marketing. As our findings indicate, intangible assets played an equally (if not more) significant role in successfully responding to the global disruption. In contrast to India's institutional system, the Chinese government has initiated a number of interventions since the early 2000s to help their textile firms develop higher-order capabilities in new product development, human resources, supply chain management, sales and marketing, including brand building, and R&D. Gu and Lev (2017) call them 'strategic assets' and argue that they are critical to building and maintaining local organisations' competitive edge. However, direct support by the state to organisations for capability development for international growth often violates WTO norms regarding subsidies (Dhingra and Meyer 2021). In this regard, our findings around the close association between international product and resource markets provide some policy implications. We have shown that in response to global institutional change, import liberalisation of know-how and intermediates played an important role in upgrading capabilities and international growth for both the Indian textile and pharmaceutical industries. Trade policies geared towards facilitating access to global resource markets accomplish two goals for policymakers in developing economies. First, they allow local firms to access global resources that are unavailable locally because of the presence of institutional voids. Second, the liberalisation of imports to facilitate exports helps smoothen global and bilateral trade relationships.

Concluding Thoughts

Increased integration of the global economy and the governance of international trade through supranational institutions such as the WTO have meant that national economic objectives and associated trade policies of individual countries need to be compatible with the norms of the global institutions. Change in institutional norms at the global level impact national economies and necessitate adaptation in a way that balances adherence to the new global norms while maintaining the broad socio-economic national objectives. Our primary objective in this book was to focus on two sector-specific global institutional changes initiated and implemented by the WTO in 2005 and examine how India's textile and pharmaceutical industries coped with these changes through coordinated efforts of the respective national institutional system comprised of the state, industry and the local organisations within each industry. The analysis shows both convergence and divergence across the two industries in ways in which each responded to global institutional change. We hope that our specific findings regarding the two industries as well as the theoretical and policy implications discussed in this chapter provide impetus to future research that enhances our collective understanding of institutional change and the interactions between global and national institutions.

Notes

1. Several studies have adopted a more critical approach to evaluating the adaptation of the two industries to global institutional change and have identified numerous factors (including government policies, strategic choices by domestic organisations, investment priories across value-chain activities, and so on) that may have hindered the full growth potential in the two industries (for example, see Abrol et. al., 2019; Abrol 2014; Deshpande 2018; Stein 2020; *The Economist* 2018). Our primary interest in this study is to examine the paths taken by these two industries in responding to global institutional change rather than to assess their eventual performance gains or shortfalls. From the available data, it is clear that the two industries in India were able to cope with the new rules of the game ushered by the abolition of a quota-based regime in the textile industry and the stronger product patent regime in the pharmaceutical industry. Whether or not they achieved the full potential is not germane to our study.

2. These upward trends are also evident in the tables and figures provided in Chapter 5. See Table 5.1, Figures 5.2–5.4.

3. The TUFS was later amended to not only incentivise technology upgrading but also to increase employment at the firm level (see Chapter 3).

4. These investments in clusters and parks, especially in the pharmaceutical industry, have been initiated in the last few years, and thus their impact on any outcome parameters is unclear at this time.

5. We modelled the effects of these historical clusters in the empirical analysis provided in Chapter 5.

6. Evidence from India's pharmaceutical industry also points to a proliferation of cross-border interfirm alliances in the industry as well as participation of India's pharma firms in existing production networks of foreign multinational corporations (Horner 2014). Given the difficulty of getting firm-level data of such alliances, especially for the whole period of the study, we did not incorporate alliance-based resources in the empirical analysis. We do, however, discuss the implication of being part of production networks of multinational corporations later in the chapter.

7. An organizational field is defined as a set of 'organizations that, in the aggregate, constitute a recognized area of institutional life: key suppliers, resource and

product consumers, regulatory agencies, and other organizations that produce similar services or products' (DiMaggio and Powell, 1983: 148).

8.   While overall the Indian pharmaceutical industry has been able to achieve price competitiveness (that is, its costs are some of the lowest in the world, and drugs in India are comparatively cheaper than in other markets) and thus adhere to price controls, there have been concerns about the long-term sustainability of India's price controls and the industry's ability to maintain its productivity. It has been suggested that only larger Indian firms with economies of scale emanating from presence in domestic and international markets have shown productivity gains to warrant lower prices, and the smaller players had to exit the domestic market. Others have suggested that price controls on certain drugs have led to companies not producing these drugs. For these viewpoints, as well as some concerns about slowdown in productivity growth, see Pradhan (2019); *The Economist* (2018, 2020); Chaudhuri (2012).

9.   Another subsegment of the industry is the garment or apparel sector, which predominantly operates as an organised sector. This segment is gaining higher importance in India's textile industry, but given its recent growth, reliable data is not available, especially related to employment.

10.   For example, Pharmexcil is a prominent industry association of India's pharmaceutical industry whose goals include making representations to the government 'and other agencies in India and abroad to get amicable solutions for the common problems of the Industry' (https://pharmexcil.com/content/role-of-council). Similarly, the Textile Committee set up by the Ministry of Textiles, Government of India, comprising both state officials and industry representatives

> has, in its ambit a vast range of functions and activities like scientific, technological and economic research, export promotion, inspection, testing, establishment of laboratories and test houses, collection of statistics for market study and research and rendering advice on all matters relating to the development of [the] textile industry and production of textile machinery. (http://textilescommittee.nic.in/history)

11.   Lee (2019: 14–15) suggests that business groups (BGs) in developing economies 'not only emerge in response to market failures but also may serve as vehicles for economic catch-up' as these groups help 'affiliate firms to enter new markets by providing cross-subsidies' and provide opportunities for 'resource sharing and knowledge spillover' among member firms.

12.   These include global value chains (GVC), global commodity chains (GCC) and global production networks (GPN) (Horner 2014). This literature is vast, and its full explication is beyond the scope of this chapter. Some representative studies that discuss the different types of global networks at some level of detail are Blazek (2010); De Marchi and Alford (2021); Gereffi (2010); Frederick and Gereffi (2011); Haakonsson (2010); Seric and Tong (2019).

13. See http://texmin.nic.in/schemes; see also Government of India, Ministry of Textiles, Annual Reports, http://texmin.nic.in/documents/annual-report (accessed 15 June 2021).

14. On the other hand, Hu, Cui and Aulakh (2019: 197–198) note that the 'power of the state and the lack of active agency of businesses are constant indications of China's state-led system', while 'there is more of a symbiotic relationship between the state and business organizations, which ascribe active agency to businesses ... to shape policy' in India's co-governed state capitalism system. The broader implication of this difference is the greater ability of organisations and industry associations to resist state pressures in India than in China.

15. The 2001 agreement, 'Everything but Arms (EBA)', provided duty- and quota-free access to least developed countries, and the 2011 agreement relaxed rules of origin for clothing imports from Bangladesh to the EU countries (Curran and Nadvi 2015).

16. For a detailed analysis of the post–Multi-Fibre Agreement productivity in the Indian textile industry, see Bhandari (2021), who identifies economies of scale and further technological upgrading as the key to maintaining its competitive advantage in export markets.

17. Data sourced from: www.fabindia.com; Chattopadhyaya et al. (2015).

18. See www.cooptex.gov.in.

19. See also Horner (2021) for the evolution of South Africa's pharmaceutical industry in relation to global value chains and global integration.

Bibliography

Abdi, Majid and Preet S. Aulakh. 'Internationalization and Performance: Degree, Duration and Scale of Operations'. *Journal of International Business Studies* 49 (2018): 832–857.

Abernathy, William J. and James M. Utterback. 'The Pattern of Industrial Innovation'. *Technological Review* 80, no. 7 (1978): 41–47.

Abraham, Balaji and Rohit Kumar. 'Dr. Reddy's Laboratories Ltd: Searching Its Glorious Days'. *South Asian Journal of Business and Management Cases* 9, no. 3 (December 2020): 359–374.

Abramovitz, Moses. 'Catching Up, Forging Ahead, and Falling Behind'. *Journal of Economic History* 46, no. 2 (1986): 385–406.

Abrol, Dinesh, Amitava Guha, Rollins John and Nidhi Singh. 'India's Domestic Pharmaceutical Firms and Their Contribution to National Innovation System-building'. *Economic and Political Weekly* 54, no. 35 (31 August 2019): 34–43.

Abrol, Dinesh. 'Technological Upgrading, Manufacturing and Innovation: Lessons from Indian Pharmaceuticals'. Institute for Studies in Industrial Development, New Delhi, Working Paper 162, March 2014.

Adelman, Martin J. and Sonia Baldia. 'Prospects and Limits of the Patent Provision in the TRIPS Agreement: The Case of India'. *Vanderbilt Journal of Transnational Law* 29, no. 3 (1996): 507–534.

Aggarwal, Aradhna. 'Strategic Approach to Strengthening the International Competitiveness in Knowledge Based Industries: The Indian Pharmaceutical Industry'. Research and Information System for the Non-Aligned and Other Developing Countries (RIP) Discussion Papers, RIS-DP #80/2004, September 2004.

Agrawal, P. and P. Saibaba. 'TRIPS and India's Pharmaceuticals Industry'. *Economic and Political Weekly* 36, no. 39 (2001): 3787–3790.

Ahluwalia, Montek S. 'Economic Reforms in India since 1991: Has Gradualism Worked?' *Journal of Economic Perspectives* 16, no. 3 (2002): 67–88.

Ahuja, Gautam and Sai Yayavaram. 'Perspective—Explaining Influence Rents: The Case for an Institutions-based View of Strategy'. *Organization Science* 22, no. 6 (2011): 1631–1652.

Alam, Md Samsul, E. A. Selvanathan and Saroja Selvanathan. 'Determinants of the Bangladesh Garment Exports in the Post-MFA Environment'. *Journal of the Asia Pacific Economy* 22, no. 2 (2017): 330–352.

Amsden, Alice H. *Asia's Next Giant: South Korea and Late Industrialization*. New York: Oxford University Press, 1989.

Andrews, Kenneth R. *The Concept of Corporate Strategy*. Homewood, IL: Irwin, 1971.

Anner, Mark. 'Two Logics of Labor Organizing in the Global Apparel Industry'. *International Studies Quarterly* 53, no. 3 (2009): 545–570.

Athreya, Suma, Dinar Kale and Shyama V. Ramani. 'Experimentation with Strategy and the Evolution of Dynamic Capability in the India Pharmaceutical Sector'. *Industrial and Corporate Change* 18, no. 3 (2009): 729–759.

Aulakh, Preet S. 'Emerging Multinationals from Developing Economies: Motivations, Paths and Performance'. *Journal of International Management* 13, no. 3 (2007): 235–240.

Aulakh, Preet S. and Masaaki Kotabe. 'Institutional Changes and Organizational Transformation in Developing Economies'. *Journal of International Management* 14 no. 3 (2008): 209–216.

Aulakh, Preet S. and Raveendra Chittoor. 'Organizational Heritage, Institutional Changes and Strategic Responses of Firms from Emerging Economies'. In *Handbook of International Marketing*, edited by Masaaki Kotabe and Christiaan Helsen, 468–489. New York: Sage Publications, 2009.

Aulakh, Preet S., Masaaki Kotabe and Hildy Teegen. 'Export Strategies and Performance of Firms from Emerging Economies: Evidence from Brazil, Chile, and Mexico'. *Academy of Management Journal* 43, no. 3 (2000): 342–361.

Aulakh, Preet S., Sumit Kundu and Somnath Lahiri. 'Learning and Knowledge Management in and out of Emerging Markets'. *Journal of World Business* 51, no. 5 (2016): 655–661.

Autio, Erkko, Harry J. Sapienza and James G. Almeida. 'Effects of Age at Entry, Knowledge Intensity, and Imitability on International Growth'. *Academy of Management Journal* 43, no. 5 (2000): 909–924.

Aw, Bee Yan, Mark J. Roberts and Tor Winston. 'The Complementary Role of Exports and R&D Investments as Sources of Productivity Growth'. NBER Working Paper Series No. 11774: NBER, 2005.

Balasubramanyam, V. N. and Yingqui Wei. 'Textile and Clothing Exports from India and China: A Comparative Analysis'. *Journal of Chinese Economic and Business Studies* 3, no. 1 (2005): 23–37.

Barkema, Harry G. and Freek Vermeulen. 'International Expansion through Start-up or Acquisition: A Learning Perspective'. *Academy of Management Journal* 41, no. 1 (1998): 7–26.

Barnett, William P. and Robert A. Burgelman. 'Evolutionary Perspectives on Strategy'. *Strategic Management Journal* 17, no. S1 (1996): 5–19.

Barney, Jay. 'Firm Resources and Sustained Competitive Advantage'. *Journal of Management* 17, no. 1 (1991): 99–120.

Baron, Reuben M. and David A. Kenny. 'The Moderator–Mediator Variable Distinction in Social Psychological Research: Conceptual, Strategic, and Statistical Considerations'. *Journal of Personality and Social Psychology* 51, no. 6 (1986): 1173–1182.

Bartlett, Chris and Sumantra Ghoshal. *Managing across Borders: The Transnational Solution*. Boston: Harvard Business School Press, 1989.

Bell, Geoffrey G. and Akbar Zaheer. 'Geography, Networks, and Knowledge Flow'. *Organization Science* 18, no. 6 (2007): 955–972.

Bell, Martin and Keith Pavitt. Technological Accumulation and Industrial Growth: Contrast between Developed and Developing Countries'. *Industrial and Corporate Change* 2, no. 2 (1993): 157–210.

Besharov, Marya L. and Wendy K. Smith. 'Multiple Institutional Logics in Organizations: Explaining Their Varied Nature and Implications'. *Academy of Management Review* 39, no. 3 (2014): 364–381.

Bhagwati, Jagdish N. *India in Transition: Freeing the Economy*. New York: Oxford University Press, 1993.

Bhandari, Anup Kumar. 'Withdrawal of the Multifibre Agreement and Indian Textile Industry: Concerns, Efforts, and Achievements'. *Review of Development Economics* (2021). https://doi/10.1111/rode.12760. Accessed 29 July 2021.

Bhaskarbhatla, Ajay. *Regulating Pharmaceutical Prices in India: Policy Design, Implementation and Compliance*. Cham: Springer, 2018.

Bhowmik, Manas Ranjan. 'Fourth Handloom Census: Government's Claims Belie Ground Reality'. *Economic and Political Weekly* 54, no. 19 (14 December 2019).

Blazek, Jiri. 'Towards a Typology of Repositioning Strategies of GVC/GPN Suppliers: The Case of Functional Upgrading and Downgrading'. *Journal of Economic Geography* 16, no. 4 (2016): 849–869.

Bohenbaum, Eva and Stefan Jonsson. 'Isomorphism, Diffusion and Decoupling: Concept Evolution and Theoretical Challenges'. In *The Sage Handbook of Organizational Institutionalism*, edited by Royston Greenwood, Christine Oliver, Thomas B. Lawrence and Renate E. Meyer, 2nd edition, 77–101. London: SAGE Publications Ltd, 2017.

Boisot, Max and Marshall W. Meyer. 'Which Way Through the Open Door? Reflections on the Internationalization of Chinese Firms'. *Management and Organization Review* 4, no. 3 (2008): 349–365.

Bouquet, Cyril and Julian Birkinshaw. 'Weight versus Voice: How Foreign Subsidiaries Gain Attention from Corporate Headquarters'. *Academy of Management Journal* 51, no. 3 (2008): 577–601.

Brandt, Loren and Peter M. Morrow. 'Tariffs and the Organization of Trade in China'. *Journal of International Economics* 104 (2017): 85–103.

Broadberry, Stephen and Bishnupriya Gupta. 'Lancashire, India, and Shifting Competitive Advantage in Cotton Textiles, 1700–1850: The Neglected Role of Factor Prices'. *Economic History Review* 62, no. 2 (2009): 279–305.

Buckley, Peter J. and Mark Casson. *The Future of the Multinational Enterprise*. London: Macmillan, 1976.

Buckley, Peter J., Surender Munjal, Peter Enderwick and Nicholas Forsans. 'Cross-Border Acquisitions by Indian Multinationals: Asset Exploitation or Asset Augmentation?' *International Business Review* 25, no. 4 (2016): 986–996.

Burgelman, Robert A. 'Intraorganizational Ecology of Strategy Making and Organizational Adaptation: Theory and Field Research'. *Organization Science* 2, no. 3 (1991): 239–262.

———. *Strategy Is Destiny: How Strategy-making Shapes a Company's Future*. New York, NY: Free Press, 2002.

Campbell, John L. *Institutional Change and Globalization*. Princeton, NJ: Princeton University Press, 2004.

Carney, Michael, Eric R. Gedajlovic, Pursey P.M.A.R Heugens, Marc Van Essen and J. (Hans) Van Oosterhout. 'Business Group Affiliation, Performance, Context, and Strategy: A Meta-Analysis'. *Academy of Management Journal* 54, no. 3 (2011): 437–460.

Chacar, Aya and Balagopal Vissa. 'Are Emerging Economies Less Efficient? Performance Persistence and the Impact of Business Group Affiliation'. *Strategic Management Journal* 26, no. 10 (2005): 933–946.

Chandler, Alfred Dupont. *Strategy and Structure*. Cambridge, MA: MIT Press, 1962.

Chandra, Pankaj. 'Competing through Capabilities: Strategies for Global Competitiveness of Indian Textile Industry'. *Economic and Political Weekly* 34, no. 9 (27 February–5 March 1999): M17–M24.

Chang, Sea-Jin, Chie-Nian Chung and Ishtiaq P. Mahmood. 'When and How Does Business Group Affiliation Promote Firm Innovation? A Tale of Two Emerging Economies'. *Organization Science* 17, no. 5 (2006): 637–656.

Chatterjee, Ashok. 'India's Handloom Challenge: Anatomy of a Crisis'. *Economic and Political Weekly* 50, no. 32 (8 August 2015): 34–38.

Chattopadhyay, Amitava, Prableen Sabhaney, Sunil Chainani and Jean Wee. 'Fabindia: Branding India's Artisanal Crafts for Mass Retail'. INSEAD Case Study, INS970-PDF-ENG, 2015.

Chattopadhyaya, Shinjee and Janet Bercovitz. 'When One Door Closes, Another Door Opens … for Some: Evidence from the Post-TRIPS India Pharmaceutical Industry'. *Strategic Management Journal* 41, no. 6 (2020): 988–1022.

Chaturvedi, Kalpana, Joanna Chataway and David Wield. 'Policy, Markets and Knowledge: Strategic Synergies in Indian Pharmaceutical Firms'. *Technology Analysis and Strategic Management* 19, no. 5 (2007): 565–588.

Chaudhuri, Sudip. 'Manufacturing Trade Deficit and Industrial Policy in India'. *Economic and Political Weekly* 48, no. 8 (23 February 2013): 41–50.

———. 'Multinationals and Monopolies: Pharmaceutical Industry in India after TRIPS." *Economic and Political Weekly* 47, no. 12 (24 March 2012): 46–54.

———. *The WTO and India's Pharmaceutical Industry: Patent Protect, TRIPS and Developing Countries*. New Delhi: Oxford University Press, 2005.

Chen, Xiangdong, Shaofang Xue, Miaochen Lv and Ruolan Wang. 'Pharmaceutical Industry in China: Policy, Market and IP'. In *Innovation, Economic Development and Intellectual Property in India and China: Comparing Six Economic Sectors*, by Kung-Chung Liu and Uday S. Rachrela, 15–250. Singapore: Springer, 2019.

Cheng, Yu-Ting and Andrew H. Van de Ven. 'Learning the Innovation Journey: Order out of Chaos?' *Organization Science* 7, no. 6 (1996): 593–614.

Cherif, Reda and Fuad Hasanov. 'The Return of the Policy That Shall Not be Named: Principles of Industrial Policy'. International Monetary Fund Working Paper, WP/19/74, 2019.

Chittoor, Raveendra and Preet S. Aulakh. 'Organizational Landscape in India: Historical Development, Multiplicity of Forms and Implications for Practice and Research'. *Long Range Planning* 48, no. 6 (2015): 291–300.

Chittoor, Raveendra and Sougata Ray. 'Internationalization Paths of Indian Pharmaceutical Firms—A Strategic Group Analysis'. *Journal of International Management* 13, no. 3 (2007): 338–355.

Chittoor, Raveendra, M. B. Sarkar, Sougata Ray and Preet S. Aulakh. 'Third-World Copycats to Emerging Multinationals: Institutional Changes and Strategic Transformation in the Indian Pharmaceutical Industry'. *Organization Science* 20, no. 1 (2009): 187–205.

Chittoor, Raveendra, Preet S. Aulakh and Sougata Ray. 'Accumulative and Assimilative Learning, Institutional Infrastructure and Innovation Orientation of Developing Economy Firms'. *Global Strategy Journal* 5, no. 2 (2015): 133–153.

Chittoor, Raveendra, Sougata Ray, Preet S. Aulakh and M. B. Sarkar. 'Strategic Responses to Institutional Changes: "Indigenous Growth" Model of the Indian

Pharmaceutical Industry'. *Journal of International Management* 14, no. 3 (2008): 252–269.

Christensen, Clayton M. 1997. *The Innovator's Dilemma: When New Technologies Cause Great Firms to Fail.* Cambridge, MA: Harvard Business School Press, 1997.

Colpan, Asli M. and Takashi Hikino. 'Foundations of Business Groups: Towards an Integrated Framework'. In *The Oxford Handbook of Business Groups*, edited by A. M. Colpan, T. Hikino and J. R. Lincoln. Oxford: Oxford University Press, 2010.

Coriat, Benjamin and Olivier Weinstein. 'Organizations, Firms and Institutions in the Generation of Knowledge'. *Research Policy* 31, no. 2 (2002): 273–290.

Corrado, Carol A. and Charles R. Hulten. 'How Do You Measure a "Technological Revolution"?' *American Economic Review* 100, no. 2 (2010): 99–104.

Craig, C. Samuel and Susan P. Douglas. 'Managing the Transnational Value Chain: Strategies for Firms from Emerging Market'. *Journal of International Marketing* 5, no. 3 (1997): 71–84.

CRIS INFAC. *Pharmaceuticals Annual Review: February.* CRISIL Mumbai, 2004.

Cuervo-Cazurra, Alvaro and Ravi Ramamurti, eds. *Understanding Multinationals from Emerging Markets.* New York: Cambridge University Press, 2014.

Cui, Lin and Preet S. Aulakh. 'Emerging Economy Multinationals in Advanced Economies'. In *The Oxford Handbook of Management in Emerging Markets*, edited by Robert Gross and Klaus E. Meyer, 609–630. New York: Oxford University Press, 2019.

Curran, Louise and Khalid Nadvi. 'Shifting Trade Preferences and Value Chain Impacts in Bangladesh Textiles and Garment Industry'. *Cambridge Journal of Regions, Economics and Society* 8, no. 3 (2015): 459–474.

Cusumano, Michael A. and Detelin Elenkov. 'Linking International Technology Transfer with Strategy and Management: A Literature Commentary'. *Research Policy* 23, no. 2 (1994): 195–215.

Cyert, Richard. M. and James G. March). *A Behavioral Theory of the Firm*, 2nd ed. Cambridge, MA: Blackwell Business, 1992.

Daemmrich, Arthur A. 'Stalemate at the WTO: TRIPs, Agricultural Subsidies, and the Doha Round'. Harvard Business School, 9-711-043, 2012.

Danneels, Erwin. 'The Dynamics of Product Innovation and Firm Competences'. *Strategic Management Journal* 23, no. 12 (2002): 1095–1121.

Dau, Luis Alfonso, Randall Morck and Bernard Yin Yeung. 'Business Groups and the Study of International Business: A Coasean Synthesis and Extension'. *Journal of International Business Studies* 52, no. 2 (2021): 161–211.

Davis, Lance E., and Douglass C. North. *Institutional Change and American Economic Growth*. Cambridge, UK: Cambridge University Press, 1971.

Dawar, Niraj and Tony Frost. 'Competing with Giants: Survival Strategies for Emerging Market Companies'. *Harvard Business Review* 77 (March–April 1999): 119–132.

De Marchi, Valentina and Matthew Alford. 'State Policies and Upgrading in Global Value Chains: A Systematic Literature Review'. *Journal of International Business Policy* (2021). https://doi-org.myaccess.library.utoronto.ca/10.1057/s42214-021-00107-8. Accessed on 24 July 2021.

Desai, Ashok V. 'Technology and Market Structure under Government Regulation: A Case Study of Indian Textile Industry'. *Economic and Political Weekly* 18, no.5 (29 January 1983): 150–160.

Deshpande, Neeta. 'Weavers Bear the Brunt as Powerlooms Displace the Handloom Sector'. *The Wire*, 7 August 2018. https://thewire.in/labour/weavers-bear-the-brunt-as-powerlooms-displace-the-handloom-sector. Accessed 12 May 2021.

Dhar, Biswajit and Reji K. Joseph. 'The Challenges, Opportunities and Performance of the Indian Pharmaceutical Industry Post-TRIPS'. In *Innovation, Economic Development and Intellectual Property in India and China: Comparing Six Economic Sectors*, edited by Kung-Chung Liu and Uday S. Rachrela, 299–323. Singapore: Springer, 2019.

Dhiman, Rahul, and Manoj Sharma. *The Textile Industry and Exports in Post-Liberalization India*. Abingdon: Routledge, 2021.

Dhingra, Swati and Timothy Meyer. 'Levelling the Playing Field: Industrial Policy and Export-Contingent Subsidies in India-export Measures'. Robert Schuman Centre for Advanced Studies Research Paper No. RSC 15 (2021).

Differding, Edmond. 'The Drug Discovery and Development Industry in India— Two Decades of Proprietary Small-Molecule R&D'. *ChemMedChem* 12, no. 11 (2017): 786–818.

DiMaggio, Paul J. and Walter W. Powell. 'The Iron Cage Revisited: Institutional Isomorphism and Collective Rationality in Organizational Fields'. *American Sociological Review* 48, no. 2 (1983): 147–160.

Dosi, Giovanni. 'Sources, Procedures, and Microeconomic Effects of Innovation'. *Journal of Economic Literature* 26, no. 3 (1988): 1120–1171.

Doz, Y. L., J. Santos and P. J. Williamson. *From Global to Metanational: How Companies in the Knowledge Economy*. Boston, MA: Harvard Business School Press, 2001.

Drèze, Jean and Amartya Sen. *India: Development and Participation*. Oxford: Oxford University Press, 2002.

Duncan, R. B. 'The Ambidextrous Organization: Designing Dual Structures for Innovation'. In *The Management of Organization*, edited by Kilmann, R. H. Pondy, L.R. and D. Slevin, 167–188. New York: North-Holland, 1976.

Dunning, John H. 'The Eclectic Paradigm of International Production: A Restatement and Some Possible Extensions'. *Journal of International Business Studies* 19 (1988): 1–31.

Dyer, Jeffrey H. and Harbir Singh. 'The Relational View: Cooperative Strategy and Sources of Interorganizational Competitive Advantage'. *Academy of Management Review* 23, no. 4 (1998): 660–679.

Economic Times. '25 Years of Reforms: When Narayana Murthy Took 3 Years and 50 Trips to Delhi Import One Computer'. 21 July 2016.

Eisenhardt, Kathleen and Jeffery A. Martin. 'Dynamic Capabilities: What Are They?' *Strategic Management Journal* 21, nos. 10/11 (2000): 1105–1121.

Elango, B. and Chinmay Pattnaik. 'Building Capabilities for International Operations through Networks: A Study of Indian Firms'. *Journal of International Business Studies* 38, no. 4 (2007): 541–555.

Ethiraj, Sendil K., Prashant Kale, Mayuram S. Krishnan and Jitendra V. Singh. 'Where Do Capabilities Come from and How Do They Matter? A Study in the Software Services Industry'. *Strategic Management Journal* 26, no. 1 (2005): 25–45.

Evans, D. 1979. *Dependent Development*. Princeton, NJ: Princeton University Press, 1979.

Evenson, Robert E., and Larry E. Westphal. 'Technological Change and Technology Strategy'. *Handbook of Development Economics* 3, no. A (1995): 2209–2299.

Fatas-Villafranca, Francisco, Julio Sanchez-Choliz and Gloria Jarne. 'Modeling the Co-Evolution of National Industries and Institutions'. *Industrial and Corporate Change* 17, no. 1 (2007): 65–108.

Feng, Ling, Zhiyuan Li and Deborah L. Swenson. 'The Connection between Imported Intermediate Inputs and Exports: Evidence from Chinese Firms'. *Journal of International Economics* 101 (July 2016): 86–101.

Filatotchev, Igor, Mike Wright, Klaus Uhlenbruck, Laszlo Tihanyi and Robert E. Hoskisson. 'Governance, Organizational Capabilities, and Restructuring in Transition Economies'. *Journal of World Business* 38, no. 4 (2003): 331–347.

Floyd, Steven W. and Peter J. Lane. 'Strategizing throughout the Organization: Managing Role Conflict in Strategic Renewal'. *Academy of Management Review* 25, no. 1 (2000): 154–177.

Frederick, Stacey and Gary Gereffi. 'Upgrading and Restructuring in the Global Apparel Value Chain: Why China and Asia are Outperforming Mexico and

Central America'. *International Journal of Technological Learning, Innovation and Development* 4, nos. 1/2/3 (2011): 67–95.

Frederick, Stacey and N. Cassill. 'Industry Clusters and Global Value Chains: Analytical Frameworks to Study the New World of Textiles'. *Journal of the Textile Institute* 100, no. 8 (2009): 668–681.

Friedland, Roger and Robert R. Alford. 'Bringing Society Back In: Symbols, Practices, and Institutional Contradictions'. In *The New Institutionalism in Organizational Analysis*, edited by Walter W. Powell and Paul J. DiMaggio, 232–263. Chicago: University of Chicago Press, 1991.

Furtado, Rebecca. 'Top Ten Acquisitions in the Indian Pharmaceutical Sector in India'. iPleaders, 11 October 2017. https://blog.ipleaders.in. Accessed 20 May 2021.

Ganesh, S. 'Textile Industry: Stifled by Warped Policies'. *Economic and Political Weekly* 37, no. 12 (23–29 March 2002): 1095–1100.

Gereffi, Gary. 'The Global Economy: Organization, Governance, and Development'. In *The Handbook of Economic Sociology*, edited by N. Smelser and R. Swedberg, 160–182. Princeton, NJ: Princeton University Press, 2010.

Gerschenkron, Alexander. *Economic Backwardness in Historical Perspective: A Book of Essays*. New York: Praeger, 1962.

Ghoshal, Sumantra. 'Global Strategy: An Organizing Framework'. *Strategic Management Journal* 8, no. 5 (1987): 425–440.

Goldberg, Pinelopi Koujianou, Amit Kumar Khandelwal, Nina Pavcnik, and Petia Topalova. 'Imported Intermediate Inputs and Domestic Product Growth: Evidence from India'. *Quarterly Journal of Economics* 125, no. 4 (2010): 1727–1767.

Gopakumar, K. M. 'MNC Patent Monopoly and Takeover of Generics in India'. TWN, Third World Network Briefing Paper 62, March 2012.

Goto, Kenta, Kaoru Natsuda and John Thoburn. 'Meeting the Challenge of China: The Vietnamese Garment Industry in the Post MFA Era'. *Global Networks* 11, no. 3 (2011): 355–379.

Government of India. *Eighth Five Year Plan, 1992–1997*. New Delhi: Government of India, 1992. https://niti.gov.in/planningcommission.gov.in/docs/plans/planrel/fiveyr/index5.html. Accessed May 2021.

———. *Ninth Five Year Plan, 1997–2002*. New Delhi: Government of India, 1997. https://niti.gov.in/planningcommission.gov.in/docs/plans/planrel/fiveyr/index5.html. Accessed May 2021.

———. *Tenth Five Year Plan, 2002–2007*. New Delhi: Government of India, 2002. https://niti.gov.in/planningcommission.gov.in/docs/plans/planrel/fiveyr/index5.html. Accessed May 2021.

———. 'Statement of Industrial Policy'. 24 July 1991. www.dpiit.gov.in/default// files/IndustrialPolicyStatement_1991. Accessed 10 April 2021.

———. 'The Patents (Amendment Act) Act, 2005'. *Gazette of India*, 5 April 2005, New Delhi.

Government of India, Department of Pharmaceuticals. 'Drug Policy 1986'. National Pharmaceutical Pricing Authority, 1986. http://www.nppaindia.nic.in/en/drug-policies/drug-policy-1986/. Accessed 31 May 2021.

———. 'Pharmaceutical Policy 2002'. Government of India, 2002. pharmaceuticals. gov.in/policy. Accessed 14 April 2021.

Government of India, Department for the Promotion of Industry and Internal Trade. *Annual Report, 2012–2013*. New Delhi: Government of India, 2012–2013. https://dipp.gov.in/publications/annual-report. Accessed April 2021.

———. *Annual Report, 2013–2014*. New Delhi: Government of India, 2012–2013. https://dipp.gov.in/publications/annual-report. Accessed April 2021.

———. *Annual Report, 2014–2015*. New Delhi: Government of India, 2014–2015. https://dipp.gov.in/publications/annual-report. Accessed April 2021.

———. *Annual Report, 2015–2016*. New Delhi: Government of India, 2015–2016. https://dipp.gov.in/publications/annual-report. Accessed April 2021.

———. *Annual Report, 2017–2018*. New Delhi: Government of India, 2017–2018. https://dipp.gov.in/publications/annual-report. Accessed April 2021.

———. *Annual Report, 2018–2019*. New Delhi: Government of India, 2018–2019. https://dipp.gov.in/publications/annual-report. Accessed April 2021.

———. *Annual Report, 2019–2020*. New Delhi: Government of India, 2019–2020. https://dipp.gov.in/publications/annual-report. Accessed April 2021.

Government of India, Ministry of Chemicals and Fertilizers. *Annual Report, 2001–2002*. New Delhi: Government of India, 2001–2002.

Government of India, Ministry of Chemicals and Fertilizers, Department of Pharmaceuticals. *Annual Report, 2020–2021*. New Delhi: Government of India, 2020–2021.

———. 'National Pharmaceuticals Pricing Policy, 2012 (NPPP-2012)'. *Gazette of India*, 7 December 2012, Government of India, New Delhi.

———. 'Scheme for the Development of Pharmaceutical Industry, 2018'. Government of India, 2018. https://pharmaceuticals.gov.in/ schemes. Accessed 20 April 2021.

———. 'Scheme for the Promotion of Medical Devices Parks, 2020'. Government of India, 2020. https://pharmaceuticals.gov.in/ schemes. Accessed 20 April 2021.

———. 'Production Linked Incentive Scheme (PLI) for Pharmaceuticals, 2021'. *Gazette of India*, 3 March 2021, Government of India, New Delhi.

Government of India, Ministry of Finance. *Economic Survey 2018–19*. New Delhi: Government of India, 2019.

———. *Economic Survey 2019–20*. New Delhi: Government of India, 2020.

Government of India, Ministry of Textiles. 'Amended Technology Upgradation Fund Scheme'. July 2016. http://texmin.nic.in/schemes. Accessed 14 March 2021.

———. *Annual Report, 2001–2002*. New Delhi: Government of India, 2001–2001. http://texmin.nic.in/documents/annual-report.

———. *Annual Report, 2009–2010*. New Delhi: Government of India, 2009–2010. http://texmin.nic.in/documents/annual-report.

———. *Annual Report, 2011–2012*. New Delhi: Government of India, 2011–2012. http://microdata.gov.in/nada43/index.php/catalog/ASI (accessed May 2021).

———. *Annual Report, 2013–2014*. New Delhi: Government of India, 2013–2014. http://texmin.nic.in/documents/annual-report.

———. *Annual Report, 2016–2017*. New Delhi: Government of India, 2016–2017. http://texmin.nic.in/documents/annual-report.

———. *Annual Report, 2017–2018*. New Delhi: Government of India, 2017–2018. http://texmin.nic.in/documents /annual-report.

———. *Annual Report, 2018–2019*. New Delhi: Government of India, 2018–2019. http://texmin.nic.in/documents /annual-report.

———. *Annual Report, 2019–2020*. New Delhi: Government of India, 2019–2020. http://texmin.nic.in/documents/annual-report.

———. 'National Textile Policy 2000'. Government of India, 2000. http://texmin. nic.in/sites/default/files/policy_2000.pdf Accessed 15 August 2020.

———. 'Progress of TUFS'. Government of India, 2019–2021b. www.txindia.gov. in. Accessed 20 June 2021.

———. 'Scheme for Integrated Textile Parks (SITP)'. *Gazette of India*, 27 March 2018, New Delhi.

———. 'Strategic Plan (2012–2017)'. February 2014. http://texmin.nic.in/sites/ default/files/policy_2000.pdf. Accessed 18 April 2021.

Government of India, Planning Commission. *Five-Year Plans*, 1987–2017. https:// niti.gov.in/planningcommission.gov.in/docs/plans/planrel/fiveyr/index5.html. Accessed 24 April 2021.

Granovetter, Mark. 'Economic Action and Social Structure: The Problem of Embeddedness'. *American Journal of Sociology* 91, no. 3 (1985): 481–510.

Greene, William. *Econometric Analysis*. New York, NY: Prentice Hall, 2002.

Greene, William. 'The Emergence of India's Pharmaceutical Industry and Implications for the U.S. Generic Drug Market'. U.S. International Trade Commission, Washington, DC, Office of Economics Working Paper 2007-05-A, May 2007.

Greenwood, Royston and C. R. Hinings. 'Understanding Radical Organizational Change: Bringing Together the Old and the New Institutionalism'. *Academy of Management Review* 21, no. 4 (1996): 1022–1054.

Greenwood, Royston, Amalia Magán Díaz, Stan Xiao Li and José Céspedes Lorente. 'The Multiplicity of Institutional Logics and the Heterogeneity of Organizational Responses'. *Organization Science* 21, no. 2 (2010): 521–539.

Greenwood, Royston, Mia Raynard, Farah Kodeih, Evelyn R. Micelotta and Michael Lounsbury. 'Institutional Complexity and Organizational Responses'. *Academy of Management Annals* 5, no. 1 (2011): 317–371.

Greif, Avner. *Institutions and the Path to the Modern Economy. Lessons from Medieval Trade.* New York: Cambridge University Press, 2006.

Grosse, Robert E. and Klaus Meyer, eds. *The Oxford Handbook of Management in Emerging Markets.* New York, NY: Oxford University Press, 2019.

Gu, Feng and Baruch Lev. 'Time to Change Your Investment Model'. *Financial Analysts Journal* 73, no. 4 (2017): 23–33.

Gubbi, Sathyajit R. 'Dominate or Ally? Bargaining Power and Control in Cross-Border Acquisitions by Indian Firms'. *Long Range Planning* 48, no. 5 (2015): 301–316.

Gubbi, Sathyajit R., Preet S. Aulakh, Sougata Ray, M. B. Sarkar and Raveendra Chittoor. 'Do International Acquisitions by Emerging-Economy Firms Create Shareholder Value? The Case of Indian Firms.' *Journal of International Business Studies* 41, no. 3 (2010): 397–418.

Gubbi, Sathyajit, Preet S. Aulakh and Sougata Ray. 'International Search Behavior of Business Group Affiliated Firms: Scope of Institutional Changes and Intragroup Heterogeneity'. *Organization Science* 26, no. 5 (2015): 1485–1501.

Guennif, Samira and Shyama V. Ramani. 'Explaining Divergence in Catching-up in Pharma Between India and Brazil Using the NSI Framework'. *Research Policy* 41, no. 2 (2012): 430–441.

Gulati, Ranjay. 'Alliances and Networks'. *Strategic Management Journal* 19, no. 2 (1998): 293–317.

Gulati, Ranjay, Nitin Nohria and Akbar Zaheer. 'Strategic Networks'. *Strategic Management Journal* 21, no. 3 (2000): 203–215.

Gümüsay, Ali Aslan, Michael Smets and Timothy Morris. '"God at Work": Engaging Central and Incompatible Institutional Logics through Elastic Hybridity'. *Academy of Management Journal* 63, no. 1 (2020): 124–154.

Gupta, Anil and V. Govindarajan. 'Managing Global Expansion: A Conceptual Framework'. *Business Horizons* 43, no. 2 (March–April 2000): 45–54.

Gupta, Anil K., Ken G. Smith and Christina E. Shalley. 'The Interplay between Exploration and Exploitation'. *Academy of Management Journal* 49, no. 4 (2006): 693–706.

Gupta, Neha. 'India's Textiles and Clothing Industry in Global Value Chains and Its Linkages with other Asian Countries'. Working Paper CWS/WP/200/33, Centre for WTO Studies, New Delhi, April 2015.

Haakonsson, Stine Jessen. 'The Changing Governance Structures of the Global Pharmaceutical Value Chain'. *Competition and Change* 13, no. 1 (2009): 75–95.

Haley, George T. and Usha C. V. Haley. 'The Effects of Patent-Law Changes on Innovation: The Case of India's Pharmaceutical Industry'. *Technological Forecasting and Social Change* 79, no. 4 (2012): 607–619.

Hall, Peter A. 'Historical Institutionalism in Rationalist and Sociological Perspective'. In *Explaining Institutional Change: Ambiguity, Agency, and Power*, edited by James Mahoney and Kathleen Thelen, 204–224. Cambridge, UK: Cambridge University Press, 2009.

Hall, Peter. A. and David Soskice. *Varieties of Capitalism: The Institutional Foundations of Comparative Advantage*. Oxford: Oxford University Press, 2001.

Halliburton, Murphy. *India and the Patent Wars: Pharmaceuticals in the New Intellectual Property Regime*. Ithaca: ILR Press, an imprint of Cornell University Press, 2017.

Hamilton, Marci A. 'The TRIPS Agreement: Imperialistic, Outdated, and Overprotective'. *Vanderbilt Journal of Transnational Law* 29, no. 3 (1996): 613–634.

Hannan, Michael T. and John Freeman. 'Structural Inertia and Organizational Change'. *American Sociological Review* 49, no. 2 (1984): 149–164.

Hanson, Gordon H. 'Who Will Fill China's Shoes? The Global Evolution of Labor-Intensive Manufacturing'. National Bureau of Economic Research (NBER) Working Paper 28313, December 2020. http://www.nber.org/papers/w28313. Accessed 19 July 2021.

Haskel, Jonathan and Stian Westlake. *Capitalism without Capital: The Rise of the Intangible Economy*. Princeton, NJ: Princeton University Press, 2018.

Hassel, Anke, Martin Höpner, Antje Kurdelbusch, Britta Rehder and Rainer Zugehör. 'Two Dimensions of the Internationalization of Firms'. *Journal of Management Studies* 40, no. 3 (2003): 705–723.

He, Zi-Lin and Poh-Kam Wong. 'Exploration vs. Exploitation: An Empirical Test of the Ambidexterity Hypothesis'. *Organization Science* 15, no. 4 (2004): 481–494.

Helfat, Constance E. and Margaret A. Peteraf. 'The Dynamic Resource-based View: Capability Lifecycles'. *Strategic Management Journal* 24, no. 10 (2003): 997–1010.

Helfat, Constance E. and Marvin B. Lieberman. 'The Birth of Capabilities: Market Entry and the Importance of Pre-history'. *Industrial and Corporate Change* 11, no. 4 (2002): 725–760.

Hitt, Michael A., Haiyang Li and William J. Worthington IV. 'Emerging Markets as Learning Laboratories: Learning Behaviors of Local Firms and Foreign Entrants in Different Institutional Contexts'. *Management and Organization Review* 1, no. 3 (2005): 353–380.

Hitt, Michael A., Laszlo Tihanyi, Toyah Miller and Brian Connelly. 'International Diversification: Antecedents, Outcomes, and Moderators'. *Journal of Management* 32, no. 6 (2006): 831–867.

Hitt, Michael A., Robert E. Hoskisson and Hicheon Kim. 'International Diversification: Effects on Innovation and Firm Performance in Product-diversified Firms'. *Academy of Management Journal* 40, no. 4 (1997): 767–798.

Hitt, Michael A., Robert E. Hoskisson and R. Duane Ireland. 'A Mid-range Theory of the Interactive Effects of International and Product Diversification on Innovation and Performance'. *Journal of Management* 20, no. 2 (1994): 297–326.

Horner, Rory. 'Beyond Facilitator? State Roles in Global Value Chains and Global Production Networks'. *Geography Compass* 11, e12307 (2017): 1–13.

———. 'Strategic Decoupling, Recoupling and Global Production Networks: India's Pharmaceutical Industry'. *Journal of Economic Geography* 14, no. 6 (2014): 1117–1140.

———. 'Global Value Chains, Import Orientation, and the State: South Africa's Pharmaceutical Industry'. *Journal of International Business Policy* (2021). https://doi.org/10.1057/s42214-021-00103-y. Accessed 24 July 2021.

Horner, Rory and James T. Murphy. 'South-North and South-South Production Networks: Diverging Socio-spatial Practices of Indian Pharmaceutical Firms'. *Global Networks* 18, no. 2 (2018): 326–351.

Hoskisson, Robert E., Lorraine Eden, Chung Ming Lau and Mike Wright. 'Strategy in Emerging Economies'. *Academy of Management Journal* 43, no. 3 (2000): 249–267.

Hoskisson, Robert E., William P. Wan, Daphne Yiu and Michael A. Hitt. 'Theory and Research in Strategic Management: Swings of a Pendulum'. *Journal of Management* 25, no. 3 (1999): 417–456.

Hu, Helen Wei, Lin Cui and Preet S. Aulakh. 'State Capitalism and Performance Persistence of Business Group-Affiliated Firms: A Comparative Study of China and India'. *Journal of International Business Studies* 50, no. 2 (2019): 193–222.

Huff, James O., Anne S. Huff and Howard Thomas. 'Strategic Renewal and the Interaction of Cumulative Stress and Inertia'. *Strategic Management Journal* 13 (1992): 55–75.

Hsueh, Roselyn. 'China and India in the Age of Globalization: Sectoral Variation in Postliberalization Reregulation'. *Comparative Political Studies* 45, no. 1 (2012): 32–61.

Hymer, Stephen H. *A Study of Direct Foreign Investment*. Cambridge, MA: MIT Press, 1976.

IBEF, India Brand Equity Foundation. 'Indian Pharmaceuticals Industry Analysis'. www.ibef.org/industry/indian-pharmaceuticals-industry-analysis-presentation-august-2020. Accessed March 2019.

India Office of the Controller General of Patents, Designs & Trademarks. *Annual Reports, 2002–2019*. New Delhi: Government of India, 2002–2019. http://www. ipindia.nic.in/annual-reports-ipo.htm. Accessed 15 July 2021.

IQVIA. 'US Generics Market-Evolution of Indian Players'. IQVIA.com, February 2019.

Jackson, Gregory and Richard Deeg. 'Comparing Capitalisms: Understanding Institutional Diversity and its Implications for International Business'. *Journal of International Business Studies* 39, no. 4 (2008): 540–561.

Jain, L. C. 1985 'Textile Policy: End of Handloom Industry'. *Economic and Political Weekly* 20, no. 27 (6 July 1985): 1121–1123.

James, Harvey S. 'Owner as Manager, Extended Horizons and the Family Firm'. *International Journal of the Economics of Business* 6, no. 1 (1999): 41–55.

Jha, Ravinder. 'Options for Indian Pharmaceutical Industry in the Changing Environment'. *Economic and Political Weekly* 42, no. 39 (2007): 3958–3967.

Johanson Jan and Jan-Erik Vahlne. 'The Internationalization Process of the Firm: A Model of Knowledge Development and Increasing Foreign Market Commitments'. *Journal of International Business Studies* 8, no. 1 (1977): 23–32.

Johanson, Jan and Finn Wiedersheim-Paul. 'The Internationalization of the Firm: Four Swedish Cases'. *Journal of Management Studies* 12, no. 3 (1975): 305–322.

Johanson, Jan and Jan-Erik Vahlne. 'The Uppsala Internationalization Process Model Revisited: From Liability of Foreignness to Liability of Outsidership'. *Journal of International Business Studies* 40, no. 9 (2009): 1411–1431.

Joseph, Reji K. 'Outward FDI from India: Review of Policy and Emerging Trends'. Working Paper 214, Institute for Studies in Industrial Development, New Delhi, November 2019.

———. *Pharmaceutical Industry and Public Policy in Post Reform India*. New York: Routledge, 2016.

———. 'Policy Reform in Indian Pharmaceutical Sector since 1994: Impact on Exports and Imports'. *Economic and Political Weekly* 47, no. 18 (5 May 2012): 60–69.

Kabir, Mahfuz, Surendar Singh and Michael J. Ferrantino. 'The Textile-Clothing Value Chain in India and Bangladesh: How Appropriate Policies Can Promote (or Inhibit) Trade and Investment'. World Bank Group Macroeconomics, Trade and Global Investment Practice, Policy Research Working Paper 8731, February 2019.

Kamiike, Atsuko. 'The TRIPS Agreement and the Pharmaceutical Industry in India'. *Journal of Interdisciplinary Economics* 32, no. 1 (2020): 95–113.

Kannan, Elumalai. 'Post Quota Regime and Comparative Advantage in Export of India's Textiles and Clothing'. *Journal of International Economics* 1, no. 2 (2010): 14–30.

Katila, Riita. 'Using Patent Data to measure Innovation Performance'. *International Journal of Business Performance Management* 2, nos. 1–3 (2004): 180–193.

Katila, Riita and Gautam Ahuja. 'Something Old, Something New: A Longitudinal Study of Search Behavior and New Product Introduction'. *Academy of Management Journal* 45, no. 6 (2002): 1183–1194.

Kenny, David A., Deborah A. Kashy and Nial Bolger. 'Data Analysis in Social Psychology'. In *The Handbook of Social Psychology*, edited by D.Gilbert, S. Fiske and G. Lindzey, vol. 1, 233–265, Boston: McGraw-Hill, 1998.

Khanna, Tarun and Jan W. Rivkin. 'Estimating the Performance Effects of Business Groups in Emerging Markets'. *Strategic Management Journal* 22, no. 1 (2001): 45–74.

Khanna, Tarun and Krishna G. Palepu. 'Emerging Giants: Building World-Class Companies in Developing Economies'. *Harvard. Business Review* 84, no. 10 (2006): 60–70.

———. 'Why Focused Strategies May Be Wrong for Emerging Markets?' *Harvard Business Review* 75, no. 4 (1997): 41–51.

Khanna, Tarun and Yishay Yafeh. 'Business Groups in Emerging Markets: Paragons or Parasites?' *Journal of Economic Literature* 45, no. 2 (2007): 331–372.

Khurana, Deepika and Sobuhi Iqbal. 'Why India Depends Heavily on China for Drug Raw Materials?' Health Analytics Asia, 3 January 2020. https://www.ha-asia.com/why-india-still. Accessed 1 June 2021.

Kim, Hicheon, Robert E. Hoskisson and Willaim P. Wan. 'Power Dependence, Diversification Strategy, and Performance in Kieretsu Member Firms'. *Strategic Management Journal* 25, no. 7 (2004): 613–636.

Kim, Hicheon, Robert E. Hoskisson, Laszlo Tihanyi, and Jaebum Hong. 'The Evolution and Restructuring of Diversified Business Groups in Emerging Markets: The Lessons from Chaebols in Korea'. *Asia Pacific Journal of Management* 21, no. 1 (2004): 25–48.

Kim, Jong-I and Lawrence J. Lau. 'The Sources of Economic Growth in the East Asian Newly Industrialized Countries'. *Journal of Japanese and International Economy* 8, no. 3 (1994): 235–271.

Kim, Linsu. *Imitation to Innovation: The Dynamics of Korea's Technological Learning.* Boston, MA: Harvard University Press, 1997.

Kogut, Bruce. 'Joint ventures: Theoretical and Empirical Perspectives'. *Strategic Management Journal* 9, no. 4 (1988): 319–332.

Kogut, Bruce and Udo Zander. 'Knowledge of the Firm, Combinative Capabilities, and the Replication of Technology'. *Organization Science* 3, no. 3 (1992): 383–397.

Kohli, Atul. *State-Directed Development: Political Power and Industrialization in the Global Periphery.* New York: Cambridge University Press, 2004.

Korhonen, Heli, Reijo Luostarinen, and Lawrence Welch. 'Internationalization of SMEs: Inward–Outward Patterns and Government Policy'. *MIR: Management International Review* (1996): 315–329.

Kornai, J. 'Resource-constrained versus Demand-constrained Systems'. *Econometrica* 47, no. 4 (1979): 801–819.

Kotabe, Masaaki, Srini S. Srinivasan and Preet S. Aulakh. 'Multinationality and Firm Performance: The Moderating Role of Marketing and R&D Capabilities'. *Journal of International Business Studies* 33, no. 1 (2002): 79–97.

Kriauciunas, Aldas and Prashant Kale. 'The Impact of Socialist Imprinting and Search on Resource Change: A Study of Firms in Lithuania'. *Strategic Management Journal* 27, no. 7 (2006): 659–679.

Kumar, Nagesh and Aradhna Aggarwal. 'Liberalization, Outward Orientation and In-house R&D Activity of Multinational and Local Firms: A Quantitative Exploration for Indian Manufacturing'. *Research Policy* 34, no. 4 (2005): 441–460.

Kuzhiparambil, Asha. 'Skills Development Initiatives and Labour Migration in a Secondary Circuit of Globalized Production: Evidence from the Garment Industry in India. In *Mobilities of Labour and Capital in Asia*, edited by Preet S. Aulakh and Philip F. Kelly, 153–171. New York: Cambridge University Press, 2020.

La Porta, Rafael, Florencio Lopez-de-Silanes and Andrei Shleifer. 'Corporate Ownership Around the World'. *Journal of Finance* 54, no. 2 (1999): 471–517.

Lall, Sanjaya. 'Technological Capabilities and Industrialization'. *World Development* 20, no. 2 (1992): 165–186.

———. *The New Multinationals: The Spread of Third World Enterprises.* New York: Wiley, 1983.

Langlois, Richard N. 'Business Groups and the Natural State'. *Journal of Economic Behavior and Organization* 88 (1 April 2013): 14–26.

Lawrence, Thomas B. 'Institutional Strategy'. *Journal of Management* 25, no. 2 (1999): 161–187.

Lee, Keun. *Schumpeterian Analysis of Economic Catch-up: Knowledge, Path-Creation, and the Middle-Income Trap.* New York: Cambridge University Press, 2013.

———. *The Art of Economic Catch-up: Barriers, Detours and Leapfrogging in Innovation Systems.* Cambridge, UK: Cambridge University Press, 2019.

Lee, Keun and Franco Malerba. 'Economic Catch-Up by Latecomers as an Evolutionary Process'. In *Modern Evolutionary Economics: An Overview*, edited by Richard R. Nelson, et al., 172–207. New York and Cambridge, UK: Cambridge University Press, 2018.

Levinthal, Daniel A. and James G. March. 'The Myopia of Learning'. *Strategic Management Journal* 14, no. S2 (1993): 95–112.

Lichtenberg, Frank R. 'Pharmaceutical Price Discrimination and Social Welfare'. *Capitalism and Society* 5, no. 1 (2010): article 2. doi:10.2202/1932-0213.1066.

Lincoln, James R., Michael L. Gerlach and Christina L. Ahmadjian. 'Keiretsu Networks and Corporate Performance in Japan'. *American Sociological Review* 61, no. 1 (1996): 67–88.

Lohr, Steve. 'The Intellectual Property Debate Takes a Page from 19th-Century America'. *New York Times*, 14 October 2002, C.4.

Lu, S. and A. M. Dickson. 'Where Is China's Textile and Apparel Industry Going?' China Policy Institute, 2015.

Luo, Yadong, and Rosalie L. Tung. 'International Expansion of Emerging Market Enterprises: A Springboard Perspective'. *Journal of International Business Studies* 38, no. 4 (2007): 481–498.

Madhok, Anoop and Mohammad Keyhani. 'Acquisitions as Entrepreneurship: Asymmetries, Opportunities, and the Internationalization of Multinationals from Emerging Economies'. *Global Strategy Journal* 2, no. 1 (2012): 26–40.

Mahindra, A. G., T. A. Stewart and A. P. Raman. 'Finding a Higher Gear'. *Harvard Business Review* 86, no. 7/8 (2008): 68.

Mahmood, Ishtiaq P. and Will Mitchell. 'Two Faces: Effects of Business Groups on Innovation in Emerging Economies'. *Management Science* 50, no. 10 (2004): 1348–1365.

Mahmood, Syed Akhtar. 'In Bangladesh's Story of Remarkable Development, Key Role of Its Government Is Often Ignored'. *Dhaka Tribune*, 17 July 2001.

Mahoney, James and Kathleen Ann Thelen, eds. *Explaining Institutional Change: Ambiguity, Agency, and Power*. Cambridge, UK: Cambridge University Press, 2010.

Majumdar, Sumit K. 'Government Policies and Industrial Performance: An Institutional Analysis of the Indian Experience'. *Journal of Institutional and Theoretical Economics* 152, no. 2 (1996): 380–411.

Majumdar, Sumit K. and Arnab Bhattacharjee. 'Firms, Markets, and the State: Institutional Change and the Manufacturing Sector Profitability Variances in India'. *Organization Science* 25, no. 2 (2014): 509–528.

Malerba, Franco and Gary P. Pisano. 'Innovation, Competition and Sectoral Evolution: An Introduction to the Special Section on Industrial Dynamics'. *Industrial and Corporate Change* 28, no. 3 (2019): 503–510.

Malerba, Franco and Keun Lee. 'An Evolutionary Perspective on Economic Catch-up by Latecomers'. *Industrial and Corporate Change* 34, no. 4 (August 2021): 986–1010. Doi:10.1093/icc/dtab008.

Malerba, Franco and Richard Nelson. 'Learning and Catching Up in Different Sectoral Systems: Evidence from Six Industries'. *Industrial and Corporate Change* 20, no. 6 (2011): 1645–1675.

March, James G. 'Exploration and Exploitation in Organizational Learning'. *Organization Science* 2 (1991): 71–87.

March, James G. and Herbert A. Simon. *Organizations.* New York: Wiley, 1958.

Mathews, John A. 'Dragon Multinationals: New Players in 21st Century Globalization'. *Asia Pacific Journal of Management* 23, no. 1 (2006): 5–27.

Mazumdar, Mainak. *Performance of Pharmaceutical Companies in India: A Critical Analysis of Industry Structure, Firm Specific Resources, and Emerging Strategies.* Heidelberg: Physica-Verlag, 2013.

Mazzi, Caio Torres and Neil Foster-McGregor. 'Imported Intermediates, Technological Capabilities and Exports: Evidence from Brazilian Firm-level Data'. *Research Policy* 50, no. 1 (2021). https://doi.org/10.1016/j.respol.2020.104141.

McLaughlin, K., S. P. Osborne and E. Ferlie. *New Public Management: Current Trends and Future Prospects.* London: Routledge, 2002.

Meyer, Alan D., Geoffrey R. Brooks and James B. Goes. 'Environmental Jolts and Industry Revolutions: Organizational Responses to Discontinuous Change'. *Strategic Management Journal* 11 (Summer 1990): 93–110.

Meyer, Klaus. E. 'Perspectives on Multinational Enterprises in Emerging Economies'. *Journal of International Business Studies* 35 (2004): 259–276.

Mingo, Santiago and Tarun Khanna. 'Industrial Policy and the Creation of New Industries: Evidence from Brazil's Bioethanol Industry'. *Industrial and Corporate Change* 23, no. 5 (2013): 1229–1260.

Ministry of Statistics and Programme Implementation, Government of India. *Annual Survey of Industries, 1990–2019.* New Delhi: Government of India, 1990–2019. http://mospi.nic.in/annual-survey-industries. Accessed 1 July 2021.

Mitsumori, Yaeko. *The Indian Pharmaceutical Industry: Impact of Changes in the IPR Regime.* Singapore: Springer, 2018.

Moodysson, Jerker and Lionel Sack. 'Institutional Stability and Industry Renewal: Diverging Trajectories in the Cognac Beverage Cluster'. *Industry and Innovation* 23, no. 5 (2016): 448–464.

Mulkern, Anne C. 'Solyndra Bankruptcy Reveals Dark Clouds in Solar Power Industry'. *New York Times*, 6 September 2011.

Musacchio, Aldo and Sergio G. Lazzarini. 'Leviathan in Business: Varieties of State Capitalism and their Implications for Economic Performance'. Harvard Business School Working Paper, no. 12-108 (June 2012).

Musacchio, Aldo, Sergio G. Lazzarini and Ruth Aguilera. 'New Varieties of State Capitalism: Strategic and Governance Implications'. *Academy of Management Perspectives* 29, no. 1 (2015): 115–131.

Narayanan G., Badri. 'Questions on Textile Industry Competitiveness'. *Economic and Political Weekly* 40, no. 9 (26 February–4 March 2005): 905–907.

Nath, Pradosh, N. Mrinalini and G. D. Sandhya. 'National Textile Policy and Textile Research'. *Economic and Political Weekly* 36, no. 5/6 (3–16 February 2001): 489–496.

Nayyar, Deepak. *Catch Up: Developing Countries in the World Economy*. Oxford: Oxford University Press, 2013.

NCAER Report National Council of Applied Economic Research. 'Assessing the Prospects for India's Textile and Clothing Sector'. July 2009.

Nee, Victor. 'A Theory of Market Transition: From Redistribution to Markets in State Socialism'. *American Sociological Review* 54, no. 5 (1989): 663–681.

————. 'Organizational Dynamics and institutional Change: Politicized Capitalism in China'. In *The Economy Sociology of Capitalism*, edited by V. Nee and R. Swedberg, 53–74. Princeton, NJ: Princeton University Press, 2005.

————. 'Organizational Dynamics of Market Transition: Hybrid Forms, Property Rights, and Mixed Economy in China'. *Administrative Science Quarterly* 37, no. 1 (1992): 1–27.

————. 'The Emergence of a Market Society: Changing Mechanisms of Stratification in China'. *American Journal of Sociology* 101, no. 4 (1996): 908–949.

Nee, Victor and Sonja Opper. 'On Politicized Capitalism'. In *On Capitalism*, edited by V. Nee and R. Swedberg, 93–127. Palo Alto, CA: Stanford University Press, 2007.

Nelson, Richard R. *Technology, Institutions and Economic Growth*. Cambridge, MA: Harvard University Press, 2005.

————. 'What Enables Rapid Economic Progress: What Are the Needed Institutions?' *Research Policy* 37, no. 1 (2008): 1–11.

Nelson, Richard R. and Howard Pack. 'The Asian Miracle and Modern Growth Theory'. *Economic Journal* 109 (July 1999): 416–436.

Nelson, Richard R. and Sidney G. Winter. *An Evolutionary Theory of Economic Change*. Cambridge, MA: The Belknap Press of Harvard University Press, 1982.

New York Times. Editorial. 'India's Choice'. 18 January, 2005, A20.

Newman, Karen. 'Organizational Transformation During Institutional Upheaval'. *Academy of Management Review* 25, no. 3 (2000): 602–619.

North, Douglass C. *Institutions, Institutional Change and Economic Performance*. Cambridge, UK: Cambridge University Press, 1990.

Oberoi, Bindu. *The Textile Industry in India: Changing Trends and Employment Challenges*. New Delhi: Oxford University Press, 2016.

OECD. 'Emerging Multinationals: Who Are They? What Do They Do? What Is at Stake?' OECD, Paris, 2006.

Office of the Development Commissioner (Handlooms), Ministry of Textiles, Government of India. Handloom Census, First to Fourth. http://handlooms.nic. in. Accessed 18 May 2021.

Oliver, Christine. 'Sustainable Competitive Advantage: Combining Institutional and Resource-Based Views'. *Strategic Management Journal* 18, no. 9 (1997): 697–713.

———. 'Strategic Responses to Institutional Processes'. *Academy of Management Review* 16, no. 1 (1991): 145–179.

Oqubay, Arkeba. 'The Theory and Practice of Industrial Policy'. In *The Oxford Handbook of Industrial Policy*, edited by Arkebe Oqubay, Christopher Cramer, Ha-Joon Chang and Richard Kozul-Wright, 17 –65. Oxford: Oxford University Press, 2000.

Oqubay, Arkeba, Christopher Cramer, Ha-Joon Chang and Richard Kozul-Wright, eds. *The Oxford Handbook of Industrial Policy*. Oxford: Oxford University Press, 2000.

Ostry, Sylvia. 'The Uruguay Round North-South Grand Bargain: Implications for Future Negotiations'. In *The Political Economy of International Trade Law. Essays in Honor of Robert E. Hudec*, edited by Daniel L.M. Kennedy and James D. Southwick, 285–300. New York: Cambridge University Press, 2002.

Pache, Anne-Claire, and Felipe Santos. 'When Worlds Collide: The Internal Dynamics of Organizational Responses to Conflicting Institutional Demands'. *Academy of Management Journal* 35, no. 3 (2010): 455–476.

Pack, Howard and Kamal Saggi. 'Inflows of Foreign Technology and Indigenous Technological Development'. *Review of Development Economics* 1, no. 1 (1997): 81–98.

Pack, Howard and Larry E. Westphal. 'Industrial Strategy and Technological Change: Theory versus Reality'. *Journal of Development Economics* 22, no. 1 (1986): 87–128.

Papaioannou, Theo, Andrew Watkins, Julius Mugwagwa and Dinar Kale. 'To Lobby or to Partner? Investigating the Shifting Political Strategies of Biopharmaceutical Industry Associations in Innovation Systems of South Africa and India'. *World Development* 78 (February 2016): 66–79.

Peng, Mike. W. 'Institutional Transitions and Strategic Choices'. *Academy of Management Review* 28 (2003): 275–296.

———. 'Towards an Institution-based View of Business Strategy'. *Asia Pacific Journal of Management* 19, no. 2 (2002): 251–267.

Peng, Mike W., Denis Y. L. Wang, and Yi Jiang. 'An Institution-Based View of International Business Strategy: A Focus on Emerging Economies'. *Journal of International Business Studies* 39, no. 5 (2008): 920–936.

Penrose, Edith T. *The Theory of the Growth of the Firm*. New York: Wiley, 1959.

Pfeffer, Jeffrey and Gerald R. Salancik. *The External Control of Organizations: A Resource Dependence Perspective*. Stanford, CA: Stanford University Press, 2003.

Pingali, Vishwanath and Chirantan Chatterjee. 'Balancing Affordability in Drug Patent Regime'. *Economic and Political Weekly* 50, no. 41 (10 October 2015): 20–23.

Polanyi, Michael. *The Tacit Dimension*. London: Routledge Kegan Paul, 1966.

Ponte, Stefano, Gary Gereffi and Gale Raj-Reichert. Introduction to the *Handbook on Global Value Chains*. Cheltenham, UK: Edward Elgar Publishing, 2019. doi: https://doi.org/10.4337/9781788113779.00005. Accessed 30 July 2021.

Porter, Michael E. *Competitive Advantage: Creating and Sustaining Superior Performance*. New York: Free Press, 1985.

———. 'Industry Structure and Competitive Strategy: Keys to Profitability'. *Financial Analysts Journal* 36, no. 4 (1980): 30–41.

———. 'Location, Competition and Economic Development: Local Clusters in a Global Economy'. *Economic Development Quarterly* 14, no. 1 (2000): 15–34.

Powell, Walter W. 'Commentary—On the Nature of Institutional Embeddedness: Labels vs Explanation'. *Advances in Strategic Management* 13 (1996): 293–300.

Pradhan, Jaya Prakash. 'Indian Outward FDI: A Review of Recent Developments'. *Transnational Corporations* 24, no. 2 (2017): 43–70.

———. 'Liberalization, Firm Size and R&D Performance: A Firm-Level Study of Indian Pharmaceutical Industry'. *Journal of Indian School of Political Economy* 14, no. 4 (2003): 647–666.

———. 'The Determinants of Outward Foreign Direct Investment: A Firm-level Analysis of Indian Manufacturing'. *Oxford Development Studies* 32, no. 4 (2004): 619–639.

Pradhan, Jaya Prakash and Abhinav Alakshendra. 'Overseas Acquisitions versus Greenfield Foreign Investment: Which Internationalization Strategy Is Better for Indian Pharmaceutical Enterprises'. Institute for the Studies in Industrial Development, New Delhi ISID Working Paper 2006/07, August 2006.

Pradhan, Jaya Prakash and Karl P. Sauvant. 'Introduction: The Rise of Indian Multinational Enterprises: Revisiting Key Issues'. In *The Rise of Indian Multinationals: Perspectives on Indian Outward Foreign Direct Investment*, edited by Karl P. Sauvant and Jaya Prakash Pradhan with Ayesha Chatterjee and Brian Harley, 1–23. New York: Palgrave Macmillan, 2010.

Pradhan, Sarthak. 'India's Price Control Policy Has Destroyed Drug Manufacturers: This Is How It Can Be Saved'. *The Print*, 20 December 2019. https://theprint. in/opinion/indias-price-control-policy-has-destroyed-drug-manufacturers-this-is-how-they-can-be-saved/338095/. Accessed 22 July 2021.

Rachrela, Uday S. 'Historical Evolution of India's Patent Regime and Its Impact on Innovation in the Indian Pharmaceutical Industry'. In *Innovation, Economic*

Development and Intellectual Property in India and China: Comparing Six Economic Sectors, edited by Kung-Chung Liu and Uday S. Rachrela, 271–298. Singapore: Springer, 2019.

Ragavan, Srividhya. 'Of the Inequals of the Uruguay Round'. *Marquette Intellectual Property Law Review* 10, no. 2 (2006): 273–304.

Ramanna, Anitha. 'Policy Implications of India's Patent Reforms: Patent Applications in the Post-1995 Era'. *Economic and Political Weekly* 37, no. 21 (25–31 May 2002).

Ramaswamy, Kannan, K. Galen Kroeck and William Renforth. 'Measuring the Degree of Internationalization of a Firm: A Comment'. *Journal of International Business Studies* 27, no. 1 (1996): 167–177.

Rao, K. S. Chalapti and Biswajit Dhar. 'Inbound M&As in India: Issues and Challenges'. Working Paper 226, Institute for Studies in Industrial Development, New Delhi, July 2020.

Rasiah, Rajah, Zhang Miao, and Kong Xin Xin. 'Can China's Miraculous Economic Growth Continue?' *Journal of Contemporary Asia* 43, no. 2 (2013): 295–313.

Ray, Saon. 'What Explains India's Poor Performance in Garments Exports: Evidence from Five Clusters?' No. 376. ICRIER Working Paper, 2019.

Reichman, Jerome H. 'From Free Riders to Fair Followers: Global Competition under the TRIPS Agreement'. *New York University Journal of International Law and Politics* 29, no. 1/2 (1996): 11–94.

Reserve Bank of India, Government of India. *Handbook of Statistics on the Indian Economy*. Yearly volumes, 2001–2020. https://rbi.org.in. Accessed various times April–May 2021.

Rindova, Violina P. and Suresh Kotha 2001. 'Continuous "Morphing": Competing through Dynamic Capabilities, Form, and Function'. *Academy of Management Journal* 44, no. 6 (2001): 1263–1280.

Rodrick, Dani and Arvind Subramanian. 'From "Hindu Growth" to Productivity Surge: The Mystery of the Indian Growth Transition'. *IMF Staff Papers* 52, no. 2 (2005): 193–228.

Rosenkopf, Lori and Atul Nerkar. 'Beyond Local Search: Boundary Spanning, Exploration, and Impact in the Optical Disk Industry'. *Strategic Management Journal* 22, no. 4 (2001): 287–306.

Roy, Tirthankar. 'Development or Distortion? "Powerlooms" in India, 1950–1997'. *Economic and Political Weekly* 33, no. 16 (18–24 April 1998a): 897–911.

———. 'Economic Reforms and Textile Industry in India'. *Economic and Political Weekly* 33, no. 32 (8–14 August 1998b): 2173–2182.

Sahay, Arvind and Saini K. Gordhan. 'Hatch Waxman Act and the Indian Pharmaceutical Firms: An Analysis'. *Foreign Trade Review* 43, no. 2 (2008): 3–35.

Salomon, Robert. M. 'Spillovers to Foreign Market Participants: Assessing the Impact of Export Strategies on Innovative Productivity'. *Strategic Organization* 4, no. 2 (2006): 135–164.

Sapienza, Harry J., Erkko Autio, Gerard George and Shaker A. Zahra. 'A Capabilities Perspective on the Effects of Early Internationalization on Firm Survival and Growth'. *Academy of Management Review* 31, no. 4 (2006): 914–933.

Saranga, H. and Rajiv D. Banker. 'Productivity and Technical Changes in the Indian Pharmaceutical Industry'. *Journal of the Operational Research Society* 61, no. 12 (2010): 1777–1788.

Sauvant, Karl P. and Jaya Prakash Pradhan, with Ayesha Chaterjee and Brian Haley, eds. *The Rise of Indian Multinationals: Perspectives on Indian Outward Foreign Direct Investment.* New York: Palgrave Macmillan, 2020.

Schmalensee, Richard. 'Inter-industry Studies of Structure and Performance'. In *Handbook of Industrial Organization,* vol. 2, edited by Richard Schmalensee and Robert D. Willig, 951–1009. Amsterdam: North-Holland, 1989.

Scott, W. Richard. 'Conceptualizing Organizational Fields: Linking Organizations and Societal Systems'. In *Systemrationalitat und Partialinteresse [Systems Rationality and Partial Interests],* edited by Hans-U lrich Derlien, Uta Gerhardt and Fritz W. Scharpf, 203–221. Baden Baden, Germany: Nomos Verlagsgesellschaft, 1994.

———. *Institutions and Organizations: Ideas, Interests, and Identities.* Fourth Edition. Thousand Oaks, CA: Sage Publications, Inc., 2014.

Seric, Adnan, and Yee Siong Tong. 'What Are Global Value Chains and Why Do They Matter?' Industrial Analytics Platform, UNIDOI, September 2019. https://iap.unido.org/articles. Accessed 10 June 2021.

Shaver, J. Myles. 'Testing for Mediating Variables in Management Research: Concerns, Implications, and Alternative Strategies'. *Journal of Management* 31, no. 3 (2005): 330–353.

Simpson, Vern, and Sundar A. Shetty. *India's Textile and Apparel Industry: Growth Potential and Trade and Investment Opportunities.* Publication 3401. Washington, D.C.: Office of Industries, U.S. International Trade Commission, 2001.

Sine, Wesley D. and Robert J. David. 'Environmental Jolts, Institutional Change, and the Creation of Entrepreneurial Opportunity in the US Electric Power Industry'. *Research Policy* 32, no. 2 (2003): 185–207.

Sitkin, Sim B. and Amy L. Pablo. 'Reconceptualizing the Determinants of Risk Behavior'. *Academy of Management Review* 17, no. 1 (1992): 9–38.

Small Industries Development Bank of India (SIDBI). *Annual Report 2008–2009.* Lucknow: SIDBI, 2009.

Smeets, Maarten. 'Main Features of the Uruguay Round Agreement on Textiles and Clothing, and Implications for the Trading System'. *Journal of World Trade* 29, no. 5 (1995): 97–109.

Smith, Wendy K. and Michael L. Tushman. 'Managing Strategic Contradictions: A Top Management Model for Managing Innovation Streams'. *Organization Science* 16, no. 5 (2005): 522–536.

Sorensen, Jesper B. 'The Strength of Corporate Culture and the Reliability of Firm Performance'. *Administrative Science Quarterly* 47, no. 1 (2002): 70–91.

Spencer, Jennifer W. 'The Impact of Multinational Enterprise Strategy on Indigenous Enterprises: Horizontal Spillovers and Crowding out in Developing Countries'. *Academy of Management Review* 33, no. 2 (2008): 341–361.

Srinivasan, T. N. 'The TRIPS Agreement. Comment'. In *The Political Economy of International Trade Law. Essays in Honor of Robert E. Hudec*, edited by Daniel L. M. Kennedy and James D. Southwick, 343–348. New York: Cambridge University Press, 2002.

Srinivasulu, K. '1985 Textile Policy and Handloom Industry: Policy, Promises and Performance'. *Economic and Political Weekly* 31, no. 49 (7 December 1996): 3198–3206.

Stein, Howard. 'Industrial Policy, Institutional Transformation, and the Development of Industrial Parks'. In *The Oxford Handbook of Industrial Hubs and Economic Development*, edited by Arkebe Oqubay and Justin Yifu Lin, 98–114. New York: Oxford University Press, 2020.

Stein, Jeremy C. 'Efficient Capital Markets, Inefficient Firms: A Model of Myopic Corporate Behavior'. *Quarterly Journal of Economics* 104, no. 4 (1989): 655–669.

Sun, Qiang, Michael A. Santoro, Qingyue Meng, Caitlin Liu and Karen Eggleston. 'Pharmaceutical Policy in China'. *Health Affairs* 27, no. 4 (2008): 1042–1050.

Tallman, Stephen, Mark Jenkins, Nick Henry and Steven Pinch. 'Knowledge, Clusters, and Competitive Advantage'. *Academy of Management Review* 29, no. 2 (2004): 258–271.

Taubman, Antony, Hannu Wager and Jayshree Watal, eds. *A Handbook on the WTO TRIPS Agreement*. New York: Cambridge University Press, 2020.

Teece, David J., Gary Pisano and Amy Shuen. 'Dynamic Capabilities and Strategic Management'. *Strategic Management Journal* 18, no. 7 (1997): 509–533.

Ter Wal, Anne L.J., Oliver Alexy, Jörn Block and Philipp G. Sandner. 'The Best of Both Worlds: The Benefits of Open-Specialized and Closed-Diverse Syndication Networks for New Ventures' Success'. *Administrative Science Quarterly* 61, no. 3 (September 2016): 393–432.

Tewari, Meenu. 'Adjustment in India's Textile and Apparel Industry: Reworking Historical Legacies in a Post-MFA World'. *Environment and Planning A* 38, no. 12 (2006): 2325–2344.

————. 'Varieties of Global Integration: Navigating Institutional Legacies and Global Networks in India's Garment Industry'. *Competition and Change* 12, no. 1 (March 2008): 49–67.

The Economist. 'A Tangled Web'. 5 May 1990, 85.

————. 'Avoiding the Dinosaur Trap'. 19 May 2014.

————. 'Drugmakers: Convalescent.' 9 May 2020, 52–53.

————. 'Knotted'. 8 February 1997, 82–83.

————. 'Pharmaceuticals: In Need of a New Prescription'. 24 March 2018, 66–67.

————. 'Special Report: State Capitalism—The Visible Hand'. 21 January 2012, 1–18.

————. 'Special Report: The Looming Revolution—The Textile Industry'. 13 November 2004, 75–77.

Thornton, Patricia and William Ocasio. 'Institutional Logics and the Historical Contingency of Power in Organizations: Executive Succession in the Higher Education Publishing Industry, 1958–1990'. *American Journal of Sociology* 105, no. 3 (1999): 801–843.

Thornton, Patricia H. 'The Rise of the Corporation in a Craft industry: Conflict and Conformity in Institutional Logics'. *Academy of Management Journal* 45, no. 1 (2002): 81–101.

————. *Markets from Culture: Institutional Logics and Organizational Decisions in Higher Education Publishing.* Stanford: Stanford University Press, 2004.

Thornton, Patricia H. and William Ocasio. 'Institutional Logics'. In *The Sage Handbook of Organizational Institutionalism*, edited by Royston Greenwood, Christine Oliver, Roy Suddaby and K. Sahlin-Anderson, 99–129. London: Sage, 2008.

Thornton, Patricia H., William Ocasio and Michael Lounsbury. *The Institutional Logics Perspective: A New Approach to Culture, Structure and Process.* Oxford; New York: Oxford University Press, 2012.

Tsang, Eric W. K. 'The Knowledge Transfer and Learning Aspects of International HRM: An Empirical Study of Singapore MNCs'. *International Business Review* 8, nos. 5–6 (1999): 591–609.

Tushman, Michael and Philip Anderson. 'Technological Discontinuities and Organizational Environments'. *Administrative Science Quarterly* 31 (1 September 1986): 439–465.

Uhlenbruck, Klaus, Klaus E. Meyer and Michael A. Hitt. 'Organizational Transformation in Transition Economies: Resource-based and Organizational Learning Perspectives'. *Journal of Management Studies* 40, no. 2 (2003): 257–283.

United Nations Industrial Development Organization (UNIDO). 'The UNIDO Approach to Cluster Development: Key Principles and Project Experiences'. Technical Paper, Department of Digitalization, Technology and Innovation. Vienna, 2020.

Vogel, Ezra F. *Deng Xiaoping and the Transformation of China*, vol. 10. Cambridge, MA: Belknap Press of Harvard University Press, 2011.

Warwick, Ken. 'Beyond Industrial Policy: Emerging Issues and New Trends'. OECD Science, Technology and Industry Policy Papers, no.2. OECD Publishing, Paris, 2003. http://dx.doi.org/10.1787/5k4869clw0xp-en. Accessed 22 April 2021.

Watkins, Andrew, Theo Papaioannou, Julius Mugwagwa and Dinar Kale. 'National Innovation Systems and the Intermediary Role of Industry Associations in Building Institutional Capacities for Innovation in Developing Countries: A Critical Review of the Literature. *Research Policy* 44, no. 8 (2015): 1407–1418.

Wazir Advisors, India. 'Foreign Direct Investment Scenario in Indian Textile Sector'. Final Study Report Submitted to the Ministry of Textiles, Government of India, July 2016.

Weiss, John. 'Taxonomy of Industrial Policy'. Research, Statistics and Industrial Policy Branch Working Paper 8/2015. United Nations Industrial Development Organization, Vienna, 2015.

Weiss, John and Adnan Seric. 'Industrial Policy: Clarifying Options through Taxonomy and Decision Trees'. *Development Policy Review*, 2020. https://doi.org/10.1111/dpr.12522.

Wells, Louis T. *Third World Multinationals*. Cambridge, MA: MIT Press, 1983.

Wernerfelt, Birger. 'A Resource-Based View of the Firm'. *Strategic Management Journal* 5, no. 2 (1984): 171–180.

White, Halbert. 'A Heteroskedasticity-consistent Covariance Matrix Estimator and a Direct Test for Heteroskedasticity'. *Econometrica: Journal of the Econometric Society* (1 May 1980): 817–838.

Whitley, Richard. *Divergent Capitalisms: The Social Structuring and Change in Business systems*. Oxford: Oxford University Press, 1999.

Witt, Michael A., Luiz Ricardo Kabbach de Castro, Kenneth Amaeshi, Sami Mahroum, Dorothee Bohle and Lawrence Saez. 'Mapping the Business Systems of 61 Major Economies: A Taxonomy and Implications for Varieties of Capitalism and Business Systems Research'. *Socio-Economic Review* 16, no. 1 (2018): 5–38.

World Intellectual Property Protection, WIPO IP Statistics Data Center, Patents. 'Patent Applications for the Top Twenty Offices'. https://www3.wipo.int/ipstats/keysearch.htm?keyId=221. Accessed 18 April 2021.

World Trade Organization. 'Agreement on Textiles and Clothing, 1995'. 1995a. www.wto.org. Accessed 17 April 2021.

———. 'Agreement on Trade-Related Aspects of Intellectual Property Rights. 1995'. 1995b. www.wto.org. Accessed 17 April 2021.

———.'Overview: The TRIPS Agreement, 1995'. 1995c. www.wto.org. Accessed 17 April 2021.

————. 'International Trade Statistics'. 1990–2018. https://stats.wto.org/. Accessed 15 April 2021.

Yiu, Daphne W., Yuan Lu, Garry D. Bruton and Robert E. Hoskisson. 'Business Groups: An Integrated Model to Focus Future Research'. *Journal of Management Studies* 44, no. 8 (2007): 1551–1579.

Yoffie, David B. 'Textiles and the Multi-Fiber Arrangement'. Harvard Business School Case, 9-383-164 (1990).

Young, Stephen, Chun-Hua Huang and Michael McDermott. 'Internationalization and Competitive Catch-up Processes: Case Study Evidence on Chinese Multinational Enterprises'. *MIR: Management International Review* 36, no. 4 (1996): 295–314.

Zahra, Shaker A., R. Duane Ireland and Michael A. Hitt. 'International Expansion by New Venture Firms: International Diversity, Mode of Market entry, Technological Learning, and Performance'. *Academy of Management Journal* 43, no. 5 (2000): 925–950.

Zahra, Shaker A., R. Duane Ireland, Isabel Gutierrez, I. and Michael A. Hitt. 'Privatization and Entrepreneurial Transformation: Emerging Issues and Future Research Agenda'. *Academy of Management Review* 25, no. 3 (2000): 509–524.

Zhang, Miao, Xin Xin Kong and Santha Chanayah Ramu. 'The Transformation of the Clothing Industry in China'. *Asia Pacific Business Review* 22, no. 1 (2016): 86–109.

Zhang, Yansheng, Darwei Li, Changyong Yang and Qiong Du. 'On the Value Chain and International Specialization of China's Pharmaceutical Industry'. *Journal International Commerce and Economics* 3 (2011): 81–108.

Zollo, Mario and Sidney G. Winter. 'Deliberate Learning and the Evolution of Dynamic Capabilities'. *Organization Science* 13, no. 3 (2002): 339–353.

Zukin, Sharon and Paul DiMaggio. 'Introduction'. In *Structures of Capital: The Social Organization of the Economy*, edited by S. Zukin and P. DiMaggio, 1-56. Cambridge, UK: Cambridge University Press, 1990.

Index

abbreviated new drug applications (ANDAs), 107
accumulation, concept of, 20–21, 24, 126
acquisitions
    mergers and, 57, 83, 91, 164, 168
    overseas acquisitions, by Indian firms, 85
    pharmaceutical industry, in, 82, 83, 86, 112*n*12, 168
    textile industry, in, 83, 87
active pharmaceutical ingredients (APIs), 173
    production of, 76
affordable drugs, 15, 29, 168
    accessibility of, 110
    availability of, 39, 166, 176
    available to the local healthcare sector, 178
    domestic demand for, 70
    goal of accessibility of, 110
    supply of, 162
    welfare goals of providing, 12
Agreement on Textiles and Clothing (ATC), 1, 4, 46, 48–54, 62, 74, 163
Annual Survey of Industries, 88, 90, 99, 112*n*14
apparel industry, 27, 94, 114, 137
apparel production, 53, 95
apparel retailers, in India, 182
asset augmentation, 35*n*3, 147
assimilation, concept of, 20–22, 24
automobile industry of India, 37*n*11

balance-of-payments crisis, 45, 80, 83
balance of trade, 8, 57, 70
bank loans, 120, 134
bilateral free trade agreement, 180
Bissell, John, 182
Bissell, William, 183
brownfield investments, 83, 87
bulk drugs, 58
    balance of trade in, 57
    cost disadvantage in manufacturing vis-à-vis China, 77
    exports and imports of, 76
    imports from China, 77
    manufacturing of, 76
    production of, 40, 76
    supply chain, 77
    trade deficit, 77
    used as raw materials for formulations, 77
business groups (BGs), 117, 128–129, 150
    affiliation with
        Indian firms, 135
        pharmaceutical industry, 167
        textile industry, 167
    in developing economies, 188*n*11
    firms affiliated with, 129
    moderating effect of, 144–145

capability development, resources for, 5
capabilities

marketing, 76, 83, 109, 123, 132, 134, 141, 143, 146, 167
R&D, 87, 123, 143, 167, 171
capital markets, in India, 117
capital subsidy, 55
  credit-linked, 54
  for technology modernisation, 56
  on various iterations of TUFS, 56
catch-up, 61
  country, 9, 20
  defined, 19
  of developing economy firms, 9, 118, 170–174, 184
  development model, 7, 51
  economic, 9
  firms, 5, 8, 170, 171
  goals, 170
  in Indian pharmaceutical industry, 173, 184
  in Indian textile industry, 173
  processes, 19
  strategic renewal and, 19–20
Centre for Monitoring of Indian Economy (CMIE), 11
  classification of firms into specific BGs, 135
  Prowess Database, 11, 15n9, 88, 132, 136
China
  export performance vis-à-vis India, 184
  pharmaceutical industry of. See pharmaceutical industry of China
  rise as 'the world's factory', 177
  textile industry of, 177, 182
cloth production, in India, 96, 98, 101–102
  decline of, 104
  segment-wise, 99
communist economies, in Eastern Europe, 32
competing logics. See also institutional logics, concept of
  accommodation of, 169, 175
  industry-level, 30
  in institutional system, 174–176

organisation-level, 28–29
state-level, 29–30
competition, in textile sector, 100
Comprehensive Handloom Cluster Development Scheme (CHCDS), 131
Confederation of India Textile Industries (CITI), 134
constraints
  embeddedness, 23, 27–28, 34
  organisational, 22–24
  resource, 17, 23, 163, 175
cotton textile export growth, 74–75
country pathways, in coping with global institutional change, 183–185
credit-linked capital subsidy, 54
cross-border interfirm alliances, proliferation of, 187n6

debt-to-equity ratio, 136
decentralised production, in the textile industry, 101
de-licensing of industrial investments, 45
Deng, Xiaoping, 177–178
developed economies
  comparison with East Asian economies, 170
  innovation capability in, 134
developing economies, 2, 9, 31, 117
  benefits of cluster formation in, 130
  business groups (BGs) in, 188n11
  characteristic of, 180
  deployment of capabilities by, 25
  differences in state capitalisms across, 32
  economic liberalisation in, 28
  economic reforms of, 16
  innovation in the context of, 126
  internationalisation of, 18, 125
  liberalisation programmes of, 16
  market economies of, 29
  mechanism for catch-up in, 21
  models of organisational change, 18
  national innovation system in, 25
  organisational transformation in, 22

resource and embeddedness constraints of, 28
south–south FDI, 85
structural separation in, 32
underdevelopment of factor markets in, 36n4
developing economy firms, institutional system and catch-up of, 170–174
division of labour, 34
domestic industrial growth, 27
drug-delivery systems, 52, 107
drug formulations, 76
  essentiality of, 58
  exports and imports of, 76, 78
  of generic drugs, 76
  'market-based' pricing of, 58
  price regulations applied to, 58
drug master files (DMFs), 107
drug price
  affordability for domestic consumers, 62
  control system, 43, 45
  cost-based pricing, 58
  for domestic market, 58
  drug policy of
    1978, 64n2
    1994, 58
  Drug Price Control Order (DPCO) of 1970, 40
  regulation of, 58

East Asian economies, 170
economic and social welfare, 14
'economic criteria/market share' principle, 58
economic efficiency, 11, 29, 61, 175
economic growth
  export-led, 7, 24
  import substitution industrialisation and, 39
  private enterprises as engines of, 32
  South Korean model of, 32
  state-directed development, 39
economic liberalisation, 38, 66, 78, 80, 114

in developing economies, 28
economy-wide, 89
impact on
  pharmaceutical industry, 43
  textile industry, 44–45
inception of, 68
of India, 4, 6, 12, 43–45, 71
institutional resources and, 118–119
post-ATC trade regime, 94
Economic Survey of India, 181, 182
economies of scale, 8, 76, 130, 169, 180–183, 188n8, 189n16
emerging economies, 8, 85
  internationalisation process of firms from, 125
  technological development in, 122
emerging market multinational corporations (EMNCs), 85, 87
employment
  balance with technology upgrading, 57
  generation and innovation, 12
  opportunities in the textile sector, 56
  in the pharmaceutical industry, 181
  subsidy linked with, 56
  in the textile industry, 53, 98
employment-intensive industries, 66
equity flows, in India's drugs and pharmaceutical sector, 83
equity joint ventures, 37n11, 85
evolutionary
  economics, 13, 21, 68
  perspective, 25
  processes, 4, 20, 35, 170
  theory, 17
explicit knowledge, codification of, 20
export intensity, 114–115, 132–133, 135, 137, 146, 160n1
export-led economic development model, of India, 7
export-led growth, 8, 12, 44–45, 51, 61, 68, 80
export promotion capital goods (EPCG), 119

fabric industry, 137
fabric production, 53
factor markets, underdevelopment of, 36n4
financial performance, measures of, 96
firms
    affiliated with BGs, 129, 144–148
    capability failure, 23
    'closed networks' firms, 132
    economies of scale, 180–183
    effect of technological shifts on, 19
    evolutionary theory of, 17
    export intensity of, 132–133
    foreign sales intensity of, 133
    global institutional change, 24
    internationalisation process of, 125
    investments in
        innovation capabilities, 134
        technology upgrading, 21
    large number of small firms versus small number of large firms, 180–183
    path-dependent adaptations, 19
    profitability of, 136
    scale effects, 148–150
    size of, 136
    Western models of international expansion, 22
Five-Year Plan
    Eighth Five-Year Plan (1992–1997), 66
    Ninth Five-Year Plan (1997–2002), 66, 70, 80, 87, 104
    Tenth Five-Year Plan (2002–2007), 70, 87
    Twelfth Five-Year Plan (2012–2017), 27
fixed capital, in the textile industry, 89, 91
food security, 30
foreign direct investment (FDI), 39, 57, 64n4, 109, 118, 133, 171, 177
    balance of payment benefits of, 83
    brownfield investments, 83, 87
    'crowding out' effect, 83
    greenfield investment, 83–84, 87
    impact on India's economic development, 80

    in India, 82
    inward investment, 81–84, 171
    mode of, 84
    outward investment, 84–87, 171
    overseas investment, 85
    relation with economic growth in developing countries, 84
    south–south, 85
    by Third-World multinationals, 85
foreign exchange
    crisis, 68
    reserves, of India, 12, 39, 44
foreign regulatory bodies, manufacturing standards of, 91
foreign sales intensity, determinants of
    investments in manufacturing, R&D and marketing, 140–141
    mediation effect of inward internationalisation, 141–144
    moderating effects of
        firms' business group affiliation, 144–148
        location in a geographic cluster, 144–148
foreign technology
    import of, 122
    transfer of, 21
foreign trade policies, 66
forum-shopping, 46
frame bending, 17

garment industry, 54–56, 73–75, 108, 130, 182
General Agreement on Tariffs and Trade (GATT), 1, 14n1, 42, 45
generic drugs
    formulations of, 76
    manufacture of, 78
geographical diversification, of India's pharmaceutical and textile exports, 79–80
geographic clusters, 129–132
    'closed networks' firms, 132

Comprehensive Handloom Cluster
    Development Scheme (CHCDS),
    131
determinants of foreign sales intensity
    in, 144–148
developed through private–public
    partnerships, 130
industrial parks, 130
influence on firms' ability to
    successfully respond to global
    institutional change, 185
location in, 135, 144–148
textile clusters in India, 135
global champions, promotion of, 59
global commodity chains (GCC),
    188n12
global institutional changes (1995–
    2005), 1
Agreement on Textiles and Clothing
    (ATC), 48–54
preparation for, 45–54
TRIPS Agreement, 46–47
globalisation of markets, 8
global production networks (GPNs), 30,
    174, 180, 184–185, 188n12
Global South, 42
global trade, in textiles, 1–2
Global Value Chains (GVCs), 68, 109,
    179–180, 184, 188n12
participation in, 183–185
government incentives and subsidies, as
    institutional resources, 119–120
Government of India, 118, 153, 181
Annual Report, 12, 15, 55, 101
Department of Pharmaceuticals,
    15n5, 50–52, 58–59, 162
economic liberalisation policies, 127
Five-Year Plan. See Five-Year Plan
'industrial parks' schemes, 130
Ministry of Commerce and Industry, 57
Ministry of Statistics, 88
Ministry of Textiles, 55–56, 102,
    188n10

Annual Reports on the power loom,
    101
Comprehensive Handloom
    Cluster Development Scheme
    (CHCDS), 131
Powerloom Cluster Development
    Scheme, 130
National Textile Policy (NTxP-2000),
    52–55
setting up of public sector organisation,
    183
TUFS subsidy, 134
government support incentives, effects
    of, 96
greenfield investment, 83–84, 87
gross domestic product (GDP), 30, 55

Handloom (Reservation of Articles for
    Production) Act of 1985, 44
Handloom Census, 102, 112n14
handloom industry, 41, 53–54, 75
Comprehensive Handloom Cluster
    Development Scheme (CHCDS),
    131
development of handloom clusters, 131
liquidation of, 64n5
per capita/per unit production, 103
production and employment in, 102
share in India's total cloth production,
    104
Hatch-Waxman Act (1984), US, 41
high-valued goods, production of, 59
Hindustan Antibiotics Limited, 39
human capital, 20–21, 68, 129
investments in, 170

import intensity of firms, 135–136,
    141–143, 145–146, 151, 167
import licensing, 45, 118
import-substitution industrialisation
    (1947–1985), 12
and Licence Raj (1947–1985), 39–42
model for economic growth, 39

of pharmaceutical industry, 39–41
self-sufficiency of, 43
of textile industry, 41–42
index of industrial production, 94–96
Indian Companies Act, 136
Indian Drugs and Pharmaceuticals Limited, 39
Indian firms, acquisitions by foreign multinationals, 83
indigenous Indian firms, competitiveness of, 57–58
indigenous new drug-delivery system, process patents for, 52
industrial clusters, 160n7
industrial licensing, 45, 51, 118
industrially advanced countries, 21
industrial parks, 130, 160n7, 166, 171
industrial policy, frameworks of, 61
industrial production, 55
  index of, 94–96
industrial zones, 160n7
industry classification, of drugs and pharmaceuticals, 132
industry-specific subsidy programmes, 119
industry value-chain upgradation, 12
information technology (IT), 119, 121, 126
innovation
  in context of developing economy firms, 126
  in developed economies, 134
  firm-level, 25
  national systems for, 25
institutional change
  first- and second-order organisational change, 17–19
  frame bending, 17
  and pathways to organisational transformation, 17–22
institutional complexity
  framework of, 28
  levels of, 26–27, 28
institutional logics, concept of, 26–27

institutional resources, 116
  act of internationalisation, 125–128
  firms' strategies based on, 115–118
  government incentives and subsidies as, 119–120
  inward internationalisation, 126
  through regulatory reforms and trade liberalisation, 118–119
institutional system
  managing competing logics in, 174–176
  national, 11, 24–25, 28, 34, 117, 163, 171, 175, 176, 179, 186
Institutional theory, 13, 17, 36, 115, 116
institutions
  economic, 25
  field-level, 27, 32–34
  formal, 111
  global, 186
  hierarchically ordered, 26
  informal, 36
  international, 61
  market-supporting, 26, 36
  national-level institution, state as a, 26, 177
  supra-firm, 36, 132, 167
  supra-national, 16, 186
  quasi, 36
Integrated Skill Development Scheme (ISDS), 56
intellectual property protection, 25, 46–47, 50, 105
  in pharmaceutical sector, 2
intellectual property rights (IPR), 46, 57, 172
  post-2005 product-patent-centred, 59
inter-connected enterprises, geographical concentrations of, 129
interest subsidies, on loans, 96
inter-firm relationships, 116
international expansion, Western models of, 125

international investments, 80–87
  balance of payment deficits, 80
internationalisation
  of developing economic firms, 11, 18
  of emerging market firms, 35
  inward, 126, 135–136, 152
  outward, 126
  process, 9, 22
  product-market, 21–22, 123, 132
  of resources, 122
International Monetary Fund (IMF), 16
international technology, 127, 141
international trade
  export-led growth, 68
  geographical diversification, impact of,
    79–80
  governance of, 1
  industry-level trade, 69–73
  and investment, 87
  overall country-level trade, 68–69
  segment-wise exports and imports,
    73–78
  textile and pharmaceutical industries,
    69–73
inter-organisational relationships, 33
inter-sector competition, 54
intra-organisational power dynamics, 33
investments
  in assets and capabilities, 87–92
    for Indian firms, 134
    manufacturing asset intensity,
      133–134, 140–141
    marketing intensity, 134–135,
      140–141
    moderating variables, 135
  location in a geographic cluster, 135
  in marketing capabilities, 167
  in physical and human capital, 170
  in plants and machinery, 123
  in research and development (R&D),
    123, 134, 140–141
inward internationalisation, mediation
    effect of, 141–144

isomorphism
  organisational, 167
  sector-level, 164

joint ventures, 37n11, 85–87, 108, 116,
    179

keiretsus, in Japan, 128, 129
knitted garments, manufacture of, 130
know-how transfer, 12, 54, 126, 141
knowledge-based resources, 19
  acquisition of, 122
knowledge sharing, 130

labour productivity, 99, 169
labour unions, logics of, 27
learning
  accumulative, 20–22
  assimilative, 20–22
  by doing, 18, 21, 68, 125–126
Licence Raj (1947–1985), 39
  abolition of licensing requirements for
    all bulk drugs, 43
  end of, 44
loans sanctioned, in the textile sector
    under TUFS, 89

man-made fibres, production of, 53, 73
man-made textiles, exports of, 73, 74–75
manufacturing assets, intensity of,
    133–134
marginalised groups, employment of, 4
marketing intensity, of firms, 134–135
medical devices, production of, 59
merger and acquisition
  of foreign firms, 85
  of local firms, 83
micro, small and medium enterprises
    (MSMEs), 148
Multi-Fibre Agreement (MFA), 1, 42,
    48, 87
multilateral trading system, 2

multinational corporations (MNCs), 2, 31, 39, 41, 49, 57–59, 78, 80, 83–86, 107–109, 113, 165, 169, 173, 176, 184–185, 187
Murthy, N. R. Narayana, 119

National Cooperative Development Corporation, 183
national innovation system (NIS), 25, 36n7
National Institutional System, 24–27, 117
  industry-level competing logics, 30
  managing competing logics in, 31–35
  organisational-level competing logics, 28–29
  overcoming resource and embeddedness constraints in, 27–30
  state-level competing logics, 29–30
National List of Essential Medicines, 58
national patent, enforcement of, 2, 105, 107
National Pharmaceutical Pricing Policy of 2012 (NPPP-2012), 58–59, 168
National Skill Qualification Framework, 56
National Textile Policy (NTxP-2000), 52–55
Nehru, Jawaharlal, 39
neoclassical economics, 20, 68
network resources
  business groups (BGs), 128–129
  geographic clusters, 129–132
  significance of, 128
networks
  closed, 128, 132, 148
  open, 132, 148
new chemical entity (NCE), 105
new drug discovery, 104, 107, 173, 176
North–South grand bargain, 2
North–South production networks, 185

off-patent branded drugs, 76
organic-inorganic mechanisms, for growth, 175
organisational capabilities, upgrading of, 120–125
organisational change
  first-order, 17–19
  second-order, 17–19, 22–24, 28, 30, 34
organisational constraints, notion of, 22–24
organisational resources and capabilities, 121
Organisation for Economic Co-operation and Development (OECD), 67
organisation-state interactions, 167
organised sector, of the textile industry, 99
organizations in social systems, 26
original brand name manufacturing (OBM), 173
original design manufacturing (ODM), 173
original equipment manufacturing (OEM), 173
ownership advantages, 125
Ownership-Location-Internalisation (O-L-I) paradigm, 125

patentable drugs, discovery of, 91
patented drugs, 78
  copying of, 49
  export of, 50
  manufacturing and selling of knock-offs of, 47, 114
patents, 105–106
  based on minor modifications, 50
  grant of, 40
  India-origin pharmaceutical patents granted by foreign patent offices, 106
  for indigenous new drug-delivery system, 52
  NCE patents, 107

Patents Act of 1970, 40, 47, 49, 113
Patents Amendment Act of 2002, 106
Patents Amendment Act of 2005, 49
pharmaceutical patents filed and
    granted in India, 105
'process patenting' for inventions, 40, 49
    legal sanctions to, 40
proposals of uniform patent laws, 46
protection for pharmaceutical
    products, 47
TRIPS agreement, 106
US Patent Office, 107
pharmaceutical industry of Brazil, 180
pharmaceutical industry of China
R&D intensity in, 179
traditional medical products, 178
Western-type chemical pharmaceutical
    products, 178
pharmaceutical industry of India, 2–3,
    29, 38, 40, 67, 148
abolition of licensing requirements for
    all bulk drugs, 43
accessibility to drugs necessary for
    public health, 49
Agreement on Textiles and Clothing
    (ATC), 49–52
competitiveness of, 54, 57–58, 104
contribution to societal health, 3
control of drug prices, 40
coping with global institutional change
    (2005–2020), 57–59
dependence on foreign technology and
    know-how, 43
Drug Price Control Order (DPCO) of
    1970, 40
effect of BG affiliation in, 167
employment capacity of, 181
equity flows in, 83
evolution of, 3
fixed capital and number of factories, 90
foreign investments in, 43
global participation of, 76–77
global position of, 6–7

growth of
    compounded annual growth rate
        (CAGR), 41
    private firms, 40
    rate of, 71, 72
impact of economic liberalisation on, 43
import of bulk drugs by multinational
    corporations, 41
imports and exports of, 3
import-substitution industrialisation
    of, 39–41
index of industrial production, 96
industrial policy framework for, 63
industry-level trade, 69–73
innovation performance outcomes in,
    104–107
intellectual property protection in, 2
international property protection, 13
inward foreign direct investments in, 82
knowledge-based competition, 9
legal sanctions to process patents for
    pharmaceutical products, 40
manufacturing of drugs, 76
mode of FDI in, 84
National Pharmaceutical Pricing
    Policy of 2012 (NPPP-2012), 58
patent-protection regime, 3
and Patents Act of 1970, 113
performance outcomes of, 93–107
policy choices in, 60
in post-2005 period, 57
in post-TRIPS period, 3
price controls of drugs, 3
product diversification of, 59
product-innovation-based, 3
product patenting, 87
profitability in, 97
public sector investment in, 70
R&D expenditures in, 90
responses to global change, 163–170
'reverse engineering' to produce drugs,
    40
sales turnover in R&D, 104

scale effect for international firms in, 148–150

segment-wise exports and imports in, 73–78

self-reliance in drug manufacturing, 41

social goals of, 50

transformation in, 113

TRIPS agreement for, 47, 49

value-added share of, 93

Pharmaceutical Technology Upgradation Assistance Scheme (PTUAS), 59

pharmacy of the world, India 68

plants and machinery, upgrading of, 99

policy
framework, 12, 38, 61–63
domain, 61, 62
instruments, 11, 14, 25, 63, 180
orientation, 61–63

power looms, 54, 75, 101
decentralisation of power loom sector, 101–102
Ministry of Textiles
Annual Reports, 101
Powerloom Cluster Development Scheme, 130

price controls of drugs, 3, 78

Price Control Order of 1979, 64n2, 65n10

private enterprises, as engines of economic growth, 32

private-label manufacturing, 18

process-engineering capabilities, 117

product development, 178, 186

product diversification, 180
importance of, 79
of Indian pharmaceutical sector, 59

product innovation, 3, 29, 52, 54, 173, 176

production technology, 89
modernisation of, 88

productive employment, 52

product-market internationalisation, 21–22, 122–123, 132, 141, 152, 165, 167, 172

product patenting, 87

product-related knowledge, 22, 125

prophylactic medicines, 43

public policy implications, 176–186
in coping with global institutional change, 177–180
dilemmas of
economies of scale, 180–183
institutional resources, trade policies and capability development, 185–186
participation in global value chains, 183–185

public–private partnerships, 59, 171
for development of geographical clusters, 130

public sector enterprises, 15n9, 39, 132

public sector investment, in the pharmaceutical industry, 70

public sector units (PSUs), 39

quota system
abolition for Bangladesh, 180
in trade of global textile and apparel industry, 114, 163, 169

ready-made garments, 6, 73–75, 108, 182
export of, 74

redistributive economies, institutional logic of, 29

research and development (R&D), 59, 62, 88, 118, 150, 165
attitude towards innovation, 87
in China, 179
expenditures in India's pharmaceuticals industry, 90, 104
expenses in, 125
importance of, 150
intensity, 134, 140–141
investments in, 123
public, 40
textile industry, 91

Reserve Bank of India (RBI), 67, 94

resource allocation, 29, 34, 163
resource-based view (RBV), 120, 160n5
resource constraint, 17, 23, 163, 175
resource dependencies, 33, 167
resources
  and capabilities, 7, 9, 13, 18, 19, 23,
    85, 113, 121, 144
  institutional, 25, 36, 109–110,
    116–119, 128, 144, 147, 152,
    166–168, 171, 185–186
  international, 12–13, 30, 125–128,
    132, 136, 143, 152–153,
    166–167, 171–172
  knowledge-based, 19, 122
  national, 45, 59
  network, 13, 110, 128, 131, 132, 152,
    166, 172
  renewal of, 19, 23
return on assets (ROA), 96–97
reverse engineering, 127
  for production of drugs, 40, 49
reverse transfer, 126

scale economies, 6, 118, 150, 152, 179,
    181–183
  creation of, 182
scale effect for international firms,
    in pharmaceutical and textile
    industries, 148–150
Scheme for Capacity Building in Textile
    Sector (SAMARTH), 56
Scheme for Integrated Textile Parks
    (SITP), 56
search
  behaviour, 22, 31
  distant, 18, 21–22, 28–29, 34, 129,
    176
  exploratory, 19, 23, 33, 117–118, 163,
    165
  local, 18, 22, 34
  proximate, 28, 117
shareholders' equity, 136
skill-development initiatives, 56

skilled workforce, in textile industry, 56
small and medium enterprises (SMEs),
    59, 130, 148
small-scale industry, 54
social welfare, 14, 49, 54, 61–62, 168, 175
societal welfare, 61
solar panel industry, 117
South–South
  FDI, 85
  networks, 173
  production networks, 185
special economic zones (SEZs), 119
state capitalism
  in terms of government ownership, 32
  types of, 32
state-directed development, for
    economic growth, 39
state-industry interactions, for managing
    competing logics, 175
state-owned enterprises (SOEs), 64n4
  importance of, 32
state-owned organisations, 29
strategic importance of the industry, 24,
    38, 41, 72, 121, 123, 160n2
strategic renewal and catch-up, notion
    of, 19–20
subsidies
  on taxes and borrowings, 96
  to textile firms, 166
supra-organisational networks, 185

Tamil Nadu Handloom Weavers'
    Cooperative Society Ltd, 183
technological and market disruptions, 122
technological development, in emerging
    economies, 122
technological knowledge, 9, 21
technological learning, process of,
    20–21, 61
technology-oriented industries, 105
technology parks, 119, 161n9
technology upgrading
  investments in, 21

projects, 120
Technology Upgradation Funds
    Scheme (TUFS), 53, 55–56, 88,
    114, 120, 134, 137, 148, 166
    Amended TUFS (ATUFS), 65n11
    loans under. See TUFS loans
    Revised Restructured TUFS (RR-
    TUFS), 65n11
Tenth Five-Year Plan (2002–2007), 70
textile clusters, in India, 144
    Ludhiana, Punjab, 135
    Tiruppur, Tamil Nadu, 135
textile-exporting developing countries, 55
textile industry of Bangladesh, 55, 114,
    177, 179–180
textile industry of China, 55, 114
textile industry of India, 3, 38
    Agreement on Textiles and Clothing
        (ATC), 52–54
    competition from English machine-
        made textiles, 41
    competitiveness of, 54, 104
    coping with global institutional change
        (2005–2020), 55–57
    cotton sector, 64n3
    decentralised production in, 101
    deregulation of, 45
    economic history of, 42
    employment in, 53, 56, 98
    evolution of, 67
    exports and imports of, 69
    fabric production, 53
    fixed capital and number of factories, 88
    fragmented nature of, 137
    global competitiveness of, 45
    handloom industry, 41
    impact of economic liberalisation on,
        44–45
    import-substitution industrialisation
        of, 41–42
    index of industrial production, 94, 95, 96
    industrial policy framework for, 63
    industry-level trade in, 69–73

investments in plant and machinery,
    R&D and marketing, 92
inward foreign direct investments in, 82
lines of credit, 44
mediating effects of imports, 144
modernisation of, 54
Multi-Fibre Agreement (MFA), 42
National Textile Policy (NTxP-2000),
    52–55
organised sector of, 99–100
performance outcomes of, 93–107
policy changes of the mid-1980s, 44
policy to protect the handloom sector,
    42
post-2005 period, 57
post-quota regime of, 3–4
power loom sector, 44, 75, 98, 101,
    104, 175
profitability of, 97, 137
rate of growth of, 72
reforms by storm, 45
reliance on foreign technologies, 44
responses to global change, 163–170
scale effect for international firms in,
    148–150
segment analysis of, 150–151
segment-wise exports and imports in,
    73–78
segment-wise production in, 98
skilled workforce in, 56
structural transformation during
    British colonial rule, 42
structure of, 52
Technology Upgradation Funds
    Scheme (TUFS), 53
technology upgrading of, 52, 54
Textile Policy of 1985, 44
underperformance of, 95
unorganised handloom sector, 41
unorganised sector of, 101–104
value-added share of, 93
during World War I, 41
textile industry of Vietnam, 180

textile production, 95
  stages of, 52
Textile Workers' Rehabilitation Fund, 54
Third-World multinationals, 85, 87
trade barriers
  and investment restrictions, 33
  lowering of, 8
trade flows, in goods and services, 71
trademarks, 14n2, 18, 46
Trade Related Intellectual Property
    Rights (TRIPS), 1–2, 46, 91,
    113, 164, 179
  adoption of, 6
  global institutional change related to, 71
  implementation of, 4, 64n7, 76
  requirements of, 50
  Uruguay Round of international trade
    negotiations, 46
TUFS loans, 120, 134, 168
  disbursements of, 89, 99
  for technology upgrading, 100

unitary-versus-pluralistic political
    system, 32
United Nations Conference on Trade
    and Development (UNCTAD),
    11, 67

United Nations Industrial Development
    Organization (UNIDO), 129
unorganised sector, of the textile industry,
    42, 53, 61, 84, 101–104, 109,
    110, 112n16, 127, 172, 175
Uruguay Round (1986–1994), 1, 15n3,
    45
  North–South grand bargain, 2
US Food and Drug Administration
    (USFDA), 107, 173
US Patent Office, 107

value-added clothing sector, 6
value-chain networks, 30
venture capital, 116, 129

Western models, of international
    expansion, 22, 125
wholly-owned subsidiaries, 85
World Bank, 16, 67
World Health Organization (WHO),
    58, 107
World Intellectual Property Organization
    (WIPO), 11, 46, 67, 105
World Trade Organization (WTO), 2–3,
    14n1, 16, 45, 113, 162